Gideon Haigh has been a journalist for more than thirty years, contributed to more than a hundred newspapers and magazines, and written thirty-one previous books and edited seven others. His book *On Warne* was the Cricket Society and MCC Book of the Year and the British Sports Book Awards Cricket Book of the Year. He lives in Melbourne, Australia.

Further praise for *Stroke of Genius*

'A cracking book . . . fabulous, thought-provoking' Tanya Aldred, *Cricketer*

'Australia's finest writer on cricket now turns his masterly prose to another legendary cricketer . . . his quest is gripping' *The Times*

'Impeccably researched . . . the book is a triumph' *All Out Cricket*

'This may be the book Haigh was destined to write. Rich and rewarding . . . this is the cricket book of the year' Paul Edwards, *Cricinfo*

'A study befitting the man Haigh describes as being the first Australian to be the best in the world at anything' *Guardian Australia*

'Brings a virtuoso's breadth of reference and perception to a famous photograph of cricketer Victor Trumper' *Guardian*

'One of his best yet . . . it is ultimately about iconography and idolatry' *Observer*

'In *Stroke of Genius*, Gideon Haigh has given *Jumping Out* and the men who created it the richly perceptive tribute they have always deserved' *The Age*

'The true stroke of genius is Haigh's, for he brings Trumper to life in a way that not even the adoring Neville Cardus was able to. In doing so, he has created a work of true genius . . . This work stamps him as the best cricket writer ever' *The Australian*

ALSO BY GIDEON HAIGH

GIDEON HAIGH

Stroke of Genius

Victor Trumper and the shot
that changed cricket

**SIMON &
SCHUSTER**

London · New York · Sydney · Toronto · New Delhi

A CBS COMPANY

First published in Great Britain by Simon & Schuster UK Ltd, 2016
This paperback edition published by Simon & Schuster UK Ltd, 2017
A CBS COMPANY

1 3 5 7 9 10 8 6 4 2

Simon & Schuster UK Ltd
1st Floor
222 Gray's Inn Road
London WC1X 8HB

www.simonandschuster.co.uk
www.simonandschuster.com.au
www.simonandschuster.co.in

Simon & Schuster Australia, Sydney
Simon & Schuster India, New Delhi

A CIP catalogue record for this book is available from the British Library

Paperback ISBN: 978-1-4711-4682-4
eBook ISBN: 978-1-4711-4681-7

Printed in the UK by CPI Group (UK) Ltd, Croydon, CR0 4YY

CONTENTS

INTRODUCTION

The batsman appears almost airborne. Only the instep of his back foot remains grounded; the front foot hovers in space, destined never to land. Yet there is no sense of strain – only energy and expectation.

His figure is spread, as if involved in a Vitruvian exploration of batting's physical limits. His bat, slim, loosely gripped, is at the commencement of its downswing. The muscles of his left forearm are taut with pent-up power. His cap is tugged low, accentuating the precision of the gaze.

His clothing is generous, yet contoured to the hips and shoulders, expressing their purposeful geometry. His sleeves are folded just so, distinctively below the elbow, a personal signature. His legs are lightly sheathed in slatted pads, but they're purely for form's sake. All that matters is the imminent interaction of the bat with a ball we're left to imagine. Nor are there fielders, stumps, crowd. Rather is he fringed by a full-grown wattle, in the corner of a vineyard.

For I am regarding not a photograph but a statue. A hundred years after the death of Victor Trumper, I've inched my way along Victoria's Mornington Peninsula to Red Hill in search of a 2.5-metre-tall bronze cast of him – to be precise of an image of him, perhaps the most famous image in all of cricket, and certainly the image famous longest.

Crafted in 1999 by the sculptor Louis Laumen at one and a quarter times lifesize, it was acquired through the auction house

Bronzed Aussie: Trumper by Louis Laumen.

Christie's by a successful bookmaker, David McLachlan. For almost as long as he has been the owner, McLachlan has been wondering what to do with it. He has no interest in cricket; he acquired it as an investment, during a dabble in collecting. Having twice failed to sell it, he lent the statue to a developer friend, Neil Bryson, who owned a vineyard with its own little cricket ground. For a few years it provided a talking point for guests at an annual match for Bryson's friends. The statue moved to its present whereabouts, by truck and crane, when that property was sold.

Other plans have come to McLachlan's quicksilver mind from time to time. Some have been grand, such as placing it in the forecourt of a residential development to be called Trumper Towers. Some have been more rococo, like drilling a hole in the sculpture's head and turning it into a swimming-pool water feature. More recently, he's thought differently. 'For a while, I was a bit embarrassed about it,' McLachlan says. 'I'd bought it to make a few grand and it was kind of a failure.' Then a note of surprise enters his voice. 'But I've got to admit, I've fallen in love with it.'

•

For more than a century, cricket's votaries have been doing the same, at first because of who the image depicted in its original two dimensions, increasingly because of what it has become – according to sources as diverse as *Wisden Cricketers' Almanack* and Wikipedia, an 'icon'.

Victor Trumper would have been an iconic figure anyway. He was the first truly Australian sporting hero, in the sense of having an actual nation to represent, and being the best at the sport that to his countrymen mattered above all. He also formed part of a profound moral and aesthetic revaluation of cricket, an awakening to its potential beauties, an invitation to appreciations deeper than runs and wickets, victory and defeat. And after his death, he became the first Australian athlete around whom a truly lasting legend was built, remaining lodged in public affection even through decades of Bradmania, despite there being no significant book about him, no public monument to him of any description, no all-encompassing mass media to inundate the senses with messages of his greatness.

What existed, however, was this photograph – the most durable, and still among the most popular, of a great sportsman in action. Trumper remains accessible through certain canonical writings –

moving elegies in the autobiographies of teammates Monty Noble and Frank Iredale, lavish panegyrics among the works of Sir Neville Cardus and Jack Fingleton. Yet Trumper is the earliest sporting luminary to have been, in the main, visually bequeathed: he is as much his picture as Sir Donald Bradman his statistics, and perhaps even more so, as what first illuminated then complemented Trumper has almost replaced him altogether, culminating in its final transfiguration into an art object, inspiring paintings, prints, plates and figurines, helping to sell beverages and bands alike.

Despite this, the achievement of the image's creator, George Beldam, an accomplished amateur batsman and self-taught photographer, has languished in near-total neglect. He was the first skilled practitioner to devote concerted attention to sport, speaking of 'Action Photography' decades before the expression enjoyed widespread usage, and his picture of Trumper predates by generations those Australian sporting images that vie with it for fame, such as the climax of the Tied Test (Ron Lovitt), Norm Provan and Arthur Summons at the SCG in 1963 (John O'Grady) and Nicky Winmar at Victoria Park thirty years later (Wayne Ludbey).

By subordinating text to illustration, Beldam's books *Great Batsmen* and *Great Bowlers and Fielders*, in which Trumper and scores of his contemporaries go through their paces, completely reversed sport's traditional descriptive economy. Then, almost as quickly, Beldam diverted his autodidact's gaze to competing enthusiasms. A photogravure of what was originally 'Plate XXVII: Jumping out for a straight drive' on page 124 of *Great Batsmen* hangs in Australia's National Portrait Gallery; artworks derived from other of his photographs hang in Britain's. Yet Beldam's oeuvre remains uncurated and uncatalogued; a sizeable proportion of his plates have never even been printed.

Partly in consequence, it remains a mystery how the paths of Trumper and Beldam originally interleaved. None of the photographs Beldam took of Trumper are dated; neither man recorded impressions of the experience; the original of 'Jumping Out' appears to have been destroyed, accidentally, by Beldam's youngest son. Mind you, when versions have reached the scale of a quarter of a tonne of silicon bronze reinforced by steel rods, that loss hardly seems so injurious. And that the image marks no special innings and relates to no particular match may account for some of its durability: it conjures an era, an attitude; it both harks back to cricket's first visual imaginings of itself and anticipates a present day where action can be arrested by a keystroke. That front foot is still to land, just as there is always, in cricket, something about to happen.

•

Although this book has biographical elements, it is not a biography of Trumper. Three biographies give chronologies of his life, collate reportage of his innings and sentiment about his personality. *Stroke of Genius* is instead, for want of a better word, an iconography, a study of Trumper's valence in cricket's mythology and imagery. E. B. White famously likened humour to a frog: 'Humor can be dissected, as a frog can, but the thing dies in the process.' The same risk may be thought to apply to sporting legend. That's far from my purpose: on the contrary, Trumper's is a legend to which I have been attached as long as I can remember.

Like many people, I encountered Trumper and 'Jumping Out' simultaneously – in my case on page 89 of one of my earliest cricket books, a slim paperback called *Great Australian Cricket Pictures* (1975). The reproduction was poor, the caption terse and uninformative. But to it I went back and back, as can be judged from the fact that my copy today falls open at exactly that page. Such a dashing stroke. Such a vivid image. Such a musical name, too. Neville Cardus wondered aloud about the rightness or otherwise of cricketers' names after reading an evening stop press of a good score by a Worcestershire wicketkeeper called Gaukrodger: 'With such a name he ought never in this world to have been permitted to score 19, let alone 91.' It gave him a renewed appreciation of his schoolboy hero: 'Had Trumper been named Obadiah he could scarcely have scored a century for Australia against England before lunch.'*

Fittingly, it was Cardus whom I first read at length on the subject of Trumper, which again I can date exactly: a chapter from *Cricket: The Great Ones* (1967) republished in the souvenir program for 1977's Centenary Test. 'I have never met a cricketer,' began Cardus, 'who, having seen and played with Victor Trumper, did not describe him without doubt or hesitation as the most accomplished of all batsmen of his acquaintance.' No doubt or hesitation in Cardus's assertion either, nor in this later personal cameo:

> As a schoolboy I at once worshipped him. He looked so like every schoolboy's idea of the perfect batsman, not too muscular; he was

---

* Others have liked the name too. Characters called 'Trumper' appear in works by cricket-loving novelists George Lamming and Jeffrey Archer. More recently, 'Victor Trumper' was a villain in the BBC's Victorian melodrama *Ripper Street* (2012), a wink from cricket-loving creator Richard Warlow.

Cricket-loving composer Tim Rice has made two uses. 'Victor Trumper' was his pseudonym for an American novelty single with MCA, 'The President Song' (1974), in which Rice recited the name of each president to a backing track, leaving a brief echo-laden silence after each one who had died violently. MCA's enthusiasm waned when a Boston radio station interpreted the silence after the name of Richard Nixon as inciting an assassination attempt. Rice's American champion in the musical *Chess* (1986) was then 'Freddie Trumper', while his right-hand man, 'Walter de Courcey', was named for Jimmy de Courcy, Australian batsman of the 1950s.

actually slender of build, but good looking of face, and of graceful movement. The problem which worried me as a schoolboy arose from the fact he was an Australian.

Every schoolboy is fanatically eager to see and to know England has beaten Australia. I would pray at my bedside at night for an England victory. Yet I always hoped Victor would play a great innings every time. A predicament! Inspiration descended on me, solving my problem. I prayed thus: 'Please God, let Victor Trumper score a century against England tomorrow . . . out of an Australian all-out score of 124.'

To an impressionable eleven-year-old, this passage opened worlds. I was a schoolboy eavesdropping on the thoughts of another school-boy three-quarters of a century earlier. I was also encountering, for the first time, the notion of the cricketer who defies the obvi-ous bounds of affiliation, whose success is transcendently enjoyable. In hindsight, despite being a diffident mediocrity of a cricketer, as unlike Trumper as it is possible to be, I was well on the way to nam-ing my cat after him twenty years later.

Revisiting those foundational documents of my interest in Trumper, I am struck by different things. In *Great Australian Cricket Pictures*, 'Jumping Out' is the only photograph of a cricketer in motion before Bodyline: a comment on the abiding challenge of reviving athletes long dead and spottily recorded for a modern visual audience. In that well-thumbed *Centenary Test Souvenir*, I can see that four cricketers were deemed worthy of profile arti-cles: Sir Donald Bradman, W. G. Grace and Sir Jack Hobbs as well as Trumper, all batsmen, all at least thirty years or so out of the game. The programme depicted their modern heirs more strik-ingly in advertisements: breaking up Cardus's black-and-white

Trumper was a full-colour page of Tony Greig eating Nutri-Grain. This tension 'twixt old and new was uneasier than the game's governors understood. A few months later it would be revealed that Greig among many others had been recruited during the Centenary Test by the agents of Kerry Packer for a brash new private venture, World Series Cricket. The first public act of the captain of Australia's 'establishment team', Bob Simpson, was to place a New South Wales Cricket Association (NSWCA) wreath on the grave of Victor Trumper, on the occasion of the centenary of his birth, 2 November 1977.

It went unnoted that this gesture, apparently affirming of cricket's loftiest traditions, contained an acute historical irony. For the second half of Trumper's career, he and his leading contemporaries had been at more or less permanent loggerheads with the NSWCA, which dominated Australia's inchoate Board of Control. The association at one stage banned recalcitrant players, including Trumper, in much the same way as the authorities in 1977 banned those players aligned with the Packer organisation. Far from being a period innocent in the ways of commerce, cricket in the time of Trumper could be as rapacious and fractious as our own.

Yet historical ironies are eluding us all the time, for it is not facts we find compelling so much as ideas, not the matter of achievement so much as the manner. Australians are expert at creating continuities, sidestepping complications, refurbishing traditions that suit us, neglecting those that do not. And what lingers vestigially in 'Jumping Out' is Australia's oldest cricket myth – Trumper was an idol figuratively long before he became one literally, and was acquired by a man who had never heard of him.

•

Trumper, as we shall see, is an elusive historical figure. He left no memoirs. He left no papers. He gave next to no interviews, made few public statements. Basic biographical information about him is missing. He was lauded as the most exhilarating batsman of his time, and loved as the foremost sportsman, described by contemporaries in almost Christlike terms for his modesty and selflessness. This subtly deepened his enigma. 'He was a hard man to know, because he made you so indebted to him for many kindnesses extended,' thought his teammate Frank Iredale. It also left nothing to adulterate or distract from his sporting reputation. Part of Beldam's success lay in capturing an image of comparable purity, full of what his *Great Batsmen* collaborator C. B. Fry referred to as Trumper's 'generous abandon'. The expressive photograph, argues the philosopher John Berger, works dialectically: it both 'preserves the particularity of the event recorded' and 'chooses an instant when the correspondences of those particular appearances articulate a general idea'. Beldam captured the idea of Trumper for generations to hand on, and it has endured into the era of Instagram.

It has had, as we shall see, numerous admirers, from Dennis Lillee to Steve Waugh, Sir Donald Bradman to Sir Michael Parkinson, all of whom hung it on their walls – Bradman's contemporary Jack Fingleton, his era's leading Australian cricket writer, would argue that 'Jumping Out' should hang in every cricket pavilion in all the world, an essay in elegance, an injunction to action. Its ubiquity persists. During the writing of this book, perhaps for having half an eye out for it all the while, I have seemed to encounter it everywhere – in the headquarters of the cricket equipment maker Gray-Nicolls in Melbourne's Cheltenham, on a museum wall at The Oval in London, in the pavilion at the Cricket Club of India's Brabourne Stadium in Mumbai, in a meeting room at the investment company

38 likes

portraitau And now one for the #cricket fans amongst us. Isn't this #photograph a beauty? This is Victor Trumper mid monster cover drive! #portrait #photography #Australia

Log in to like or comment.

Insta-Vic: Trumper via the National Portrait Gallery.

Wellington Management in Boston. In October 2015, *Cricinfo* published a lengthy profile of A. B. de Villiers, probably the world's most admired cricketer, illustrated with a photograph of de Villiers from side-on, taking a huge stride, bat upraised. 'Victor Trumper would have been proud,' read the caption: few readers would have needed further elaboration. Now I recall a reproduction hung in the chambers of my late friend Michael Shatin QC, who recruited me for the cricket club where I'm now a life member. *Now I recall* . . . who knows on what we might stumble in rummaging the locker of memory?

If David McLachlan knows precious little of cricket, John Goff, now a retired farmer in Tamworth, knows a good deal. He can remember when it started, too. In June 1948, he was a boy at Chatswood West Public School whose class had just graduated to ink pens. His teacher Miss Pennington, a small but severe spinster, was encouraging their efforts by caning everyone who made a blot. John was in line for encouragement again one day when he raised his hand so she could not reach, and for this was sent for additional chastisement to the headmaster's office. A kindly man, the headmaster limited the penalty to John's having to sit outside said office at lunchtime for a week.

On the opposite wall was a photograph, old and faded but thrilling, of a batsman jumping out to drive. There was nothing for seven-year-old John to do but stare at that photograph, the storming front foot and the brandished bat against the murky skyline, and the faded name underneath it: 'Victor Trumper'. It sounded vaguely familiar: a pavilion bore the same name at nearby Chatswood Oval; in fact, Trumper had been a local resident and player. Well, whomever he was, John decided, *that* was the way to bat, with a hawk eye and a headlong launch. At Chatswood West Public School, cricket was played with a crude bat and a tennis ball, and special fame awaited anyone who could hit over a two-storey building that segregated the boys' play area from the girls'. When next he was free to do so, John succeeded. It earned him another week outside the headmaster's office. More time to study the photograph – till he knew every lineament and shade.

Chatswood West shaped John Goff's life. He became a teacher, headmaster and administrator, dedicating forty-two years to the

New South Wales Education Department. He also never forgot Trumper's pictorial example. Whether in the bush on his early teaching rounds, or during the more than 300 games he played for Lane Cove CC in Sydney's Shires competition, he hit hard, straight and often. His son Jeremy, who introduced us, has childhood memories of watching his father hit six after soaring six at suburban parks on the North Shore through the 1970s. 'I always thought that was the way to play cricket,' said John when we talked. And despite never having done it that way, I had to agree.

I

'THE MEMORABLY PERCEIVED PHASE'

'My great aim is to discover whether this splendid game is or is not connected with some of the beautiful laws of motion as to deserve the appellation of a science; and if so to institute a few inquiries to ascertain what are the laws that regulate such honourable appellation.'
— NICHOLAS FELIX, *Felix on the Bat* (1845)

Cricket was devised to be played, not watched. Much of the action occurs very fast, almost all of it very far from the spectator. In the twenty-first century we take for granted television's enrichment of our visual experience, how it effectively imbues us with superhuman powers of perception: the profusion of powerful cameras that draw us into the centre of the action from every angle, including from through the middle stump and the umpire's hat; the pitch microphones that permit our eavesdropping on every grunt and oath; the multiplicity of replays that turn back and slow down time for our delectation; the super slo-mos that decrypt the most complex skills, and are now used so indiscriminately that fielders simply bending down to pick up a ball can appear to have been choreographed by Sam Peckinpah; above all, perhaps, the Decision Review System, augmented by Hawk Eye, Hot Spot and Snickometer, now forming cricket's ultimate appeals court. But the chief purpose of the foregoing is to counteract the obstacles that speed and distance place in the way of watching, interpreting and adjudicating cricket.

Now consider cricket without all this. To obtain a sense of it, a good place to begin is at Lord's. In the collections of the Marylebone Cricket Club is a single 28 cm × 33 cm page from the notebook of a Surrey cricketer, George Shepheard Snr, featuring watercolour sketches of a dozen prominent players of about two and a quarter centuries ago. They are the oldest surviving images of cricketers involved in an actual match, striking what the artist has called 'characteristic attitudes', such as taking block, crouching in the field, leaning on their bats. The only hint of technique is in the cameo of the eminent Hambledonian David Harris, who appears to be taking aim preparatory to an underarm delivery. The images are precious precisely because of their rarity; they also attest the elusiveness of cricket 'action'. The colours are soft, the brushstrokes quick and delicate. But hits, deliveries, catches? For even the raciest recording media, these were too fleeting and far off. In his enchanting chronicle of Hambledon, *Cricketers of My Time* (1832), Richard Nyren paused over Silver Billy Beldham to elucidate the visual treat of his batting: 'It was a study for Phidias to see Beldham rise to strike. The grandeur of the attitude, the settled composure of the look, the piercing lightning of the eye, the rapid glance of the bat, were electrical. Men's hearts throbbed within them, their cheeks turned pale and red. Michael Angelo should have painted him.' But he didn't. Nobody did.

Because it was difficult to capture moments, artists preferred to gather up games in topographic views, positioning cricketers in meadows, on greens, by churches and cathedrals; then, as cricket began drawing crowds, amid onlookers too. By the 1830s and 1840s, as illustration was democratised by new printmaking technologies and 'art' ceased to be the prerogative of the wealthy, these conventions in cricket were well established. In probably the finest and certainly the most popular example, 'A Cricket Match between the Counties of Sussex and Kent, at Brighton' (1849), the game is a backdrop to the crowd – although what a crowd. Brainchild of W. H. Mason, an occasional cricketer who expanded his Brighton stationery premises into a 'Repository of Art', it features portraits of no fewer than seventy-one individuals – selected, interviewed, sketched, painted separately then grouped together by artists William Drummond and Charles Basebe, and finally engraved on copper by George Henry

Madding crowd: Mason's 'A Cricket Match'.

Phillips. Six years in the making, some of the subjects were dead by the time it appeared.

It is as much a social as a sporting study. While the XIs represent the finest flower of their era, we are left in no doubt that the likes of bowler William Lillywhite, a bricklayer, and batsman Fuller Pilch, a tailor, appear by the grace of the Earls, Sirs, Hons and Esqs posed languidly in the foreground. The detailed skyline, meantime, attests Brighton's burgeoning as a seaside resort thanks to royal patronage and rail service. Yet the most fascinating feature of 'A Cricket Match' became its sheer ubiquity, in original and pirated versions. The antiquarian Alfred Taylor, who spent a lifetime researching the print and its variations, noted its hanging in 'every clubhouse in the kingdom' and beyond, from 'the wilds of northern Canada' to 'the wastes of Western Australia'. His classic monograph, *The Story of a Cricket Picture* (1923), rejoiced in tales of its fame:

> A Brighton youth wishing to experiment in a newer and brighter land was financed by his parents and packed off to Australia when immigration was at fever heat. Sad to relate, misfortune dogged his footsteps; but one eventful day he entered a saloon in Ballaret [sic], with scarcely a sou in his possession, and noted the familiar engraving in a prominent position. Only natural that he should be lost in contemplation. 'Good old Brighton,' he muttered. 'Know it?' queried the proprietor. 'Know it! My people live within the shadow of that church,' he said, pointing to the edifice of St Peter.
>
> The rest can be gathered. A freemasonry was established, and the traveller helped on his way. This time he made good, and in after years returned to Brighton a wealthy man, where he spent the remainder of his life, and where he never tired of telling the story related.

What enchanted Taylor most was his tale's testament to public suggestibility. For the match depicted never took place: that is, while the players all represented their respective counties, they never took the field against one another in these specific formations. Yet due to its sheer familiarity, Taylor encountered an 'astonishing number of old gentlemen' who claimed to have been eyewitnesses to the occasion – adamantly so, and in spite of all evidence to the contrary. One man wrote claiming to have inherited the ball; another claimed that his father had been at all three days of the match, and enclosed 'a cutting from an old newspaper' to prove it. Taylor recalled: 'Modesty forbade me to mention that same was from the defunct *Sussex Evening Times* of thirty years ago, had nothing to do with the imaginary match, and was penned by yours truly.' Even when the image was relatively scarce, perhaps even *because* it was relatively scarce, visual 'evidence' already had a cut-through to which print could only aspire. In its way, then, 'A Cricket Match' also anticipated 'Jumping Out', which likewise would decorate pavilions round the world, and likewise convince observers of its absolute verisimilitude.

•

While action lurked beyond the reach of illustrators, some groped for it, introducing a semblance of animation to their artworks by concentrating on what the historian Alexander Sturgis has called the 'memorably perceived phase' of motion – that is, 'when the direction of a movement changes'. You do not, observes Sturgis, illustrate a pendulum's swing halfway through, when it is pointing downwards; you illustrate the instant at which it begins reversing. In a batting stroke, these 'memorably perceived' phases are the beginning and the end. A bat upraised, exuding possibility, was to become a recurrent motif in cricket art, thanks in large part to one of the figures in the foreground of 'A Cricket Match'.

Nicholas Wanostrocht was a polymath schoolmaster from Blackheath who rejoiced in music, languages, art, science and cricket. His nom de plume, Felix, was a nod to Virgil's Georgics: *Felix, qui potuit rerum cognoscere causas* ('Fortunate is he who is able to know the causes of things'). He invented the original batting glove; he invented the first bowling machine; above all, he invented the study of cricket technique. There had been tutors before him, but none so comprehensive and matter-of-factly ambitious: 'My attempt is merely to prove that we may treat the subject with the same courtesy as any other scientific or skilled inquiry, and not ascribe to bad luck all that happens to the chance-surrounded batsman.'

In his explorations, Felix had an unlikely collaborator: painter and sculptor George Frederic Watts, pre-Raphaelite master in the making, but then the teenage son of a friend. From Watts, Felix commissioned pencil sketches demonstrating different shots, which were published as a series of popular lithographs, then adapted for Wanostrocht's masterwork *Felix on the Bat* (1845). They remain strikingly informative. In 'Play', for example, the batsman takes his stance, looking over his left shoulder, knees slightly bent, bat on the ground, feet at ten-to-two. The images of action then concentrate on 'memorably perceived' phases. In 'The Cut', 'Leg Volley' and 'Leg Half-Volley', the legs are wide apart and the bat being flourished; in 'Forward', 'Home Block' and 'The Draw' the stroke has been carried to completion. The comparison Felix draws in the text is between a right-handed batsman and a left-handed fencer moving between defence and attack. But he doesn't just tell – thanks to Watts, he also demonstrates.

Felicitous: Watts' 'The Leg Volley' and 'The Cut'.

Watts' images had a remarkable afterlife, informing almost every depiction of cricket action for the rest of the nineteenth century: as talented an artist as John Corbet Anderson, for instance, simply mimicked them when he assembled 'Cricketing Postures' in 1860. And when George Beldam captured Victor Trumper in 'Jumping Out', how did he convey potential drama but by a bat flamboyantly flourished?

•

'A Cricket Match' and *Felix on the Bat* are fruits of a period of great, if chaotic, growth in cricket, thanks to a long peace, the ceaseless spread of industry, the growing reach of rail, and the expansion of education, literacy and the franchise. Cricket was so busy expanding, in fact, that it had no particular need to cohere, and came under three overlapping spheres of influence: that of the emergent counties like Sussex, Kent, Surrey and Nottinghamshire; that of amateur Marylebone, the country's most prestigious club; that of the professional All-England XI, the country's most illustrious team. The amateur was not yet quite the hegemon he became; the professional still enjoyed the stature of a semi-independent artisan; some cricketers, like Felix, flitted between categories. If anything, the great travelling troupe of the All-England XI predominated, thanks to the energy and avarice of its impresario William Clarke. The summit of the amateur and professional rivalry, the Gentlemen v Players match at Lord's, regularly reiterated professional superiority, being won by the amateurs only seven times in forty-six matches between 1831 and 1865.

Except that professional cricket was a house growingly divided. After Clarke was succeeded on his death by George Parr, the All-England XI found itself rivalled by defectors and epigones competing for the same fixtures. Amateur talent emanating from the public schools reinvigorated both the indolent MCC, which had traditionally abbreviated its season so members could head for the moors in August, and the counties, whose controllers craved gentility in the newly industrialised landscape. Above all there loomed the figure of Dr W. G. Grace, who would seek the privileges of amateurism and the profits of professionalism, and contrive, such were his gifts, to secure them both. By the late 1850s and early 1860s, as professional cricketers clambered over one another in search of new markets, a new technology, the steamship, abruptly placed them within reach. In October 1861, a dozen venturesome professionals led by H. H. Stephenson of the All-England XI and Surrey boarded the SS *Great Britain*, whose screw propulsion and iron hull had halved voyage time to Australia. And in the spirit of newness they first paused in the stableyard of the Anglesea Hotel in the Haymarket, put on their creams, blue waistbelts and bow ties, and posed for a photograph.

Mr W. B. Mallatt.
Merrick. Mudie. Bennett. Famreson. H. B. Stephenson. Cuffey. Griffith. Hearne. Iddison. Sewell. F. Stephenson.
FIRST ENGLAND ELEVEN IN AUSTRALIA

Pioneers on parade: Stephenson's 1861 Englishmen.

•

Twenty years since Fox Talbot's patent of the calotype and Louis Daguerre's launch of the daguerreotype, photography had been thoroughly popularised – and, some felt, utterly debauched. Like cricket, it strained to distinguish amateur from professional. Its amateur pioneers had been a tight circle of gentleman scientists, antiquarians and artists, who debated photographs as well as taking and exchanging them, especially whether it was the purpose of the medium 'to avoid awkward forms, and to correct the unpicturesque', or merely to capture the 'beautiful and unconscious pose'. Wet collodion had then brought photography within reach of professionals with rudimentary knowledge, in particular those who specialised in *cartes de visite*, a genre of small images on albumen paper pasted onto cards so stunningly popular that their vogue was called 'cardomania'. Queen Victoria and Prince Albert bestowed their patronage when Roger Fenton founded the Royal Photographic Society in January 1853, and commissioned from him a dozen private works; but their greater royal impact would be participating in *carte de visite* portrait albums that sold in hundreds of thousands, especially after Albert's death. The versatile Fenton, a barrister with sufficient artistic pretentions to train as a painter in Paris, would experience tugs both ways.

In March 1854, Britain slid into a murky, maladministered war in the Crimea, joining an allied force that besieged Sebastopol. Prime Minister Lord Aberdeen was in turn besieged by the columns of the *Times* correspondent William Howard Russell describing dreadful casualties and indicting incompetent leadership. Whether for profit, public spirit or both, Fenton turned on the war his mechanical and chemical eye. It was as yet a blinking eye. His horsedrawn wagon of apparatus and ten-second exposure times were unequal to the action; his collodion dried in the heat almost as soon as he spread it on the plate; his Victorian sensibilities precluded his photographing casualties. His 350 usable negatives were thus mainly landscapes and panoramas, portraits of commanders and vignettes of soldiers well behind the lines, plus one cameo of a brooding Russell. Yet, seemingly independent and unmediated, these foundational 'war photographs' were critically acclaimed as 'actualities'.

Returning home, Fenton embarked on six frenetic years photographing an astonishing range of subjects: landscapes and lightscapes, still lives and stately homes, archaeological artefacts and orientalist tableaux. Striving to be neither dilettante nor hack, he found himself increasingly out of sympathy with his old amateur colleagues, who opposed members having 'any connexion with photography as a commercial speculation', and out of step with the customs of professionals, whose proliferation had caused the price of photographs to plunge. When the organising committee for the 1862 International Exhibition decided to bump photography from its accustomed place among the arts to among the lowlier crafts, otherwise reserved for machinery, tools and instruments, Fenton gave up: as Stephenson's team toured Australia, he was in the process of selling his equipment and portfolio.

In the meantime, however, Fenton had started something else. During 1857, when he was otherwise busily documenting the Elgin Marbles, cathedrals in Ely, Peterborough, Lincoln and York, and the crags, ravines and valleys of North Wales, he paused on 25 July at Islington's Artillery Ground and took five similar pictures of the Royal Artillery Cricket Club playing Hunsdonbury Cricket Club: cricket's oldest surviving photographs. It's unclear why Fenton did so when in his whole career he took no more than a handful of photographs of activities that could be called recreational. The Artillery Ground, too, was well past its heyday a century earlier; it more closely resembled a village green, rimmed with mature trees. Perhaps, like those painters who had incorporated cricket in their landscapes, Fenton regarded the game as straightforwardly scenic; perhaps he simply knew some members of the Royal Artillery XI from the Crimea.

In any event, Fenton faced similar perplexities to those earlier illustrators: unable to freeze the action with his camera, he had to curtail it by request; unable to ford the boundary, he had to make the best of his distance. Some effort was made at simulating action: the batsman stooped over his blade; the fielders faced toward the centre. But the chief activity around this photograph would have been Fenton's: first coating the plate with emulsion in his portable darkroom, hurrying to insert it in the holder, exposing it for five to ten seconds, then hastening to process the negative in its silver bath before the emulsion dried, all the while trying not to inhale too much ether vapour from the collodion, and this on a summer's day to boot. For Fenton, then, cricket and the Crimea posed surprisingly similar challenges.

Nor, it had to be said, was being photographed other than an ordeal, which accounts in some degree for the solemnity of Victorian portraits. 'Many people have remarked to me that George Parr had rather a morose and sullen expression as judged from the portraits seen of him,' recalled teammate Richard Daft of his All-England XI captain:

But I can assure the reader that he had a much pleasanter expression in reality than that which he often assumed when standing to be photographed, especially in those portraits taken of him with the rest of the XI, on which occasions the long time it took to arrange our positions, and the length of time we had to remain perfectly motionless, was most trying on the nerves . . .

Black and white green: Cricket's oldest photograph.

The local photographer would generally appear on the scene when we were at breakfast at an hotel, and send the waiter to request an interview with Mr Parr to make arrangements for our photos to be taken later in the day.

'Mr Parr, the photographer's here,' the waiter would announce.

'What, again!' George would exclaim with a look of disgust as he would reluctantly leave the table.

Soon enough it would be an ordeal there was no avoiding, wherever in the world you were.

•

There is a regularly published but still remarkable sepia photograph of a stagecoach containing H. H. Stephenson's Englishmen pulling up in Melbourne's Bourke Street on Christmas Eve 1861. Taken by a local specialist in theatrical *cartes de visite*, William Davies, it shows the cricketers perched atop the vehicle, purportedly the largest in the colony, which seems to be bobbing in a sea of hatted heads. Onlookers seeking better vantages prop on steps, peer out windows, mass around a lamppost, and in one case perch atop a sign advertising pantomime at next door's Theatre Royal; from the facade, broken by Tuscan columns, blare the names CAFÉ DE PARIS and THE VESTIBULE.

In this very first image of English players in Australia, then, are discernible two distinctive characteristics of colonial cricket: giddying public enthusiasm and brash commercialism, for the Café and the Vestibule signify the premises of Spiers & Pond, the tour's sponsor. It could hardly have been further removed from Fenton's tranquil scene with its sylvan fringe, but nor, really, could the Antipodes.

Englishmen abroad: Stephenson's team arrives.

Here lay few traditions – in cricket or illustration. Australia's oldest surviving cricket image dates from 1834, a rough pencil drawing of a batsman and bowler from the field book of a surveyor operating north-east of Perth. Among a large collection of local views and streetscapes by John Rae, Sydney's first town clerk, are three 1842 watercolours of cricket on Hyde Park. But with the advent of intercolonial competition in the 1850s, artists had to turn for inspiration to the best-known depiction of the nearest English equivalent, Mason's 'A Cricket Match'. It became a model for factual depictions such as the coloured lithograph by Joseph Fowles and the watercolour by S. T. Gill of the inaugural intercolonial between New South Wales and Victoria on the Domain in January 1857, in which the crowd is foregrounded, the players distant. In further homage to Mason's print, Fowles provided explanatory listings, Gill an outline of the advancing conurbation.

Photography, however, was already well established in Australia, where none were troubled by England's occupational distinctions:

they photographed what they could sell. When Victoria won the 1859 intercolonial, the team was captured in collodion by the brothers Freeman, William and James, in front of a painted background of Sydney Harbour. At the intercolonial a year later in Melbourne, Barnett Johnstone took the first photographs of an actual Australian cricket match – two of them now residing unassumingly in a box at the State Library of Victoria. Johnstone's first subject was the crowd, lying thick on the slopes surrounding the undeveloped Melbourne Cricket Ground, and moving in some instances too fast for him – the foreground is stalked by the ghostly passers-by, the view of the play largely obscured by trees. His second subject was the players, who stood still for roughly a minute, through which the crowd excitedly cheered, enjoyment enhanced by New South Wales being nine for 26 chasing 111 in the fourth innings. Johnstone's self-deprecating annotation suggests he was lucky to obtain any image, thanks to the hot northerly wind blowing: 'The governor of the colony [Sir Henry Barkley] was present in his Box in the Stand, and the game was stayed in situ for the photograph – but the Silver Bath not in an amiable mood just then!!!' Barkley's shape and gubernatorial regalia can be discerned at dead centre.

The epoch-making English visit two years later was extensively recorded at the MCG by the prolific government and police photographer Charles Nettleton, and on Sydney's Domain by Freeman Brothers and a Pitt Street rival, Thomas Glaister. An engraving of the Freemans' 22 cm × 32 cm image published in the *Illustrated London News* in May 1862 was probably the first glimpse of Australian cricket seen abroad; Glaister's 2.7 m panorama, which was actually six photographs conjoined and reliably reported as 'the largest photographic picture yet produced in the colony', unfortunately does not survive. Yet in their entwined ambitions, cricket and photography in Australia already made a cheerfully outsized pair.

•

A subgenre of the visual documentation of Australian cricket has today more pathos. These are the images of cricket played by Indigenous Australians, which are surprisingly profuse, given that this cricket was usually so isolated and temporary, though that, perhaps, is the point – by making a record, by providing 'proof', those responsible could demonstrate progress, fire enthusiasm.

Quite what they evince can be ambiguous. John Crossland's famous 1854 portrait of wistful Nannultera is Australia's earliest painting of a cricketer. Yet records are too scant for us to know whether the star pupil of the Poonidie missionary institution near Port Lincoln actually played the game, or whether he was required to pretend that he did for illustrative purposes. Nearly two decades later, the mission's team was photographed in the field during a game against St Peter's College, an encounter that Adelaide's Anglican archbishop Augustus Short flourished as proof 'that the Anglican aristocracy and England and the "noble savage" who ran wild in the Australian woods are linked together in one brotherhood of blood – moved by the same passions, desires and affections . . .' These exchanges, however, were shortly to cease.

Images were integral to the best known of all Indigenous cricket strivings – the talented team hailing from Victoria's Western District, whose journey from Edenhope to England made them the first Australian cricket tourists, a decade in advance of an official team. The team's station-owner organisers, William Hayman of Lake Wallace and Thomas Hamilton of Bringalbert, substantiated their application for a match with the Melbourne Cricket Club by sending a handsome set of studio photographs of the team members, dignified and resplendent in their whites, taken by J. C. A. Kruger of Warrnambool in March 1866. By the time these photographs were used as the basis of a promotional engraving by Samuel Calvert in the *Australian News* nine months later, one of the players, Sugar, had actually died. But he rejoined his comrades one last time around a set of stumps beneath an imagined pennant for the 'A. C. C.' – the Aboriginal Cricket Club, perhaps.

Ahead of their Boxing Day fixture, the team sat for a real team photograph, since widely reproduced, encased this time in jackets and waistcoats, white pot hats doffed. To the left stands King Cole, leg propped on a chair, elbow resting on a knee, almost parodic of the leisured gent. In the back row stands the coach provided by the club, Tom Wills, left hand at his breast, perhaps a touch uncomfortably, for this coming-together is as artificial as it is hopeful. 'These men are literally and truly the last of their race,' Hayman prophesied confidently in *The Australasian*, 'and in a few years the aboriginals [sic] will have ceased to exist in the West Wimmera district.' The

Men apart: Aboriginal cricketers at the MCG, 1866.

first plan to mount an Aboriginal tour of England fell foul of a con
man. The second was regarded with deep suspicion by the Central
Protection Board. They made their way in England by playing up to
the exoticism of a second team photograph, taken by Warrnambool's
Patrick Dawson, featuring half the members with bats and balls,
the other half with hunting implements: their games were punctuated by displays of athletic prowess and tribal skills featuring
traditional weapons, some of them left behind at Lord's and Exeter's
Royal Albert Memorial Museum. Also left behind, in Victoria Park
Cemetery, were the mortal remains of King Cole, he of the languid
stance, after his death from tuberculosis in Guy's Hospital.

Not long after the team's dissolution, an English naturalist, Henry Nottidge Moseley, was seeking wildlife north-east of
Melbourne, near present-day Healesville. Though he could not persuade the 'incorrigibly lazy' Aborigines to aid him in his quest, he was
a fascinated observer of both their cricket prowess and their phreno-
logical endowments, which he undoubtedly regarded as linked:

> We found the cricket party in high spirits, shouting with laughter,
> rows of spectators being seated on logs and chaffing the players
> with old English sallies: 'Well hit!' 'Run it out!' 'Butter fingers!'
> &c. I was astonished at the extreme prominence of the supraciliary
> ridges of the men's foreheads. It was much greater in some of the
> Blacks than I had expected to see it, and looks far more marked
> in the recent state than in the skull. It is the striking feature of the
> face. The men were all dressed as Europeans; they knew all about
> Mr W. G. Grace and the All-England XI.

Moseley had encountered one of the most remarkable of all
Aboriginal settlements, Coranderrk, created in June 1863 after leaders

of the Kulin met Sir Henry Barkly at a birthday levee for Queen Victoria and successfully petitioned for 150 acres (61 hectares) of land around the Yarra's meeting with Badger Creek. Over the next decade, the station became more or less self-sufficient, growing wheat and running livestock, surrounding a school and church with fifteen cottages, and playing sport. By the time Moseley visited, however, their land was attracting covetous pastoral eyes, and the classic 1877 image that endures of Coranderrk cricket is an artefact of their response. Fred Kruger, an accomplished photographer from Berlin, was commissioned by the Protection Board to document features of daily settlement life, emphasising their European clothing, Christian rectitude and civilised pursuits. That cricket was the only recreation Kruger chose to feature says something of its status among both the subjects of the photograph and the intended audience. Much effort has gone into the participants' poses – the back-leaning umpire, the forward-leaning non-striker, the alert fielders, the orderly spectators. Cover point, by contrast, stares at the camera, probably out of curiosity, but almost through it as well, as if to make eye contact with posterity.

The quivering arm: Aboriginal cricketers at Coranderrk, 1877.

For all the contrivance, the image retains a disarming intimacy. Kruger has taken advantage of the game's informality to draw comparatively close; you can imagine events in progress before the erection of his tripod and proceeding after his scurrying retreat to the darkroom. The batsman looks like he knows what he's doing; the bowler seems to be aching to roll his arm over. Look closely and you can detect a blur, in all likelihood from the effort of holding his arm out straight for the period of the exposure – it feels like both the strain of the mimetic exercise and of photography's trembling on the brink of motion.

Eighteen seventy-seven itself was a brink: the year of the inaugural Test match, at the MCG, and of the first game at the Association Ground, later to be renamed the Sydney Cricket Ground. It was the year of the first total of 500 and the first seasonal aggregate of 1000 runs in any class of Australian cricket. It was the year in which Dave Gregory's Australian cricket team commenced the lengthy preliminaries to a journey that would take them to England, climaxing in a game that changed cricket history. And it was the year Victor Trumper was born.

•

To a greater degree than at any stage in its history, cricket at the time of Trumper's birth could be condensed to a single figure. Not yet thirty, W. G. Grace was in the process of transforming batting from a precarious occupation on surfaces of sometimes lethal unreliability – he had been involved in the 1870 game at Lord's when a delivery rebounding from a pebble on the pitch struck George Summers a mortal blow – into a practice of skill, power and patience. In doing so he was securing for batsmanship a priveleged status. Boosters such as Rev. James Pycroft in *The Cricket Field* (1851) and Thomas Hughes in *Tom Brown's Schooldays* (1857) had already ascribed the game certain moral excellences; as Grace traversed England setting record upon record, he was establishing 'the batsman' as the hero of its pageant. Batting contained values with a deep Victorian appeal: the authority of the strong; the endurance of the stoic; the defiance of the outnumbered. By identifying with Marylebone, moreover, Grace seized that prestige for the amateur creed. Not a public schoolboy, and the graduate of an unglamorous medical school rather than an elite university, Grace was hardly the stuff of which amateurs were usually made. But he was reinforcing a set of class relations that would outlast him for generations, whereby batting was perceived as an occupation commensurate with gentlemanliness, bowling a trade in the nature of skilled manual labour.

In 1877, Grace was at one of multiple peaks in his fifty-year career. He and his brothers had made their native Gloucestershire into a leading county. His renown in this imperial heyday had been extended by visits to Canada then Australia. Gluttony was beginning to take its toll on his physique, initially lithe and athletic; yet this growing bulk, along with his luxuriant beard, would enhance his visual identity. The spectator arriving at a county ground might struggle to distinguish one distant cricketer from another, but there was no mistaking ursine, hirsute, appealingly rustic Grace. That year he became the first cricketer to be sketched by *Vanity Fair*; his features adorned the first issue of the *All-England Cricket and Football Journal*. Its spread unimpaired by notions of commercial copyright or intellectual property, his image was widely appropriated by advertisers and promotors. In perhaps the most famous representation, he filled a pavilion gate, ready to advance, Marylebone colours artfully tinged to correspond with the relevant condiment: 'Colman's Mustard Leads the Field'.

That visual identity did not, however, extend to representation of his actual skill. W.G.'s image makers were engaged chiefly by his presence and reputation, reflecting the preferences of his journalistic chroniclers, only a handful of whom addressed Grace's technique in other than plain and rather uninformative terms. Descriptions of Grace went on emphasising his monumentality, his assuredness, his steady pervasion of the crease, his avidity for great scores, his zeal for competitive advantage; he was, in other words, interpreted heroically rather than aesthetically; now and again, in fact, an admirer confided to posterity that his batting appeared rather cumbersome, power vested in broad shoulders and brute strength. By the time MCC commissioned his portrait, Grace was over forty, weighed about 140 kg, and took months to coax into the Chelsea studio of artist Archibald Stuart Wortley, where he stood stiffly, weight anchored on the back foot, a cocked left toe and cautiously lifted bat the only accommodations with action, superimposed on a background copied from a painting of a Varsity match.

Grace is survived by his figures – and astonishing they are, stretched across decades. But cricket's descriptive grammar, written and pictorial, had as yet no real means of distinguishing players on the basis of style. Grace himself was a practical cricketer, who shed little light on his methods. His official biographer later described the painful business of extracting his reflections. Asked how he had felt during this innings or what he had thought during that, Grace would reply in puzzlement . . . why, he'd been watching the bowling, the fielders, hadn't he? That left no scope for feeling or thought. Against new and mettlesome opponents especially, one could hardly afford such distraction.

•

The eleven Antipodean cricketers who stepped forth in London on 14 May 1878, their capacious canvas 'caravan' of equipment marked in whitewash with the legend 'Australian Eleven', did so in a spirit of pure colonial bravado. Their impresario, journalist John Conway, promoted them as a team 'thoroughly Australian in character' of 'the best cricketers in Australia without respect to colony' under 'the Australian flag' – and assembled six New South Welshmen, four Victorians and a solitary Tasmanian under a flag fluttering nowhere but in the imagination. They had no backing from any of the fledgling cricket associations of the fissile colonies, who scorned an enterprise so obviously commercial, in that the team members were stumping up £50 each to defray expenses then splitting gate takings at the end. They lacked even the backing of Conway's newspaper, *The Australasian*, which said severely: 'It cannot be denied that it is nothing more than a speculation which the promotors hope to carry through without a loss and possibly with a fair margin of profit.' But speculation was part of the colonial way of life, of gluts and scarcities, of booms and bigger booms. Conway was selling cricket as others sold wool, wheat, copper and gold, and struck lucky. For just a fortnight after arriving, the Australians beat mighty Grace-led Marylebone on a hectic afternoon of 105 runs and thirty-one wickets, eleven of these wickets for 20 to their Mephistophelean opening bowler Fred Spofforth, eight for 17 to his henchman Harry Boyle.

It wasn't the original Australian sporting triumph. Two years earlier, Ned Trickett had overpowered Englishman James Sadler in the World Sculling Championship on the Thames stroking a boat called *Young Australia*. But he had been a New South Welshman, bound to engender twinges of jealousy in other colonies; in Australian cricket's first foreign triumph, three colonies could claim a share. The

'A speculation': the 1878 Australians.

effect was magnified by a new miracle of the age, the telegraph, which, as yet succinctly because of its expense, encapsulated events abroad almost as they happened. Amazingly, readers of Melbourne's *Argus* learned of the rout within a day of its occurring.

THE AUSTRALIAN CRICKETERS IN ENGLAND.
[BY SUBMARINE CABLE.]
(FROM OUR OWN CORRESPONDENT.)
LONDON, MAY 27.

To-day the Australian cricketers played against an eleven of the Marylebone Club on Lord's ground. There was a large attendance at the match, which excited considerable interest. The result of the play was as follows: -

Marylebone Club, first innings . . . 31

Marylebone Club, second innings . . . 19

Total . . . 50

Australian Eleven, first innings . . . 41

> The Australians in their second innings obtained the requisite
> number of runs with the loss of one wicket, and therefore won the
> game by nine wickets. The bowling of the Australians was very
> effective.

International cricket? Not quite, but it felt like it. 'Australia is advancing, indeed in sports as in everything else,' said *The World*. 'She has beaten the country on the Thames and now she beats *England* at Lord's. [my italics] At the present rate we shall soon have nothing left of our boasted athletic pre-eminence.' The response of *Vanity Fair* was to accord Spofforth the honour of being caricatured by 'Spy' that among cricketers had only previously been accorded Grace, reinscribing him in an English narrative: Spofforth, it reported reassuringly, was 'of a good English family', and 'like all the better kind of Australians . . . not distinguishable from an English gentleman'.

Yet were these Australians *really* 'gentlemen'? Conway's confederacy now set themselves to cornering their new market: the decisive day of their tour was arguably a week after their Lord's triumph, when they played Surrey at The Oval. What *Sporting Life* called 'the largest gathering of spectators that we ever saw assembled to witness a cricket match' ignored the turnstiles, forced the carriage gates and trampled the wooden fencing in their rush for seats. The Australians reacted by upping their ticket prices from sixpence to a shilling, and in doing so collided with English strictures against professionalism.

For the Australians were claiming the status of amateurs, entitling themselves to such niceties as an honorific prefixing their name on scorecards. Intercolonial cricket had not the same rigid demarcations as county cricket; a mix of public servants and bank officers plus one solicitor, the Australians little resembled English professionals, who were increasingly the indentured servants of their counties. In the tour they were investors, and viewed the profits they planned to divide as necessary to cover expenses incurred in absences from work. Yet to English cricketers, amateurs and professionals alike, a £750 dividend for each Australian looked awfully like being paid to play – especially when someone like twenty-year-old Tom Garrett earned £140 a year as a legal clerk.

Things got ugly. When the Australians returned to The Oval on 2 September to meet Professionals of All-England, nine of the home team, including its stars Alfred Shaw and Arthur Shrewsbury, demanded that Conway double their match fee to £20. They were replaced with the consent of the county's canny secretary Charles Alcock, no fonder of restive professionals than the visitors. But unrest about the Australians' status was now spreading to the press. 'Let us not be misunderstood; we do not blame them in the least for looking after the main chance – we find no fault with them for exhibiting their skill for gain, and making profit out of their prowess,' said *Sporting Gazette* with self-conscious broadmindedness. 'There is nothing derogatory to man's dignity in making money by his proficiency in any art or sport – he has a perfect right to do so if he is so disposed; only he must allow himself by so doing to be classed among professionals, not amateurs.'

Why did Australian cricketers hold so fast to their status as amateurs in England? The colonial sense of upward social mobility, resistant to challenge? The colonial inferiority complex, confronted by pejorative associations of professionalism? Because they actually *did* subscribe to the notion that only amateurs could provide cricket with its moral leadership, and they were determined be part of that *corps d'élite*? Perhaps, in one way, simply because they could, daring the English to call their bluff.

Every so often, the English threatened to. In November 1878, Marylebone took the matter on, issuing a proclamation concerning the 'definition and qualification of amateur cricketers' deeming 'that no gentleman ought to make a profit by his services in cricket'. That left ample wriggle room – ample enough for Grace to wriggle through soon after when a group of Gloucestershire members protested his 'special scale' for expenses. And he was far from alone: it was an open secret that a goodly number of English 'shamateurs' not only pocketed expenses with both hands but held paid secretarial posts at counties.

The English, however, were not about to condone colonials doing openly what their upper crust did privately – not without a show, anyway. When Conway brought his next team in 1880, they were scorned. In May, June and July, Billy Murdoch's team could arrange only three first-class games. 'We could not be treated worse if we were a set of blacklegs,' griped Harry Boyle. The ranks of disapproval were broken by Grace, in whom antipodeans brought out magnanimity as well as competitiveness. He offered the visitors a game against Gloucestershire, which they won, and opened doors at The Oval. Four times an Australian application for a fixture had come before Alcock and the Surrey committee; four times they had said no; a fifth time, the answer was maybe; a sixth time, the answer was yes. It was a coup. Grace and Murdoch starred in England's inaugural Test match, which drew the greatest cricket attendance to that time – nearly 70 000 in three days. The visitors had learned valuable lessons. Planning an 1882 return, Murdoch's team veiled their mercenary instincts, accepting a smaller share of gate takings and, instead of stumping up their own money, having public-spirited businessmen, bankers and lawyers make the initial £1500 outlay. Manager Charles Beal then deferentially solicited the approval of Marylebone's secretary, Henry Perkins, with success. 'I received a cable telling me Lord's would gladly receive us as amateurs, and then we arranged the tour,' Beal recalled. 'The team would not have gone had Lord's cable been different.'

The Test match that gave rise to 'the Ashes', then, was only made possible by colonial obeisance to English class niceties. From the ensuing spirit of amity then sprang the charming gesture of the urn to go with it, the next English team to visit the colonies featuring only four professionals alongside eight 'genial and unassuming' amateurs under the auspices of the Melbourne CC. It was during this temporary abatement of commercial rapacity that cricket's status as taking 'first place among Australian sports' was famously attested by the journalist Richard Twopeny in his widely read *Town Life in Australia* (1883): 'As Napoleon's soldiers remembered that they carried a marshal's *bâton* in their knapsacks, so the young Australians all remember that they have a chance of becoming successors of that illustrious band of heroes who have recently conquered the mother-country and looted her into the bargain, though the idea of gain certainly never enters into their heads in connection with cricket.'

In fact, when Murdoch led the fourth Australian team to England in six years, imputations of avarice reared their heads again. *Illustrated Sporting and Dramatic News* deemed the visitors to be outwearing their welcome: 'The present generation of lovers of the once noble game must have seen enough of the Australians to last them for life, and their intrusion into the mother country will henceforward be regarded as a veritable nuisance, carried out to its bitter end.' When Shaw and Shrewsbury brought another team south in 1884–85, the model collapsed. Murdoch's Australians antagonised everyone with their financial demands – the visitors, the local associations, Conway, even esteemed colleagues such as Spofforth and Tom Horan, now Melbourne's most influential cricket columnist, writing for *The Australasian* under the reminiscent pen name 'Felix'. Controversy roiled all summer, crowds shrank, profits plunged. Returning to England from eight years sojourning in the colonies to tilt at Westminster, Harold Finch-Hatton was typical of English opinion in his *Advance Australia!* (1885): 'Much as I admire the indomitable pluck of the Australian cricketers who have met England both at home and in their own country, beyond their skill in handling the weapons of their trade there is little to be said for their conduct. While arrogating to themselves the title of amateurs, they make it perfectly plain that they follow cricket as a lucrative profession, and do not care to play except for sufficient plunder . . .'

Call it the spirit of the times: the 1880s were as gaudy and greedy as the corresponding decade a century hence. Murdoch was a representative speculator, who staved off creditors by marrying a mining magnate's daughter after being bankrupted in a South Seas trading venture. There were no real rules, little constituted authority. England's counties met once annually; Australia's colonial associations not at all. Marylebone enjoyed respect but not deference. And when the Melbourne CC stepped gingerly into the Australian fray in an attempt to 'replace Australia on a good footing in England', it was with mixed results.

The club had flourished in the boom – thanks to its savvy secretary, Major Ben Wardill, it also led the way in Australian Rules football, tennis, baseball and lacrosse. Wishing to strike a blow for amateur ideals, it embarked on organising a team to visit England without 'any desire for gate money'. Accoutred in smart Melbourne blazers of red, white and blue, hosted to dinner in the House of Commons, guests of the Prince of Wales and his cricket-mad son Prince Albert Victor, the 1886 Australians were the best dressed and socially smoothest of the nineteenth century. They were also among the weakest, losing all three Tests by increasing margins. Yet, being gentlemen, they were welcome in perhaps the most prestigious vision of cricket yet.

•

'The Imaginary Cricket Match: England v Australia' (1887) now hangs in the Writing Room at Lord's, the only room in the pavilion big enough for its dimensions of 310 cm × 166 cm. It was executed by two accomplished portrait artists, Sir Robert Ponsonby Staples and George Hamilton Barrable, during two years of imperial cele- bration, containing the lush Colonial and Indian Exhibition, Queen Victoria's silver jubilee, the inaugural colonial conference and, by happy coincidence, Marylebone's centenary.

Its exact origins are a mystery, although it was almost certainly hatched in collaboration with Staples' cousin, Sir Coutts Lindsay, founder of the Grosvenor Gallery, bastion of the 'art for art's sake' aesthetic movement. The Grosvenor's aesthetes welcomed being satirised in the cartoons of George du Maurier in *Punch* and in Gilbert and Sullivan's *Patience*: after all, in the view of a gilded youth who attended the gallery's opening in a costume inspired by a cello, the only thing worse than being talked about was not being talked about. Notoriety was lucrative, too. During the Colonial and Indian Exhibition, which marked 'the development of the empire in the arts of civilisation', Lindsay was invited to organise a touring display of modern British art for Australian audiences.

The 158 canvases Lindsay assembled were suitably rich and dec- orative, from G. F. Watts' symbolist masterpieces 'Love and Life' and 'Love and Death' to Edward Burne-Jones's racy full-length male nude 'The Depth of the Sea'. Throwing in the painting of a cricket game at Lord's smacks of providing something comfortingly familiar for the lay visitor. The inspiration was Mason's indestructible 'A Cricket Match', for again it depicted a match that never took place: it was reported that the two 'ideal elevens', whose faces appear in the predella, had been chosen by 'competent judges' from England and the colonies, and the fielders positioned in consultation with Spofforth, who had 'taken a great interest in the picture'. To the visitors, too, the compliment was unmistakable: the presences at the wicket of W. G. Grace and the Surrey amateur W. W. Read subtly accorded social parity to the colonial cricketers, and to the Melbourne CC whose colours they wore.

As with Mason's 'A Cricket Match', further burnish was imparted by the 'A' enclosure crowd, nobility and royalty reinforced by celebrity: the actress Lillie Langtry, coyly averting her eyes from former paramour the Prince of Wales; the hostess and enchantress Lady de Grey, receiving a note, perhaps from one of her lovers; numerous other society belles. Tucked away to the right, colonials were also accorded their due, including several of the commissioners to the Colonial and Indian Exhibition, all identified in a detailed key. An Indian Premier League crowd festooned with Bollywood stars and business moguls could hardly rival such density of glamour.

The sheer number of figures is likely because Ponsonby Staples, an impecunious eccentric with a marked aversion to shoes, badly wanted a sale. He even included the face of his father, to whom he was heavily indebted. Cause for optimism existed when the painting, after attracting admiring notice at Marylebone's centenary dinner, was praised by the colonial press for its 'graphic representation of our national game', enhanced as it was by 'the charming toilettes of the ladies, among whom will be easily recognised some of our most popular English beauties'. Alas, everyone liked the painting except those with money, who disdained it in favour of wooded glens and blasted heaths. 'It is "the thing" at present in Melbourne, to take, or to pretend to take, an interest in art,' wrote 'Our Lady Correspondent' of the *West Australian*. 'It is curious to listen to the comments of "Young Australia" on the pictures. He does not like Burne-Jones, and G. F. Watts is beyond him. But he is much interested in a daub by Messrs Staples and Barrable, called "England v. Australia." It is a picture of a cricket-match at Lord's cricket ground.' A 'daub'! A 'picture of a cricket-match'! Returned unsold, Marylebone did not acquire until 1927 what may now be cricket's most valuable painting.

What's usually overlooked in the general richness of the vision is that 'The Imaginary Cricket Match' *does* represent an advance in the representation of cricket. The action matters: the unnamed young woman at right, binoculars to her eyes, attests it. And if far away and fictionalised, the activity in the middle *is* well chosen: bowler Spofforth *is* looking convincingly chagrined; Grace *is* refusing a call for a run from his partner Read, his arresting of the action an analog of painting itself; the fielders are variously arrayed for action. The stooping figure in the foreground is actually copied from an older engraving, Valentine Bromley's 'At the Eton and Harrow Match' (1877). But he, too, is well chosen: Tom Garrett, a veteran of the very first Test match, and a harbinger of Test drama to come. For he was, *inter alia*, a mentor of Victor Trumper.

2

'ONCE YOU SEE HIM THERE WILL BE NO DOUBT'

'Before he had batted for half an hour it was obvious
that a new star of unsurpassed brilliance and charm had
joined the cluster of the Southern Cross.'
– H. S. ALTHAM, *A History of Cricket* (1926)

For an Australian so prominent, much basic information about
Victor Trumper is lacking. His birthdate and birthplace, for
instance; even his true parents. Despite several valiant efforts,
his birth certificate has never been located. The polite convention is '2 November 1877, Sydney', because it is the information
Trumper gave when Tom Garrett helped him obtain a public-service job. At that time, however, his ostensible parents,

Charles and Louise, would have been only fourteen years old.

The mystery has discomfited his biographers. In the research notes for *The Immortal Victor Trumper* (1978) that form part of Jack Fingleton's papers in the State Library of NSW is an extract of Charles and Louise's marriage certificate with the date 15 May 1883 insistently underlined. Could Trumper have been illegitimate, he wondered? If so, was it prudent to say so? Fingleton solicited the advice of his friend Sir Robert Menzies, saying he was tempted to mention it: it would be, thought the devout Catholic, a 'wonderful plug against abortion'. Menzies counselled against, believing it would 'do more harm than good', and Fingleton tastefully obscured the matter. While writing *Victor Trumper: The Illustrated Biography* (1985), Ashley Mallett made the same discovery and posed a similar question of Sir Donald Bradman. Bradman also advised against, on grounds it might 'cast a shadow over the Trumper family'. Peter Sharpham alone spelled it out in *Trumper: The Definitive Biography* (1985), positing that Trumper was adopted, perhaps from another branch of a widespread family. But nobody knows – maybe not even Trumper himself.

Where did he spend his first six years? Who introduced him to cricket? Who were his boyhood heroes, his playmates? None of these basic facts have come to light either. Knowable only is the intensely local landscape of his life. Save for some later years in Chatswood, Trumper lived and died within a scalene triangle of about 12 square kilometres bounded by Darlinghurst, Paddington and Surry Hills – a seedy, sooty neighbourhood of lower-middle-class tradesmen and working-class labourers taxed by overcrowding and poor sanitation. In her novel of the vicinity, *Foveaux* (1939), Kylie Tennant describes a populace 'with one foot in gentility and a desperate other boot sliding downhill towards the workers of the terraces and the flotsam of the alleys'. Charles Trumper, a clicker, knew boots well: if he always seems to have been gainfully employed, he lost his father and two infant daughters to tuberculosis in 1890.

The only glimmer of Trumper the boy in his own words is feint and reflected, in an article under his name in *C. B. Fry's Magazine* in May 1905 – not a memoir but a description for English readers of Australian cricket's various levels. His tribute to cricket in streets and lanes is redolent of Surry Hills' slums and rookeries, with their myriad back alleys for nightsoil disposal. It bred, he thought, not only a certain self-sufficiency but skills more widely applicable:

Any piece of timber roughly fashioned with a hatchet does service for a bat, and as for stumps – well, a kerosene tin is splendid, or a chalked-off space on the wall of a house, or a given area of a friendly fence . . . The 'wicket' is freely studded with metal, and

Trumper writes: a unique glimpse.

37

the ball pursues the most peculiar courses, there being always the chance of it getting up suddenly and disastrously. An inexorable rule in these games is 'over the fence out', a rule which came into existence by the deep-rooted objection of the occupiers of the adjoining houses to act as auxiliary fieldsmen. Therefore, our young batsman gets an early lesson as to the advisability of keeping the ball down, because, once it goes over the fence, not only is his innings over, but frequently the game has to be abandoned for the want of a ball.

Although the vocabulary ('inexorable', 'auxiliary') suggests a degree of editorial assistance, it is a homely passage, of scarcity and adaptation, and also a glimpse of Australian urban living before the hankering for private space and the growth of private transportation, before the ideal of every man his quarter-acre block. The article reminds us, too, that while Australian cricket myth is thick with tales of the bush and backblocks, cricket was first of all a game of cities and towns, where children faced particular challenges. 'In some parts of the metropolis these street games have become a nuisance, and an occasional broken window comes under the notice of the authorities,' reported Trumper. 'Only the other day sixteen young cricketers, who insisted on playing in the street of a popular suburb, were proceeded against in the police court, each desperado being fined to the enormous extent of one shilling.'

Trumper, in fact, would go on being identified with just such improvised games – the kind immortalised as 'the back lane cricket association' in Ken G. Hall's classic featurette *That's Cricket* (1931), with its scenes of barefoot urchins batting, bowling and bantering. That same year a solicitor in a Parramatta court representing a score of boys of whose street cricket a local woman had complained invoked Trumper's example in defending them: 'Victor Trumper learned half of his cricket in the street and at the expense of many broken windows.' In later dramatising parts of Trumper's life, the radio serial *They Were Champions* (1953) revelled in the sound-effects possibilities:

> NARRATOR: From an early age he showed a keen interest in sport of every kind, particularly in cricket, and he missed few opportunities of demonstrating his skill with bat and ball in neighbouring backyards. [sound of breaking glass] Yes, many a window paid the price of young Victor's enthusiasm. It was a relief to his parents and neighbours alike when Victor's cricketing activities were transferred to the playing fields of Crown Street State School. [sound of bat hitting ball] Oh nice shot, Trumper, nice shot!

In reality, Trumper's Crown Street School had no 'playing fields' as such – instead it made use of the verdant expanses of Moore Park, named for the Sydney mayor who had far-sightedly set it aside as public parkland twenty years earlier. Trumper regarded the expanse as a second home: in a 1913 interview with *The Referee*, Charles Trumper dated Victor's 'passionate devotion to cricket' as dating from the ages of 'nine or ten years old' when they would practise together for two hours from 6 a.m. in 'that magnificent playground'. In explaining Australian cricket to English readers, Trumper recalled Saturdays at Moore Park where there could be 'twenty-five or thirty matches going on simultaneously and without any lines of demarcation between the playing areas':

> There in one corner are a number of young players in spotless costume fighting out a keen match on a matting wicket. Next

> to them, and not forty yards [37 metres] between the pitches, is
> a contest between barefoot urchins on a wicket formed by just
> chipping the surface of the turf. A few yards further off the young
> men belonging to some church are playing away keenly. And so on.
> There is nothing like the democracy of a sports ground.

This was more than simply a congenially demotic image. It registered a shift in Australian cricket that Trumper would step into.

Everything in the colonies crashed at the climax of the febrile 1880s, including cricket. The *aestas horribilis* was 1887–88 when the Melbourne CC and SCG Trustees each brought their own visiting teams from England. As six different versions of an Australian XI met four mix-and-match English combinations, the public shrugged and turned away – the only Test match, in Sydney, drew a wretched 2000 spectators. Cricket waned; rival pursuits advanced. 'Soon it will be the football that is called noble while cricket descends to a mere plebeian diversion,' forecast the Frenchman Oscar Comettant in his travelogue *In the Land of Gold Mines and Kangaroos* (1890). Arthur Streeton's painting 'The National Game' (1889) and Tomasso Sani's ebullient bronze 'We Won' (1891) likewise celebrated the games of winter. In the years of economic blight, just one cricket team visited, and only because its patron, Lord Sheffield, could afford to lose heavily on the venture, which he duly did.

His lordship's largesse, however, extended to a considerable parting gift: £150 to stimulate intercolonial competition, which gave impetus to a first conference of representatives from the cricket associations of Victoria, New South Wales and South Australia. In September 1892, they formed an 'Australasian Cricket Council' – less a controlling body than the aligning of one Australian cricket faction, excluding as it did the Melbourne CC, the SCG Trustees, and also the players. But its members had, like those colonial politicians toying with a draft Australian constitution, serious federal ambitions – nothing less than 'the regulation of visits of English or other teams' and 'the regulation of visits of Australasian teams to England or elsewhere'. The council began positively with a vote, albeit by the narrowest possible margin, to turn his lordship's sterling into 160 oz (4.5 kg) of symbolic silver – the Sheffield Shield.

Like the Federal Council of Australasia that the colonies had conceived of in 1883, the Australasian Cricket Council's title was as grand as its actual powers were small. It controlled no grounds, had neither income nor reserves. Players abided its constituting a selection panel, but resented its appointment of a manager on their next two tours of England; it was the Melbourne CC and the SCG Trustees who organised the next two tours by English teams. What the council would do over eight fitful years was hint at how a federal structure might work, while the associations themselves took other internal steps, such as the promotion of local pennant competitions along 'electoral' lines – that is, with players drawn from within defined residential boundaries, fostering local rivalries and more equal competition. Trumper's comment that 'there is nothing like the democracy of a sports ground', then, had quite particular resonances – ironically, as we shall see in Chapter 8, it would be his playing generation who ended up resisting the last step in that process.

•

The Australian summers of 1894–95 and 1897–98, when local teams for the first time met visiting teams across the expanse of five Test matches, set new standards in scale and scope. The wholesome blending of colonial cricket could be interpreted as preluding statesmen's efforts towards actual union: thus *The Bulletin*'s oft-quoted remark about Australian cricket success doing 'more to enhance the cause of Australian nationality than could be achieved by miles of erudite essays and impassioned appeal'. Never before, too, had so many people been able to follow cricket. If daily newspapers were slow to exploit the development of the dry plate and the halftone block, weeklies such as *The Australasian* and *Australian Town and Country Journal* were now thickly lined with photographs, line drawings and engravings, and accorded Test and Sheffield Shield matches lush visual coverage. The accent remained on event rather than action – the distant white-clad figures might have been a flea circus. But in crowd panoramas, regularly spread over double pages, the 'democracy of a sports ground' was thoroughly in evidence. Other things, too.

In a vast, thinly populated land, the thronging to a Test match was a remarkable phenomenon. What explained it? Not only the craving for success, some thought; the spectacle itself formed part of the allure. Cricket exerted an 'unmeasured power of attraction', thought a *Sydney Morning Herald* contributor: 'It is an abiding joy to the participants, and a picture of grace and skill to the spectator. All its surroundings are delightful to the eye, and refreshing to the brain. Its geometric precision and the flashing celerity of polished movement are blandly exhilarating, and, without any extra charge at all, every onlooker may be a critic. And he generally is.' Cricket was restrained, refined, civilised, civilising – a game, thought a leader writer in *The Australasian* after a Melbourne Test, to 'delight the eye of the artist':

What athletes in classic games and times could surpass in swiftness and grace of movement, in skill of wrist and quickness of eye and enduring pluck, the white-clad figures that make up the players in a great cricket match? The movements of a famous bowler like Richardson or Turner are in the highest degree picturesque; and a fine batsman like Gregory, or Darling, or Brockwell resembles a fencer with his bat for rapier meeting with quick-turning parry and lunge the attack, now subtle, now furious, of the bowler.

To an artist perhaps, the vast crowd of spectators, silent and vigilant, is as picturesque and almost as interesting as the play. Nearly twenty thousand spectators watched the play on New Year's Day, and the floor of green turf was literally framed in a mighty curving slope of human faces. No other sport produces exactly the sort of crowd which a great cricket match attracts. A race meeting is a sort of picnic, flavoured with tiny and intermittent doses of intense excitement – excitement packed into a few seconds – when a race is being actually run. A football match is two hours of mere tumult, but the crowd at a [Test] match like that which has just taken place will sit patiently from twelve o'clock till six for four days in succession. It is for the most part silent and grave-faced; the interest is too intense for frivolity! Every eddying turn and change in the game is watched with fixed vigilance, punctuated by short, sharp, and businesslike expressions of approval . . . The youths whose faces made a living frieze above the curving pickets could not perhaps give the kings of England, but they know with familiar knowledge the names of every Australian player, and the records of all the Australian Elevens.

These were unusual appeals. It was a common complaint of Australians in colonial times that their jubilant materialism had rendered them philistines, indifferent to civilising indulgences. Thus Richard Twopeny: 'It cannot be understood too thoroughly that Australia is before everything a money-making place.' Thus J. A. Froude: 'They [Australians] aim at little except what money will buy; and to make money and buy enjoyment with it is the be-all and end-all of their existence.' Thus Francis Adams: 'To speak of "culture" and "society" in Australia, in the sense that one does of the greater European capitals, would be like speaking of the snakes of Iceland. Disinterested study is unknown in a country where every one is still in haste to gamble, grab land, or create a business.' But in cricket, some were now arguing, lay a form of aesthetic and intellectual redemption – it was the stylish game, the cerebral game, where a subtle critic might discern worlds by a look.

•

This change also reflected the impress of English ideas, and the influence of English personalities. By the late Victorian age, the English regarded their summer game, diffused by mass transportation and promoted by the print media, with deep satisfaction. Test matches were less frequent but more meaningful; the County Championship was firmly established. Unlike rugby, cricket had not fissured along class and regional lines; unlike football, it retained an inviolable amateur primacy, the professional XIs having long disbanded. There was also a growing corpus of popular literature. Guides and collections abounded, the majority of them cheap, but some expensive and lavishly illustrated with lithographs, woodcuts and portrait photographs such as the first edition of *The Badminton Book of Cricket* (1888), tenth and most prestigious in the Duke of Beaufort's *Badminton Library of Sports and Pastimes*. Despite his deeming writing 'not a recreation I care for', Grace's *Cricket* (1891) weighed in at 500 pages, bulked up with advices such as 'do not go into the field with a cigarette or pipe in your mouth'; his old rival Billy Murdoch's *Cricket* (1894), part of 'The Oval' series, extended to a more modest ninety-five pages. Most splendid was Charles Alcock's *Famous Cricketers and Cricket Grounds* (1895), published in eighteen instalments by the *News of the World*: 272 full-page portraits of 110 amateurs, 105 professionals, sixteen Australians, nineteen teams, three administrators and two umpires, some at the wicket, some posed as if waiting to be painted while gazing wistfully into the middle distance. Grace took precedence, the ageless guru, beard still youthfully dark. The assemblage was also flecked with glamour, two figures standing out.

Resembling a young Byron was Oxford University's Charles Burgess Fry. By 1895, he was the epitome of the all-round Englishman, already heavy with academic and athletic laurels: a first-class classicist, a triple captain in cricket, football and athletics. He was playing amateur football for Corinthians, amateur rugby for Barbarians. He had equalled the world long-jump record. He had also leapt into the pages of *Vanity Fair* as a subject, 'Spy' stressing the noble profile of the 'dark blue hero', and into the pages of *Isis*, *Badminton* and *New Review* as a writer, where he espoused reliably high-minded opinions ('a strong leaven of amateurism is absolutely necessary for the good of the game').

The other, dark features accentuated by his billowing silk shirt, was the figure from whom Fry's name would become inseparable: Cambridge's Kumar Shri Ranjitsinhji. 'Kumar Shri,' Alcock added helpfully, 'it may be useful to add signifies Prince.' Up to a point: Ranji was actually a village farmer's son adopted as an heir by the Jam Saheb of a tiny Indian statelet, Nawanagar, as a precaution

Cricket magnifico: C. B. Fry.

against that potentate's inability to father an heir of his own. That status had been revoked with the arrival of an heir four years later, and Ranji had arrived in England uncertain of his future. Cricket had embraced him, and Fry too, when Ranji whisked him to the mid-wicket boundary in a game at Hove. 'To me,' Fry recalled, 'the stroke was a revelation of an entirely new technique only possible to a player with a quickness of eye, a nicety of poise, a surety of foot and a control of hand far superior to the best English practice.'

Fry was intrigued by technique. His own, he thought disapprovingly, was limited and mechanical, set into ruts by coaching at Repton from a master who 'offered a few general sarcasms' and a 'fat old professional' who knew 'just exactly nothing about the art of batsmanship'.

His serene majesty: Ranjitsinhji.

Fry had been raised, for example, to regard the leg side as positively vulgar: 'If one hit a ball in an unexpected direction to the on-side, intentionally or otherwise, one apologised to the bowler . . . The opposing captain never by any chance put a fieldsman there; he expected you to drive on the off-side like a gentleman, even if his bowlers presented stuff which . . . one could turn into long-hops to leg.' When they teamed up with Sussex the following season, Fry studied Ranji as intently as a naturalist alighting on a new species. Noting Ranji's supple wrists, prehensile fingers and quicksilver reflexes, he deemed himself inferior in every respect, and strove to improve.

The moment was ripe. Grace was approaching fifty, his star quietly waning. Ranji's 1896 debut for England, an unbeaten 154 against

Australia at Old Trafford, established him as cricket's coming man. 'Grace has nothing to teach him as a batsman,' pronounced the *Manchester Guardian*. 'And none of the men of renown of thirty years ago could have exhibited a more thorough mastery of every point of the game.' And although Ranji remained showily deferential to the cricketer he simply called 'The Champion', his style of batting clearly represented an exquisite advance. Slim, lithe and athletic, his backswing a twirl, his batspeed a flash, his leg glance a signature, he revealed batting possibilities never previously divined. The pace of a bowler could be turned against them by an artfully angled bat; the traditional concentration of fielders to the off side could accordingly be foiled. These were subversive, even revolutionary ideas: in a sense Ranji's difference was licensed by his exotic origins, even as misgivings about these were allayed by his overt imperialism. 'It has always been, and will always be, my endeavour in my humble way to bring about real brotherly love between the two nations,' he said at the Cambridge banquet in his honour at the end of that season. 'From the very beginning I have been connected with the English people, and have a great liking and enthusiasm for their high social and intellectual qualities.'

The Englishman to whom he most closely connected was Fry, who when they batted together was regarded as providing a kind of rational, occidental counterpart to Ranji's venturesome oriental speculations. In common they had improvidence – living effortlessly, as amateurs were expected to, was extraordinarily hard work. Ranji had at least an erratic stipend and a supply of oriental baubles and regalia; once a modest Oxford scholarship ceased, Fry had no income to speak of. Cricket, fortunately, was holding forth new possibilities. Ranji was invited to monetise his fame by producing a cricket guide; Fry, lumbered with a teaching job at Charterhouse that he cordially despised, was the perfect amanuensis. *The Jubilee*

Book of Cricket (1897), dedicated 'by her Gracious Permission, to Her Majesty the Queen-Empress', was a detailed *tour d'horizon* of the English game, and also a manifesto for amateur supremacy. Heaven forfend that cricket should emulate football's trend towards professional control: 'Facts show that the majority of elevens composed entirely or even principally of professionals do not succeed . . . There is no doubt that if the high standard of what may be called "sportsmanship" is to be maintained, amateurs must continue to form a fair proportion of the entire body of first-class cricketers.'

The *Jubilee Book* was an immediate craze, establishing Ranji and Fry as to cricket what Walter Pater and John Ruskin were to literature and art – setters of standards, arbiters of beauty. It traded first of all on Ranji's eastern singularity but was enriched by the ring of Fry's classical learning, in praise for The Champion ('He [Grace] turned the one-stringed instrument into a many-chorded lyre, and, in addition, he made his execution equal to his invention') and for 'the heroic' more generally ('I can imagine Agamemnon, Achilles and their peers not unbecomingly engaged in a cricket-match'). Helped by constant publicity from the collaborators' piling up 22 000 first-class runs at an average of more than 60, royalties over the next five years exceeded £7000.

In the year of the *Jubilee Book*, Ranji also paid his first visit to Australia as a member of Drewy Stoddart's English team, making 1154 runs in a dozen first-class matches, and proving so popular that colonial governments waived their taxes on coloured persons. 'The prospect of meeting the princely author of *The Jubilee Book of Cricket*, and of seeing a dark prince batting and bowling like any other cricketer, may . . . account for the vast number of ladies present at the intercolonial cricket match on the new grounds at Woolloongabba,' reported *The Queenslander*. 'All eyes were centred on Prince Ranjitsinhji; little boys followed him about, little girls longed to do so, too.' Watching crowds outside his office at *The Australasian* awaiting telegraphed updates of the cricket scores caused 'Woomera' to wonder at his fellow citizens' priorities:

> Why do they come with one accord,
> Together in one place?
> Why do they gaze upon that board,
> Whilst joy illumes each face?
> Why do the youngsters babble so?
> Why do the old men shout?
> Is federation carried? No;
> But Ranjitsinhji's out.

Colonial audiences were in thrall to Ranji's every stroke, almost his every word – for his reports in the *Australian Review of Reviews* were voluminous, sometimes provocative. One view that met widespread approval was of a junior batsman representing New South Wales against the tourists. 'He created a very favourable impression on me from the way he was shaping at the wickets,' reported Ranji. 'He seemed to be all there, and the confidence with which he played the bowling, although it was for a very short time, makes me firmly believe that he will be a very great batsman in this country, and at no very distant date. Indeed, I have seen very few beginners play the ball so well, and show the same excellent style.' This was a remarkably fulsome prophecy for a batsman who made 5 and 0 in the match. Yet Ranji was far from the first to so respond to Victor Trumper.

·

The story of the emergence of every sporting champion is an invitation to speculate on *that* moment when special qualities proclaimed themselves. In the case of Trumper, this is more than usually difficult. The great early scores are not really there. A chronicle of his junior career at Crown Street School and Carlton CC published in 2015 by the assiduous historian Alf James divulged no legacy of stupendous records. But what was unmistakably present, contemporaries insisted, was a 'look', first discerned by his father during their dawn practices: 'Every day I would note some degree of improvement in his skill with the bat and in his style of play, which needless to say was a source of much gratification for me.' The effect was enhanced by his willowy figure. He was 'short, spare, narrow-shouldered', inspiring nobody 'with the idea of athleticism in any direction'. He was the smallest boy in a line drawing of the Crown Street team; he was an incongruously slim youth in shorts among Carlton's hardy, hirsute men, who numbered among them the legendary Charles Bannerman, Test cricket's first century maker. But put a bat in his hands and he seemed to have intuited batting from first principles.

How and why did Trumper stand out so in the colonial cricket of the 1890s? The game was only just being regularised. Techniques remained homespun. Batting was unenterprising. Distances precluded more than half a dozen Sheffield Shield fixtures per season, each played to a finish, which made for long phases of austerity. If a bowler pursued the prevalent 'off theory' – a line wide of off stump to a packed off-side field – a batsman could in theory forswear strokes indefinitely. Trumper, it is clear, never played this way. Twenty years after events, a contemporary recalled Bannerman's early efforts to train Trumper to no avail: 'For a time all went well, but young Trumper, having mastered the defensive tactics of the game, began to do a little original work in the way of the most daring strokes.

In vain Bannerman called out, "Leave it alone, Vic; that wasn't a ball to go at.'" It seems to have been decided quite early, in fact, that Trumper's cricket called simply for encouragement. What he acquired rather than coaches were advocates.

With the thinness of club facilities in Sydney, the practice pitches at the Randwick end of the SCG were heavily used, and Trumper exposed to an ever wider circle. Tom Garrett, the captain of New South Wales in the Sheffield Shield, was a first important patron, ensuring that there was never question of the youngster's availability for cricket by bringing him into his public-service office, the registry of probates and curator of intestate estates. He also spread word by introducing Trumper to other knowledgeable judges as 'the most promising boy in the world', including the captain of the Test team, Jack Blackham. After studying a few strokes, Blackham apparently agreed. 'My word, Tom,' he said. 'Isn't he like Charles Bannerman?'

When the advent of electoral cricket in Sydney delivered Trumper to Paddington CC, he impressed himself on two other influential judges, then serving as that club's delegates to the NSWCA. One was John Corbett Davis, Sydney's encyclopedist of sports journalism, who at *The Referee* wrote cricket as 'Not Out' and rugby as 'The Cynic', and also published the *Australian Cricket Annual*. A trim, dapper man always attired in dark blue, affecting a bowler hat and *pince-nez*, he was a fixture at the SCG nets whomever was practising. Davis was instantly agog: 'Everyone soon knew the phenomenal boy who batted and bowled and fielded, without a word, without an atom of self-consciousness, as though he were born an international player . . . It was a tonic to spend ten minutes watching him play.' It was a tonic for which Davis never lost the taste – over the next fifty years, nobody would write more about Trumper.

The other Paddington clubmate was Monty Noble, an alumnus

of Crown Street four and a half years Trumper's senior. He was handsome, manly, a fine all-round cricketer, and a sportsman dense with moral fibre: 'Cricket teaches you to be clean. The exercise and environment promote clean thoughts. It discountenances boastfulness, shady tricks, and unhealthy practices, and sets high value on quiet demeanour, gentlemanly conduct and modesty.' One sight of Trumper was sufficient for Noble to come away convinced that he was beyond instruction: 'You could talk to him, and coach him. He would listen carefully, respect your advice and opinions and, leaving you, would forget all you had told him, play as he wanted to play.'

Here, then, was an early example of that faith, still common among athletes, fans, coaches, commentators, talent scouts and player agents alike, that the best are set apart, not only quantifiably, but somehow by how they look, or how they move, or how they prepare – a quality more compelling for being sometimes beyond description. In Trumper's case, the basis of this general conviction can never truly be known. There remained no practical means of capturing and representing 'action': the only surviving photograph of Garrett bowling shows him, aged seventy-nine, by then the very last survivor of the very first Test, delivering the first ball of a match at the SCG in February 1938 to mark the sesquicentenary of white settlement in Australia, wearing dark trousers, a waistcoat and the hat he removed not even at mealtimes. What does endure is the utmost confidence of the claims for him. In their inference that a player could be distinguished by 'style', they reflect a step in the game's aesthetic evolution, a ramifying of Ranji's impact on entranced crowds.

This 'style' of Trumper's, of course, had first to be seen. And seeing, as the nineteenth century ended, required being in the right place at the right time. In his late teens, Trumper began piling up runs for Paddington, especially at its home ground, Hampden

Mentor: the sole surviving 'action' photograph of Tom Garrett.

Park. For New South Wales, too, he compiled bulging double hundreds against two weak opponents, Tasmania and New Zealand, at the SCG. But in fourteen other first-class matches over four years, Trumper made only three half-centuries, and eighteen scores under 20. When boosters championed Trumper's inclusion in the Australian team to tour England in 1899, they encountered what Noble admitted was entirely legitimate scepticism:

> Most of the opposition to his inclusion came from Victoria and Adelaide, for, they said, and with plenty of justification: 'We have good young cricketers with records to prove their ability. And, in any case, we just haven't *seen* Trumper.' That was just what we had been telling them. They had not *seen* him; 'but once you do,' we declared, 'there will be no doubt in your minds.' [my italics]

During the first of three trial matches for the team, in Sydney, Davis cornered its manager, Major Ben Wardill, and submitted him to a passionate advocacy. One glimpse of Trumper, Davis insisted, was all it would take. He felt Wardill's scepticism harden: 'The Major was a most genial man, and I remember as we parted he remarked, "You Sydney people are married to Trumper. What has he done to justify it?" To that I answered, "Good-bye, Major. If you had him in Melbourne you'd soon understand it."' But Trumper did nothing out of the ordinary in the first two of the games, and went unnamed in the thirteen-member squad.

Deliverance came at the eleventh hour. In the last trial match, at Adelaide Oval, the day after which the team was due to depart, Trumper made 75. It must have been very good. It was no small thing for the Australians to welcome an additional member, for it diluted their profit pool. But the selectors reconvened and decided to expand their squad with a fourteenth member doubling as an assistant manager, on a fixed stipend rather than a full share. As Noble recalled it:

> Major Wardill, the manager, came to me towards the end of
> the third trial match in Adelaide and said: 'Do you want Victor
> Trumper to go to England?'
> 'Rather,' I replied.
> 'Well,' he said, 'you can go and tell him that he is selected.'
> I could hardly believe my ears.

But his colleagues, as implored, had believed their eyes.

•

This 1899 tour, the first in England to feature as many as five Tests, was unusually freighted with expectations. With the second Federation referendum scheduled to seek public endorsement while the team was away, Joe Darling's men were a kind of aspirational symbol: the pithy suffrage advocate Rose Scott, in fact, had derided the whole federalist campaign a 'glorified cricket match'. A few weeks prior to departure, the core of the team attended a Sydney Town Hall benefit concert for Trumper's erstwhile club teammate Charles Bannerman, where they were addressed by Edmund Barton and George Reid, long-time political rivals recently reconciled in the federal cause, who also doubled as vice-presidents of the NSWCA. It was the politicians being honoured by the presence of the cricketers rather than the other way around, thought a correspondent of *The Australasian*: 'The sight of those manly heroes in ordinary garb, sitting so modestly in the body of the hall, as if hardly conscious of the honour they were conferring upon the rulers of the coming Australian nation, was an intoxicating sight, calculated to turn the soberest head.' Reid and Barton duly laid on the blandishments:

> The remarks which followed were a charming blend of Federation and cricket. Mr. Reid implored the departing Eleven not to think, as was the custom 20 years ago, that all the people in the other colonies were rogues and swindlers. He said – with tears in his eyes – that he knew the Victorians were honest men; he had said so before, and he now said it again.
>
> Mr. Barton called on the Eleven to remain true to the nation which they would belong to on their return. If defeated they were to bear defeat nobly, and if victorious to bear it modestly. In any case, the hearts of Federated Australians would beat as one over

the issue. Mr. Barton concluded by hoping that in conduct, manners, and morals the Eleven would prove themselves worthy of the great Australian nation.

Joe Darling stepped forward, with his hand upon his heart, and declared that that should be their only endeavour.

The irony is that in the organising of their tour, Darling and his comrades were undertaking what was still a private speculation. Contemptuous of the colonial associations' pretensions to governing the game, they had partnered with the Melbourne CC, whose advance on the tour's proceeds enabled them again to visit England as cricket's best-compensated amateurs. This tolled the knell on the Australasian Cricket Council, shortly wound up with all of £10 in the bank, survived by a single idea that the players appropriated – a recent suggestion, by South Australian council member Mostyn Evan, that the Australian team settle on a uniform set of colours. Rather than adopt the red, white and blue Melbourne raiment favoured by the 1886 team, Darling's team had blazers tailored and boaters banded in Evan's idea of green and gold; they hoisted a green-and-gold standard from the flagpole above their London base, the Inns of Court Hotel in High Holborn; they presented a green-and-gold bouquet to the contralto Ada Crossley when she performed for them in Eastbourne. With an allusion to the tour's likely profitability, the *West Australian* reported: 'The colours of the Australian team are sage green with gold-braided edge. More gold than green about the wearers, though.'

Whether on proto-national or personal account, the team played like men on a mission, determined to outlast where they could not outplay. They won the only Test decided; the rest they dourly drew, thankful that Tests in England lasted only three days. All the while they kept a watchful eye on the bottom line. During the Test at Manchester, the local county secretary half-jokingly offered Ben Wardill £250 if Darling would declare the innings closed and make a game of it. 'Make it £500 and we'll consider it,' Darling replied. Still nursing a soupçon of irritation about the Australians' professional amateurism, the English lapsed occasionally into mockery. After Noble dawdled eight hours over 60 not out and 89 at Old Trafford, an anonymous donor posted him a leather medal inscribed in honour of his landmark of '1000 runs in 1000 years'. When Darling took three hours over 39 at Lord's, the crowd whistled 'We Won't Get Home Till Morning' and the 'Dead March' from *Saul*. As a mute protest against the visitors' professional amateurism, the *Daily Mail* and *Daily Telegraph* withheld the 'Mr' from before their names on scoreboards.

Complaints about Australian obstinacy, however, also had to be qualified by reference to Trumper. For Trumper took chances, lots of chances – sometimes too many. Equally, it emerged, he could scatter and demoralise an attack in half an hour. In the decisive Test at Lord's, Trumper made an unbeaten 135 after Australia had slipped to three for 59 in pursuit of 206. Five weeks later his undefeated triple century against Sussex at Hove – 380 minutes, thirty-six boundaries – was the first by an Australian in England. Only the sternly safe Noble and Darling scored more runs on the tour, and Noble took satisfaction in Darling's becoming a Trumperphile just as ardent. 'What do I think of him?' Darling responded when Noble asked him one day. 'I thought I could bat!'

It was not only for his batting that teammates promoted Trumper to a full profit share – the gesture was also a personal tribute. Eight months of more or less constant travel and play revealed natures reliably. 'The Kid', as comrades called him, became a team favourite – polite, kind, ingenuous. Jack Worrall: 'A more obliging or sweet-tempered boy never lived. Nothing was a trouble to him: everything was a pleasure, and he endeared himself to all of us by his disposition alone.' Frank Iredale: 'He had one of those natures which called to you, and in whose presence you felt it was good to live.' Clem Hill: 'Trumper was a most loving and unassuming champion ... No batsman ever played more for his side.' Hugh Trumble: 'What an inspiration he was!' Noble, always Noble, with tales to be endlessly repeated: 'Coming out of the London Coliseum one cold wet night he saw a boy shivering in a doorway selling music. Victor broke away from the rest of us, spoke to the lad, bought the whole of his stock-in-trade and sent the youngster home happy.' The captain? One of his eight sons he would christen Victor.

•

For his own part in 1899, Trumper bequeathed no memoirs, letters or diaries. The fragmentary actualities that survive do so almost by accident. Since the opening of the new Lord's pavilion a decade earlier, for example, occupants of the visitors' dressing-room on the second floor had taken to carving their initials in the balcony. The Australians joined in. There is a solemnly precise 'M. A. Noble', a cheerfully informal 'Eva' and 'Lightning' – the nicknames of Hugh Trumble and Charlie McLeod respectively. On the fourth brick from right in what is now a members' bar, one still finds the etched abbreviation 'VT99'. There is no pecking order here: nearest by his is the name 'E. Reeves', who made o not out and did not bowl representing London Playing Fields against MCC four years later.

A few weeks after Trumper's triple century, Darling recalled, he opened his bag and saw a bat he did not recognise. It was the bat, a 'W.G.G.' made in Birmingham by W. G. Grenville, that Trumper had used at Hove, slipped in surreptitiously with the polite dedication: 'To Joe Darling with/V. Trumper's compliments/300 not out v Sussex/29/7/99'. It reposes today behind glass at Melbourne's National Sports Museum, fresh as the day it was last used, reflecting the care and honour with which Australia's captain treated it, with a family rededication: 'To Victor/From/Father/25/3/35/Joe Darling'.

The outline of the mechanical means by which memories would be laid down was also just visible. In the museum of the Melbourne CC are more than 1000 photographs taken by Frank Laver, who shared a cabin with Trumper and Noble aboard the *Ormuz* at the outset of the journey – the beginning of a friendship that would profoundly influence Australian cricket history. About 100 photographs survive from this trip, when Laver was simply a twenty-nine-year-old all-rounder from Castlemaine and 'inveterate snapshotter'. In the swirl of figures, only the cricketers have remained identifiable, the names of their hosts, guests, friends and acquaintances lost to time.

Laver's teammates were actually not overfond of photography. During the 1897–98 series against England, Darling and Clem Hill had been persuaded to pose for photographs while not out overnight, then been dismissed soon after play resumed, nourishing a superstitious aversion to cameras. Laver, however, was one of their own number. He mixed easily, and his images as a result are disarmingly candid. Nobody mugs. There are no silly poses or uneasy rictuses. Instead players breakfast in their pyjamas, cavort in a swimming pool, skip rope and play deck games on board ship, savour beauty spots and historic sites. Trumper is captured as a tourist in Portsmouth, on the deck of HMS *Victory* near where Nelson fell – visiting colonial, loyal Britisher.

Darling's Australians even had a brush with the newest of all technologies. Playing out their tour after the Fifth Test, they stopped at Cheltenham to play Gloucestershire, lost the toss and filed onto the College Ground on a bright, sunny day in front of a full house. We know this because we can see it, in the oldest surviving film footage of Australian cricketers.

The emergent motion-picture industry had been stalking cricket a while. On their visit to Australia eighteen months earlier, the magnetic Ranji and his teammate Tom Hayward had played 'some imaginary cricket for the special benefit of the cinematograph' in the nets at the SCG, footage shown in England with the sound effect of bat on ball synchronised. Later that same year a camera was set up in the assistant secretary's garden at Lord's so that the teams in the Gentlemen v Players match, made special by the coincidence of W. G. Grace's fiftieth birthday, could sweep past in smoothly curved lines – vanishing from view, Grace ceremoniously doffs his cap.

The Australians exhibited a variety of responses to British Mutoscope's presence. Trumper even appears slightly nonplussed, walking on with Darling, burly Ernie Jones and diminutive Syd Gregory, pausing to exchange a word with his skipper, back turned shyly – seemingly a characteristic attitude. As Trumper moves out of frame, Darling pauses to look at the cameraman before stagily beckoning his men on. Iredale points cheerfully towards the device. Wardill appears for a last-minute conference. Before the twenty-five-second sequence ends, Laver, Noble, Jim Kelly and Hugh Trumble have also been glimpsed. It is raw footage, without intertitles, credits or, of course, soundtrack. It's unclear whether it was even shown.

Examining such artefacts today, one is struck mainly by the miracle of their survival, so much else having perished between times. Apparently there was distant film footage of the Fifth Test at The

Oval, including of Ranji and Darling – a 'marvellous reproduction of the principal events in connection with the test matches played in the old country' according to an *Advertiser* report of attractions at Adelaide's Theatre Royal at Christmas 1899. Along with ninety-five per cent of the moving picture film stock shot before the World War I, it is long gone. Yet such fragments of fragments as do endure testify to a deeply felt impulse to leave a trace, out of a sense of participating in deeds of lasting significance. They are the harbinger of a recording century to come, in which the necessary means and media would be increasingly within everyday reach, and Victor Trumper would provide one of cricket's most indelible motifs.

3

'THE FIRST BATSMAN
OF HIS TIME'

'I am not above suspicion in my use of words
when it comes to writing of Trumper.'
– NEVILLE CARDUS, *The Summer Game* (1929)

After the Fifth Test of Australia's series with England in 1902, London's *Daily Express* came up with a charitable notion. The *Express* would seek the bats of famous cricketers from home and abroad, England and Australia, and auction them for the benefit of England's Cricketers' Fund Friendly Society, a charity for broken-down old pros on hard times. Items were widely forthcoming, with an implement volunteered by W. G. Grace taking pride of place.

Except that the bat that everyone wanted belonged to the Australian Victor Trumper: at £42, it was sold at thrice the price of the next most valuable, that of the redoubtable Ranjitsinhji. Although Gilbert Jessop had just made a record-breaking seventy-five-minute century at The Oval, his bat fetched just £8.

Pride was at stake. A flurry of telegrams and telephone calls were necessary to flush out an anonymous, face-saving £50 bid for the bat of The Champion. Unaware of the backstage machinations, the Antipodean press thought the tribute sufficient. 'There is peculiar source of satisfaction for Australians in the fact that Trumper's piece of willow was so eagerly sought after,' reported the *Wellington Times*. 'It is a recognition of his magnificent prowess in the cricket field, and that he is held so near the purchasing power of Dr. Grace, the still famous hero of nearly half a century's cricket, speaks volumes.' Grace was, in any event, a hero of yesteryear. As *Cricket of Today* stated quite simply, 1902 had stamped Trumper 'as unquestionably the first batsman of his time'.

Even in Scotland: *Edinburgh Evening News*, 2 August 1902.

That made him, effectively, the first *Australian* of his time – the first to be the best in the world at *anything*. His only true rival was Dame Nellie Melba, appearing that summer in *Rigoletto* at Covent Garden. But Melba had spent sixteen years abroad – in a pursuit at which Australians measured themselves, Trumper went forth and returned as ascertainably the best. Australia, moreover, had been a nation barely a year and a half, and even then in name rather than substance: it had no anthem of its own, no coinage, official flag or heraldry; it deferred to British legislation and vice-regal authority; it had no power to declare war or peace, conclude treaties or be represented diplomatically. Trumper, then, also incarnated Australian possibilities.

In 1899, the tour's backdrop had been Federation; in 1902, it was coronation, counting in some respects for more, as Australians' imperial loyalty was rather stronger than their incipient nationalism. Henry Lawson urged his countrymen to combine the two in 'From the Bush' (1902): 'Hold up your heads in London/Tread firm in London streets!/We come from where the strong heart/Of all Australia beats.' Some took him up on the idea. Prominent expatriates formed London's Austral Club in the Bayswater drawing room of the *Daily Chronicle*'s chief foreign correspondent, Sydney-born Martin Donohue – members included actor Oscar Asche, composer George Clutsam, artists Arthur Streeton and John Longstaff, and novelists Rosa Praed and Mary Gaunt. They had much success to toast: the Australian rifle team won the Kolapore Cup at Bisley; Manly's Fred Lane swam 100 yards (91 metres) in less than a minute at Leicester. But none quickened hearts like the cricketers.

Trumper would change the way the English saw Australians too. Darling's team arrived with baggage, regarded as canny opponents but still not quite on social or cultural par. In *The Lighter Side of Cricket* (1901), Captain Philip Trevor, an army officer who wrote shrewdly as 'Dux' for *The Sportsman*, was politely scathing about Australian batsmen – 'difficult . . . to get out', but from whose 'masterly inactivity' the English had 'absolutely nothing to learn'. 'They have great patience and great stamina, and in their own country, when a match is played to a finish, even if it lasts for a fortnight, these qualities stand them in good stead,' wrote Trevor. 'But in England we manage matters differently, and the object of every sportsman is to inflict rather than avoid defeat.' Not to put too fine a point on it, Trevor thought the Australians, tenacity and defiance rooted in gate-money mindedness, had generally been bad for the game: 'The Australians have reduced to a fine art the practice of making the English three-day match last its full three days, and in doing so they have dealt a severe blow to the best interests of English cricket.'

Interestingly, Trevor's opinions were not based on his actually having seen the Australians play in 1899 – he had been on duty in South Africa. They reflected, rather, opinion stubbornly hard to shift. Which makes what followed all the more remarkable – here would be a first rehearsal of the idea, now deeply rooted in both countries, that Australian cricketers are innately aggressive, and set a tempo for the English to follow. In 1902, then, Victor Trumper was not simply playing cricket for his country; he was helping to invent it.

•

Trumper and 1902 elide in cricket history in the same way as Grace and 1895, Denis Compton and 1947, Viv Richards and 1976, Ian Botham and 1981 – great players in their purest avatars. Yet Trumper's golden summer also differs from these. It can be measured not just by the excellence of Trumper, but by the mediocrity

of others. *Wisden*'s first-class averages present the case straightforwardly: in 1902 just six batsmen made 1000 runs at an average in
excess of 40, while twenty-seven bowlers took at least fifty wickets at less than 20. From this Trumper's record stands out as if in
copperplate: 2570 first-class runs with eleven hundreds, both records
by a visitor, at an average of 48.49 uninflated by a single not out.
Only Arthur Shrewsbury, the indefatigable Nottinghamshire professional, slightly headed Trumper in the averages, with half as many
runs and seven not-outs; only Bobby Abel, Surrey's eternal favourite, came near him for runs, with 2229 in eleven more innings.

The reason was rain, not so much the amount, actually slightly
below average, as the sheer frequency. Rainy days in May, as the
Australians arrived, were a third greater than usual. June, July and
August were nearly as bad. When it wasn't raining, it looked about
to rain, the worst possible conditions for batting: lots of disrup-
tions, few outright washouts. On the era's uncovered pitches, the
Australians endured some grim days: England bowled them out for
36 at Edgbaston, Yorkshire for 23 at Bramall Lane. But all the while,
the normally staid *Wisden* observed, Trumper seemed to be *playing
another game*:

> Trumper stood alone among the batsmen of the season, not only
> far surpassing his own colleagues, but also putting into the shade
> everyone who played for England ... Having regards to its many
> wet days and soft wickets, it is safe to say that no-one – not even
> Ranjitsinhji – has been at once so brilliant and so consistent since
> W. G. Grace was at his best. Trumper seemed independent of the
> varying conditions, being able to play just as dazzling a game after
> a night's rain as when the wickets were hard and true. All bowling
> came alike to him and on many occasions, notably in the Test

matches at Sheffield and Manchester and the first of the two games
with MCC at Lord's, he reduced our best bowlers for the time
being to the level of the village green.

The year 1902 was on its way to becoming the gateway myth of the
Trumper legend, with the advantage of being anchored in reality – in
conditions as alien to him as could be, a twenty-four-year-old from
Sydney established himself as batting's foremost exponent. Yet this
also raises fundamental questions. *How* did Trumper bat? What
did he *look like*? He was clearly an improved version of the gifted
stripling who had visited three years earlier, but in what respects
had he advanced? And these questions are disconcertingly difficult
to answer. 'Pages might be written about Trumper's batting without exhausting the subject,' *Wisden* claimed – and they were. But
to revisit the contemporaneous reportage of the tour is to be disappointed. Cricket was still at the stage where it was reported rather
than genuinely written; newspaper journalism was about the con-
veyance of information rather than of impression. To search for
images from 1902 is likewise to leave dismayed. There was not even
Frank Laver on this tour to capture the Australians backstage, as
it were. Still as far off as ever, action remained largely the domain
of newspaper sketchers – versatile men like Frank Gillett, Ernest
Prater and S. T. Dadd who might be asked for a line drawing of a
regal occasion one day, to recreate the drama of a shipwreck the next.
The *Daily Graphic*, for example, had Gillett at each day of the summer's big games, and his facile pen provided the nearest thing to a
surviving visual record of Trumper's startling century in the first session of the Fourth Test at Old Trafford.

A few tentative conclusions can be drawn. Trumper was a
rapid scorer – his runs per minute, then the standard measure, are

TRUMPER AND DUFF DO WHAT THEY LIKE FOR THE FIRST HOUR AND A QUARTER

R.A.DUFF

A NEAR THING FOR TRUMPER

FRED TATE

LILLEY CATCHES DUFF

BRAUND'S SAD MISTAKE

FRANK GILLETT. MANCHESTER.

Action penmanship: Day one at Old Trafford.

appreciably faster than any other Australian's. Trumper was a versatile strokemaker – no writer stresses a particular strength or signature stroke. His batting was unconstrained by circumstance, such as state of game, quality of bowling, placement of field, and he seems to have been loath to play defensively *at all*. 'It is necessary for most batsmen to play the game for a few overs before unfolding their strokes,' wrote Noble. 'Not so with Victor.' And these factors challenged the stereotypes. England, where the flower of cricket was amateur, freed from the dull cares of earning a living, had always been the home of pedigree batsmanship; lacking gentlemanly polish and refinement, Australia had conventionally been seen as the forge of a grim cricket efficiency. Yet Trumper at the crease did not suggest preoccupation with the gate money of the day, or his share of spoils at tour's end. Writing in *The Strand* magazine in 1902, C. B. Fry, cricket's *arbiter elegantiae*, struggled to incorporate Trumper's nationality into an appreciation: 'Trumper appears to unite in his person the utilitarian virtues of Australia with the artistic virtues of the old country; or, perhaps, it is fair to say he is more like a very good English batsman than a very good Australian.' By batting like the very carefree amateurs that Australians had always purported to be, and which a certain English school had held they were not, he became a freak of cricket nature.

One of the most perceptive appreciations of Trumper, composed with the zeal of the convert, came from the pen of the aforementioned Trevor, who described how difficult it was 'to follow exactly what he [Trumper] was doing with his bat':

> I will try to substantiate that statement at the risk of being prosaic. Extend the bowling-crease to the boundary on both sides of the ground; then bowl to Trumper an ordinary, medium-paced, good-length ball. Trumper could hit that ball to any spot on the boundary in front of that extended white line . . . You would watch these successful strokes, and you could not tell accurately as the bat came onto the ball the exact direction in which the batsman intended the ball to go. Trumper knew it himself almost to the 'minute of the degree'. His knowledge, indeed, of batting angles was too exact for the ordinary eye to follow.

I am still blessed with good ordinary eyesight. I can read figures and names on hoardings in a way that ought to make advertisers feel that they have not spent their money in vain. The bull's eye at Bisley 1000 yards [914 metres] away is to me a clear and finished piece of work, though the sights of my rifle would now have to be adjusted with the aid of field glasses.

But I was made to stop swaggering about my long-distance sight when Trumper put his bat to the ball. I used to find myself guessing and I nearly always guessed wrong. I predicted a square cut as the ball flashed through the air, and then the ball would go in the air in front of cover-point. I was worse fogged by the strokes to the 'on' and hopelessly baffled by the square leg hits . . . As I watched, I got desperately anxious to analyse the inner workings of the batsman's mind, or the thing it was that was causing the man's mood.

Guessing; fogged; hopelessly baffled: in Trumper's hands, batting has become a mystery, inscrutable even to a purported expert, 'too exact for the ordinary eye to follow'. It is not a passage that Grace could have inspired, or really any contemporary bar Ranjitsinhji – admiration tinged with wonder and psychological speculation. It is a step beyond even the insistences of Noble and Davis, that to see Trumper was sufficient to grasp his greatness. The more Trevor sees, the less he feels he understands. Unable to make sense of the method, he falls back on contemplation of the man, in whom there must be something, in his 'mind' or in his 'mood', to make him play in such a way.

•

Was there? Funnily enough, for once in the annals of this enigmatic cricketer, there *is* an accompanying, corroborative record – personal, contemporaneous, utterly authentic, and read in its life span by only a handful of people. Trumper's diary of the 1902 tour, a tiny volume bound in limp black morocco, is now kept in conditions of exacting hygiene at the Melbourne Cricket Club Museum. To read it, one must visit a cold underground room at the MCG where a gloved museum staff member turns the pages.

Handed down the generations of the Trumper family, it was first publicised by Ashley Mallett, who drew on it for his *Trumper* (1985), describing it as a cricket find equivalent to 'stumbling on the Lost City of Atlantis'. In fact, the diarist was almost comically succinct about his experiences. After the first day's training in the Nursery at Lord's, for example, the Australians attended the biblical epic *Ben-Hur*, a Drury Lane replica of the Broadway production that ran twenty-one years. The famous chariot race involved 30 tonnes of horseflesh and vehicles: the horses galloped on treadmills and the chariot wheels were turned by electric rubber rollers while a cyclo-rama revolved in the opposite direction and fans swirled clouds of dust. The production was also noted for its 'bright-haired and buxom damsels' wearing 'leopard-skin bodices' including gorgeous, pouting Nora Kerin as Esther. Trumper: 'Thursday 1 May: Practice all day. Went to Ben-Hur at night – Drury Lane.'

For the coronation, the cricketers had a premium vantage: out of several invitations, Wardill accepted one from eighty-eight-year-old Baroness Burdett-Coutts, whom the new monarch regarded as 'the most remarkable woman in the kingdom' after a lifetime applying her private banking fortune to charitable works in the East End. She and the Australians now leaned out the same windows in Piccadilly from which the baroness had watched Victoria's corona-tion in 1838; afterwards she presented each player with a Coronation Medal, which caused excitement in Australia. 'Why should not the

Baroness Burdett-Coutts adopt Vic Trumper?' asked a columnist in *The Arrow*. Trumper: 'Saturday 9 August: Coronation. Baroness Burdett-Coutts. Good view of show. Disappointed. Had lunch there. Saw decorations. Not nearly as good as ours' (presumably a patriotic reference to the 8-kilometre parade to the Federation Pavilion in Centennial Park for the proclamation of the Commonwealth of Australia on 1 January 1901).

Yet there *is* a glint of a man here – and, perhaps surprisingly, it is of a certain steel. Trumper enumerates his likes and dislikes briefly but frankly. Rain, mentioned on half the first fifty days, is a curse ('Nothing but rain'; 'More rain. Miserable'; 'Spent rather miserable day'; 'Rained all day . . . played cards'). Theatre and music hall were tersely reviewed ('Good show'; 'Not bad'; 'Passable'; 'Horrible'; 'Rotten'). There is excitement, especially after Test victories at Bramall Lane ('Hurras. Won match. Glorious. All drunk. Left for Birmingham. Arrived 12 p.m.') and Old Trafford ('Glorious time', then the next day 'all have sore heads'). There is also boredom and weariness ('Very tired'; 'All dog tired'; 'Too tired to go out'; 'Dodged about and done nothing'; 'Glad Tests all over').

Of his own performances, Trumper is typically economical. What did he make of his triumph at Old Trafford? 'Thursday 24 July: Wet wicket. Fourth Test. Won toss, made 299. Self 104. RAD 50. 1st W 135. England 5 for 70. Tate 1st Test. Fire G Peak and Coy.'[*] But he cares all right. That terse 'Self 104' recalls Donald Bradman's matter-of-fact diary entry after the first day of the Headingley Test twenty-eight years later, when he emulated Trumper in scor-

---

[*] 'RAD' was Reg Duff, whose opening partnership with Trumper was worth 135 in seventy-eight minutes; 'Tate' was Fred Tate, playing his only Test, at the end of which he would be bowled to give Australia a three-run victory; 'G Peak' was the name of a warehouse next to the Australians' Grand Hotel lodgings that went up in smoke overnight, rather interrupting their preparations.

ing a hundred before lunch, then expanded it into a triple hundred: 'Archie [Jackson] out for 1. I followed and at stumps was 309 not out, breaking the previous highest score in Anglo-Australian Tests. Reached my 2000 runs for the season. To hotel in evening for dinner and wrote letters, thence to bed.' Nor does the comparison with Bradman end there: Trumper emerges as similarly achievement-driven. For much of the 1902 season, he and the Englishman Abel were neck and neck in the aggregates: Abel was first to 1000, Trumper first to 2000. Trumper was aware of Abel's progress, annoyed that he 'missed [the] bus' when he got out for 92 in a high-scoring game against Gloucestershire, vexed to follow 105 with 86 against MCC because he 'wanted double century', and not entirely displeased when Monty Noble against Sussex fell 17 runs short of surpassing the score he had made at the same venue three years earlier ('MAN out for 284 . . . Still have record'). That absorption of Trumper into an anglicised amateur tradition, then, was very much in beholders' eyes; at least at this stage, he was a young man of ambition, striving to make his name.

In general, of course, the diary is valued for what it is rather than what it contains – such is the nature of the trade in historic relics. When it was auctioned at Christie's in Melbourne in August 1997, the diary attracted several aggressive bidders, including Steve Waugh, then on tour in England. The successful purchaser was also from the far side of the world, the prodigious English collector John McKenzie outlaying nearly $30 000. But before McKenzie could secure his investment, the Australian Ministry for the Arts placed the diary on the Movable Cultural Heritage Prohibited Exports Register, which exists for 'objects of exceptional cultural importance, whose export would significantly diminish Australia's cultural heritage' – on par with the shoulder guard from Ned Kelly's armour, the

'King of the West' gold nugget, and a cat-o'-nine-tails once wielded by the master of the brig *Supply*. Which is curiously fitting: because among many things on which the diary provides no information is how close Trumper came in 1902 to being culturally exported himself.

•

Australia's tour was in the black by early July 1902 – that is, the team had repaid its £900 advance from the Melbourne CC, and was busily building the bank balance it would distribute among its members. With news of the cessation of hostilities in the Boer War, the team also felt able to entertain an invitation to play three Tests in South Africa on the way home, at a guaranteed profit of £2000. Other possibilities were also opening. After the game against Sussex finished at Hove on 2 August, Trumper lingered on his own for a spell at Markwell's Royal Hotel in Brighton amid a sibilance of whispers that he was being courted by various English counties, notably Lancashire and Surrey – which would entail him serving a period of residential qualification before playing, and essentially require him to give Test cricket up. The weekly magazine *Cricket* aggregated the rumours comprehensively, and whimsically:

    a. That Trumper has had two offers, each worth £350 a year, on condition that he will qualify for a certain county;

    b. that he intends to return to Australia, where his income is £150 a year derived from an office under Government;

    c. that he will play in 1904 for Surrey;

    d. that he will qualify for Lancashire, for which he will play in 1904;

e. that he will qualify as a professional; that he will certainly remain an amateur; and that no offers whatever have been made to him.

Not that you would sense any of the foregoing from the cheerfully mundane tone of Trumper's diary around this time:

> Sunday 3 August: Went down to pier and heard band on promenade. Windy and cold.
>
> Monday 4 August: Monday, pier. Heard band, Devil's Dyke in afternoon [an earthwork on the South Downs, a noted beauty spot]. On pier at night.
>
> Tuesday 5 August: Swim. Heard band. Bus ride to Chalk Cliffs of Old England. Band 11.30, 3.30, 7.45.
>
> Wednesday 6 August: Left for Southampton. Arrived 5.10. Saw King's train leaving Portsmouth. Good hotel. New and smells of paint. Team arrived 9 p.m. Letters at G sent for.

Only the very last line hints at other than innocent amusements. Yet the very next morning, a number of articles appeared bruiting Trumper's recruitment by a county club – the favourite seemed to be Surrey, with the bait of an assistant secretaryship. By the press the idea was received unenthusiastically, albeit not because Trumper might be lost to Australia, but because he might play in England *as an amateur* – worse, one of those amateurs paid by their county as an official. The arguments were various. London's *Daily Telegraph* exclaimed that such positions should be the prerogative of *Englishmen*: 'It is one thing for a county to find a position for one of its own men who, without some assistance, could not afford to give up the summer months to first-class cricket, but quite another to bid high for the services of a cricketer quite unconnected with the county because he happens at the moment to be the best bat in the world.' Sheffield's *Daily Telegraph* complained that such positions were *professional* in all but name: 'Surely the MCC will step in and with so clear a case before it will declare that any man who takes over what is virtually an honorary post as the reward of his qualifying must play as a professional or not at all. Shoddy amateurism has begun to stink in this country very much, and there is no wish to increase it in any way. Trumper would do well for the sake of his popularity were he to promptly give the lie to the present rumour.' The gossipy Home Gordon in *The Sportsman*, who reported 'good reason for thinking that the great Australian cricketer will in 1904 appear for Surrey', thought that Trumper would be welcome, but only as a professional – not, ahem, that there was anything wrong in that:

> I am expressing the opinion of more than one prominent
> amateur when I say it is believed he is too good a sportsman to
> be ashamed of owning he is earning a living as a cricketer, and
> to that honourable calling he will give new lustre. To add here
> any panegyric on his ability would be superfluous, but it may be
> mentioned that he is personally a real good fellow, full of generous
> enthusiasm, keenness and a healthy manliness which wins for him
> lots of friends.

Trumper made a scratchy 18 that morning and diarised that he felt 'horribly out of form'. His failure was regarded by others as signifying an uneasy mind. In addition to approaches from counties, he was said to be under offer from Joe Darling for South Australia and Ben Wardill for Victoria. Reports grew openly contradictory. The *Manchester Courier* reported Trumper himself as confirming the probability 'that he would accept one of the offers made to him', there being 'no reason why he should not better his position'. The *Nottingham Evening Post* heard the opposite, adapting Gilbert and Sullivan: 'In spite of all temptations/To belong to other nations/ He remains an – Australian (at least so one hears).' Cartoonist 'Rip' caricatured Trumper scorning moneybags dangling from extended hands.

Gold rush: Trumper declines.

In fact, Trumper was still appraising his options, and quite coolly. This we know from a letter in his fluent, round hand in the archives of the Worcestershire County Cricket Club. Dated the first evening of the Fifth Test at The Oval, it was composed in reply to inquiries about his services by that county's hard-working secretary, Paul Foley. Worcestershire was a recent but ambitious addition to the County Championship. Foley, the scion of ironmasters from Stourbridge, had hauled the club up from among the minor counties by ceaseless endeavours, transforming three sheep pastures in

the shadow of Worcester Cathedral into one of England's most picturesque grounds: Trumper had diarised of Worcester as a 'pleasant
little city' and of a 'beautiful drive' to nearby Malvern. Foley aimed
high: three years earlier he had courted Monty Noble, on the basis
of a rumour of the Australian settling in England. Trumper was now
disarmingly receptive.

> My Dear Mr Foley,
> I am much obliged to you for your courteous letter. I have not
> decided yet whether I shall stay here or not. Certainly not as a
> professional with all respects to Home Gordon, who has written
> us down on all occasions. Should I remain I would just as soon play
> for your county as any as not only do I like the team both amateur
> and pro's[sic] but also the town & surrounding district. You have
> the nucleus of a very good side.

Trumper was dismissive of the reports in circulation: 'The papers
are having a lot to say about myself & the strange part of it is that
not one of the writers came to me for any information whatsoever &
the general public know all about the different articles just as soon
as I do.' He was further approving of a sweetener that Foley appears
to have offered, probably an assistant secretaryship: 'I am pleased
that if I should accept the position I will have something to do in
the winter for on no account should I be contented loafing about.'
There was, Trumper warned, a potential delay to the beginning of
any qualifying residence: 'Our Articles of Agreement state that all
the team must go where the majority decide so that should we go to
S.Africa or play in Australia on our return I would have to go with
them. Our articles are very stiff[;] for instance if we turn up late at a
match we are fined £5 for the first offence & stand a chance of being

sent home for the second.' Nonetheless, Trumper solicited specifics: 'Could you make me a definite offer with a guarantee for a certain number of years & also let me know what qualifications it would be necessary for me to put in.'

It is a friendly, frank, intelligent letter, socially aware in its dismissal of professionalism, culturally comfortable with the idea of his services being pursued. The little asperity about garrulous Gordon and the knowing jest about the press strike a note of confidentiality, but the words are confident, assured – the same spirit, one presumes, that Trumper took into his next such encounter, with Allen Taylor.*

Taylor was a self-made hardwood timber magnate who had just ended five years as lord mayor of Annandale and would twice serve as lord mayor of Sydney – part of his legacy, perpetuated in the square bearing his name, would be clearing Trumper's Darlinghurst of its worst slums. A visitor to England that summer, Taylor was evidently disquieted by what he was reading. On 14 August, Sydney's *Evening News* reported that Taylor had cabled his business partner good news: 'Glad to say, private offer to Trumper to come back and remain in Sydney, has been accepted to-day.' However, 'no details' could be given, and they never were. On returning to Australia, both parties briefly acknowledged an agreement. Taylor divulged that 'in about another hour' his offer 'might have been too late'; Trumper stated that rather than sign a contract he had accepted his benefactor's 'word as a gentleman'; *Wisden*'s editor, Sydney Pardon, expressed satisfaction that the initiative had fallen through, as it 'would have

---

* It was not the end of Trumper's involvement with Worcestershire, for he recommended to the county Toowoomba-born Jack Cuffe, a left-arm medium-pacer who had played once for NSW. After a two-year residency, Cuffe, playing as a professional, served worthily as the county's first overseas player, taking 738 wickets and making 7476 runs over a decade. After the war, as for many an ex-pro, the pickings were slimmer. Shortly after taking a position as coach of Repton School, C. B. Fry's alma mater, Cuffe drowned himself in the River Trent, aged fifty.

been a paltry and unworthy thing to deprive Australia, by means of a money bribe, of her finest batsman'. It was when Trumper returned to Australia that he opened his first sporting-goods store – with, it's possible, financial support from Taylor. But the biographical trails hereabouts are cold and dead: the diary peters out altogether at this very point, with more than a month of the tour to go.

Why did Trumper shrink from playing county cricket? Was it a reluctance to leave Australia? Was it an aversion to playing openly as a professional, when Australians had scrabbled so hard for social parity? The peace in England was clearly uneasy. While Trumper's batting had delighted and enchanted, there remained clear reservations about his levitating above his station. The pragmatism of Trumper's correspondence with Foley suggests that when it came to it, the simplest explanation is best: he accepted what was, for all sorts of reasons, a better offer, from which he and his chroniclers then turned away, almost by mutual agreement, gentlemen not discussing other gentlemen's financial affairs. And into the spaces left by unsaid words were deposited the sentiments, assertions and conclusions of others.

•

Much of what has been handed down about Trumper at this peak of his career is actually not contemporaneous at all: it was set down in the tranquillity of later memoirs and musings, partly by participants, but most importantly by one eyewitness, who made it a motif in his emergence as cricket's most acclaimed writer.

Neville Cardus's writing about Trumper was of a special intensity: the Australian was, he said, 'first of my heroes – first in point of time, first in affections for all time'. He saw Trumper, he admitted, 'only three or four times', but never tired of describing him, and in a very particular way, for not a word did he compose while his hero was alive. In the summer of 1902, Cardus was fourteen, just growing aware of the music, art and literature that would shape his critical sensibilities and baroque prose; not for another seventeen years would he become 'Cricketer' of the *Manchester Guardian*, by which time Trumper was dead. Cardus was fated, then, always to write about Trumper in the nostalgic tense – and in so doing, to look back on his unformed self:

> As I look back on my boyhood and try to think of all the formative influences that made me a man of some awareness to the things of the imagination, I realise the power of three strangely diverse forces, each evocative of colour and romance – the music of Wagner, Turner's canvas 'The Fighting Temeraire', and Victor Trumper. I do not hesitate, at this high prime of my life, to write the name of Victor Trumper along with those two immortals of a higher plane of artistic activity. Victor was as much an artist in cricket, as much an inspiration to an impressionable urchin of Manchester, as any Turner or Wagner. It doesn't matter, really, in what direction or calling the spirit of genius takes its flights; I would no more forget Trumper's batsmanship than I would forget gorgeous sunsets, cloud-capped mountains, sonorous cadences of verse and symphony, or the full bloom of the rose.

Cardus's origins are as obscure as those of his Australian hero: he barely knew his mother, a prostitute; he never knew his father, her client; he was raised first by grandparents, then by a colourful aunt, in a slum quarter of Manchester. How Cardus came to see Trumper at the Old Trafford Test on 24 July he explained over and over with variations, starting with *The Summer Game* (1929). In *Good Days* (1934), he 'played truant from school to see it'. In *Australian Summer* (1937), he colourfully described obtaining his sixpence for the turnstile by selling 'a volume of Coleridge's poems' from his grandfather's library: 'I remember that when I went to sell the volume, feeling a criminal, I noticed one of the poems was called "Remorse"; to this day I cannot understand how the poems got into my grandfather's library, which began with the Bible and ended with the *Sporting Chronicle Handicap Book*.' In *Autobiography* (1947), he still more colourfully recalled his cricket watching being enabled by his aunt winning a breach-of-promise suit against Manchester's Turkish consul.

Given his admitted tendency to write what was 'true to character' rather than true to fact, whether Cardus was at Old Trafford *at all* may be open to some doubt. But that day at Old Trafford was particularly appealing to Cardus for pitting two of his great favourites against one another. England's captain was the superbly haughty Archie MacLaren, one of those permanently impecunious English amateurs with champagne tastes on a beer budget. Balzac, Carlyle, Wagner, Sir Henry Irving, Sir Thomas Beecham: Cardus would invoke them all in his various descriptions of MacLaren, who 'lighted a fire in me never to go out'. A favourite story, repeated at intervals with the usual variations, involved a dinner, circa the 1920s, at which Cardus and other guests chaffed MacLaren about being too defensive on the first morning at Old Trafford those many years before:

> We challenged MacLaren: 'Why Archie, you must have slipped a bit when you allowed Trumper to win the 1902 rubber on a turf nearly waterlogged in the outfield. Did you place too many men deep, and allow Victor to pick up the runs through the gaps near the wicket?'

MacLaren, who adored an argument, rose to the bait; he took lumps of sugar out of the basin and set them all over the table, saying 'Gaps be damned! Good God, I knew my man – Victor had half a dozen strokes for the same kind of ball. I exploited the inner ring and outer ring – a man here, a man there, and another man covering him.' (He banged the lumps of sugar down one by one, punctuating his luminous discourse.) 'I told my bowlers to pitch on the short side to the off; I set my heart and brain on every detail of our policy. Well, in the third over of the morning, Victor hit two balls straight into the practice ground, high over the screen, behind the bowler. I couldn't very well have had a man fielding in the practice ground, now could I?'

To Cardus, Trumper was a 'comet that flashed into my ken': 'Trumper, when I was young, made me fall in love with Australia. When I was 14 or 15, my chances of getting to Australia seemed as remote as my chance of becoming Lord Chancellor.' When this changed, and Cardus became England's most feted cricket writer, that first sight took on the quality of an omen, and of Trumper he remained ever protective. By the time Cardus commenced writing his own life story, the attachment was the keener for him actually being in Trumper's old neighbourhood: the slum boy, the prostitute's son, was sojourning in Kings Cross as music critic for the *Sydney Morning Herald* and host of the ABC's Sunday night 'The Enjoyment of Music', his bolthole from the privations of World War II. Visiting places that were part of the Trumper story was for Cardus like touring his own imagination: 'I never trod the grass of Paddington Oval without a warming of the heart.' By then, as we shall see, Cardus had elevated the cricket of his youth to a glorious and unsullied idyll, with Trumper its supreme stylist.

Perhaps it was also the identification of one young man who had transcended his unpromising circumstances by virtue of a special flair with another. 'He could not, had he tried, have played a plebeian stroke,' thought Cardus of Trumper – just as Cardus had hoisted himself by the bootstraps of his prose. 'I once called Neville the "Victor Trumper of cricket writing",' recalled his friend Jack Fingleton. 'He thanked me for the compliment.'

•

Victor Trumper and 1902: so inseparable, so ungraspable, so historic, so mythic. And with a last set of relics we have yet to grapple. Two years after events, two photographs of Trumper in action *were* published, small and indistinct, in *C. B. Fry's Magazine*. You would not know they were of Trumper were it not for their captions, so minuscule does his figure appear from the camera's vantage on the pavilion balcony at The Oval on 11 August, the first day of the Fifth Test. In one, Trumper looks to be going back and across; in the other, he seems to have hit over the top of the ball. Like Trumper's diary, they are of interest primarily because of their association with him; unlike Trumper's diary, they portended a revolution.

4

'THE CHAMPION THEORIST'

> 'I don't think you can really say you have seen something
> until you have taken a photograph of it, which reveals all the details
> you would not otherwise have noticed – and which in most
> cases cannot even be seen.'
> – EMILE ZOLA (1901)

In E. W. Hornung's short story 'Gentlemen and Players' (1899), the cricketing amateur cracksman A. J. Raffles and his offsider Bunny Manders are guests at a Dorset country house. The weekend centres on games of cricket organised by their host Lord Amersteth; Raffles and Bunny have eyes only for the priceless sapphire adorning Lady Melrose. Nervous and edgy, Bunny finds himself after dinner in wearisome company:

Lastly in the billiard room they had a great and lengthy pool table, while I sat aloof and chafed more than ever in the company of a very serious Scotchman, who had arrived since dinner, and who would talk of nothing but the recent improvements in instantaneous photography. He had not come to play in the matches (he told me), but to obtain for Lord Amersteth such a series of cricket photographs as had never been taken before; whether as an amateur or a professional photographer I was unable to determine. I remember, however, seeking distraction in little bursts of resolute attention to the conversation of this bore. And so at last the long ordeal ended; glasses were emptied, men said goodnight and I followed Raffles to his room.

The locquacious photographer proves to be a detective in disguise. Inspector Mackenzie of the Yard is on the trail of *another* thief with designs on the sapphire. The character's real-life inspiration is unknown: Hornung was himself much taken with photography, later blending it into a murder mystery, *The Camera Fiend* (1911). But it's tempting to imagine his having had an early encounter with George Beldam.

Descended from Huguenots who had crossed the Channel from Picardy in the seventeenth century, Beldam was born 1 May 1868. His father, Asplan, was a maritime designer in a Thames shipyard, and shortly established his own engineering company to address a very particular problem. Most boilers were then poorly insulated, and unable to operate at more than 30–40 pounds per square inch. In May 1876, Asplan patented a form of 'packing', combining canvas, felt and folded metal interleaved with grease, that increased boiler pressure three and four times. He advertised his Beldam Packing & Rubber Company with the SS *Stirling Castle*, which won the Great Tea Races of 1882 and 1883, steaming from

'He must know how it is done': George Beldam.

China while bulging with tea in record times. By then, Asplan and wife Elizabeth were raising two sons and two daughters in a large house and grounds near Brentford, Acton Lodge. George, the oldest, went to study engineering at Cambridge, where he attended St Peter's and captained Peterhouse at cricket, football and tennis before joining the family firm.

By class and inclination, then, Beldam was an amateur. He played amateur cricket for Luton CC, amateur football for Brentford FC, amateur golf at Walton Heath and Royal Mid-Surrey golf clubs. He would remain all his life a serial enthusiast for pastimes, from fly fishing to watercolour art, his canvases exhibiting a partiality to moody landscapes and majestic windjammers – ironically of the kind his company was helping to render obsolete. Then there was photography.

Photography was then making a comeback as an amateur pursuit, thanks to the invention of the easy-to-use dry gelatine plate and pre-mixed developing chemicals. The new amateur photographers were unlike the pioneers of old; their bible, *Amateur Photographer*, aimed at hobbyists, dispensing technical advice at a beginner's level. But the magazine also became a home for debates around amateurism itself, rather like those in cricket. 'The distinction between an Amateur and Professional is, the latter lives by his art, and the former does not,' pronounced the editor, with a Marylebone-like qualification. 'The payment of expenses is a side question.' Photography should be approached, another correspondent thought, with a sporting spirit: 'Well to us amateurs, photography is but a relaxation – a scientific Sport, but a Sport all the same.' He might well have been speaking for Beldam.

These new amateurs tugged photography in unforeseen directions. In December 1890, one enthusiast, civil servant George Davison, exhibited his famous 'The Onion Field': a misty, pastoral vision captured through a pinhole in a piece of sheet metal rather than with a conventional lens, then printed on rough paper so that it resembled an impressionist painting. Its effect was galvanising: Davison would lead a secession from the Photographic Society called the Linked Ring Brotherhood, the vanguard of a movement known respectfully as pictorialism and less respectfully as 'the fuzzy wuzzies' for the way practitioners used substances like gum bichromate and carbon pigment to soften reality's hard edges.

Beldam corresponds to no movement, and never seems to have fraternised with other photographers – his overlapping social circles would be athletes, artists and businessmen. When he first took up a camera in his mid-twenties, his subjects were friends and family, and his earliest cricket photograph a joke on his uncle, infamous in games on the family lawn for never accepting an lbw dismissal:

One day I took a snapshot of him, with my father standing behind the wicket in an attitude of appealing to the umpire. I told my father how to stand, and then turning to my uncle I said, 'There is no need for me to tell you what to do. Just imagine that you have been given out leg-before-wicket.' The result was a snapshot in which the ball is just hitting his leg (placed well in front of the wicket) while he looks up with an air of greatest surprise and indignation.

It is a charming photograph, and a foreshadowing one. For although a jest, it concerns those instants in cricket that otherwise impress only on the mind's eye; and while it is contrived, it seeks after a spontaneity, a naturalness ('There is no need for me to tell you what to do'). The wicketkeeper and batsman are oppositely engaged; the ball, having struck the pad, floats incriminatingly; the photographer is, as it were, the umpire. And if he was as yet unaware, Beldam the photographer had his subject. That subject was movement.

'A snapshot': Beldam's first cricket image.

•

In photography's foundational days, movement had cheated the camera because of the prolonged exposures necessary to obtain a satisfactory image. Movement had, of course, always cheated art, too, but traditional forms of painting, drawing, printmaking and sculpture had evolved an intricate visual language to convey motion, like the aforementioned concentration on 'memorably perceived' phases. Photography was condemned to repeat reality, in all its unpredictability.

A small vernacular movement, 'instantaneous photography', took this as a challenge, yielding erratic but evocative results. In October 1862, for example, an adventurous commercial photographer, Valentine Blanchard, exhibited an image of London's New Oxford Street, captured by means of a wide-aperture stereo camera mounted on a 'mobile studio' – a carriage with a viewing platform and a darkroom. 'Omnibuses, carts, cabs, wagons, and foot-passengers in shoals in active movement, are all "arrested",' reported the *British Journal of Photography*:

> In the immediate foreground is a man, without his coat, wheeling a barrow, his left leg poised in mid-air, in the act of stepping ... One individual in a black suit, with his hands in his pockets, and looking on excellent terms with himself, is sauntering towards the spectator. The whole scene is full of life, and the photography leaves nothing to be desired.

The instantaneous also touched Victorians sentimentally. Two hundred and fifty thousand copies were sold of a bizarre curio of a crying baby that first appeared as a plate in Charles Darwin's *The Expression of the Emotions in Man and Animals* (1872): Oscar Rejlander's small, indistinct, redrawn and rephotographed image came to be known as

'Ginx's Baby', from the title of a popular satire on urban poverty and its relief by Edward Jenkins.

Even then the photographer who would do most to unlock the instant was starting out in the United States. In 1872, émigré Englishman Eadweard Muybridge was hired by Californian railroad magnate Leland Stanford to ascertain whether all four hooves of a moving horse were ever simultaneously airborne. Equine painters had traditionally presented their subjects *ventre à terre* (belly to the ground), legs fore-and-aft like a rocking horse. Within a year, Muybridge had captured, on a wet plate at one-500th of a second, a silhouette of Stanford's champion racehorse, Occident, in 'unsupported transit'; he carried on his experiments at Sacramento Bay Track and Stanford's Palo Alto estate until he had proof in photo sequences from a battery of twelve cameras. 'The machine cannot lie,' Stanford felt able to pronounce.

The findings caused a sensation, not least among equine painters, who either fell repentantly in line or looked studiously the other way on the grounds that a mechanical view was inimical to a human artwork; they also caused a *froideur* between photographer and patron over credit for the discovery. Muybridge relocated to the University

Shotmaker: cricket gets the Muybridge treatment.

of Pennsylvania, where he used another battery of cameras for a sweeping survey of human and animal motion generating tens of thousands of 'seriates': bison cantering; big cats prowling; boys leap-frogging; ballet dancers pirouetting; baseballers slugging; discus throwers propelling; chickens 'startled by a torpedo'; a 340 lb (154 kg) nude woman rising to her feet. Muybridge used nudes extensively, including one identified as 'the best all-round cricketer in the University of Pennsylvania', purveying overarm and round-arm bowling, playing the back cut and the straight drive – the last uncannily anticipated one of Beldam's later Trumper images. Whether Beldam was actually aware of Muybridge's 'seriates' is obscure, but moot. He was certainly, as we shall see, exercised by questions of actuality and beauty – the point of intersection between photography's documentary and artistic impulses. And his work would run entirely against the grain.

•

By the 1890s, photography had made inroads into a number of sports, but in the main those where action was predictable and proximate, such as the finishes of horse and cycle races, athletics meetings and rowing events. In cricket, photography flourished in only one corner: portraiture. The Brighton firm of E. Hawkins & Co., for example, had established itself in the old premises of Mason's 'Repository of Art', and gained the patronage of Lord Sheffield, who regularly hosted cricket teams, including Australians, on his nearby estate. It became the custom for cricketers visiting Hove to pose for Hawkins & Co.'s Thomas Foster, usually standing by a set of stumps, sometimes in a batting stance, sometimes holding a ball high in an extended hand. Reproduced as cabinet cards, the bigger, thicker successor to *cartes de visite*, these photographs became the chief way by which cricketers were popularly known. Hawkins never had a greater seller than Foster's 1893 photograph of Grace stooping weightily over his bat, which the old-timer Richard Daft acclaimed as cricket's definitive image: 'When Dr Grace is no more, future generations must be shown these portraits, for it will be the next best thing to having seen the player himself.' All the same, Daft was conscious of such pictures stopping short of true action. He looked forward to the day when 'good, large instantaneous photographs may be taken of players in the field, and actually taking part in a match', which would 'do more to describe the play of the men them-selves than pages of writing would do'.

Until then, cricket would have to wait, somewhat frustratedly. In 1895, the artist Harry Furniss went to Lord's for the Gentlemen v Players match and saw forty-six-year-old Grace peel off the seventh

Still life: Hawkins' Grace.

of the nine hundreds of his 'Indian summer'. Furniss returned to his studio 'with the massive form of "WG" well imprinted upon my brain', and dashed off 'a hundred sketches from memory' that would compose *A Century of Grace* (1896) – probably the liveliest and most charming of all such illustrations. Furniss confessed disappointment nonetheless. It was, he concluded, 'impossible to make a satisfactory picture of our national game' from 'a crowd of ordinary sightseers in the foreground and also in the distance, and between these a large expanse of green grass, with a few white spots'. Worse, nor was photography up to the mark:

> Of course, the ordinary photograph of the cricketer, whether he sits or stands at ease, is a portrait. But what about him in action? If he is told to pose before a camera – if he is a batsman, he fails to get the proper swing, as he is only watching the lens, and not inspired to the correct action by seeing the ball flying towards him from the muscular arm of a Lohmann or a Richardson ... No, the photograph must be taken unawares, and perhaps before this little preface is published we may find depicted by the Cinematograph some of our well-known cricketers at play. But these have to be taken at a distance, when the game is in progress, and then enlarged; and I would like to see anyone venture on to a cricket field during the progress of some good match! The poor photographer would have to provide himself with dummy camera, as used when photographing at the Zoo.

But others were now being exercised by these challenges – including the two most glamorous names in the game.

•

Sketch life: Furniss's Grace.

The cricket celebrityhood conferred on Ranjitsinhji and C. B. Fry by their feats and by *The Jubilee Book of Cricket* (1897) brought complications. In 1897, Ranji fathered an illegitimate child with the daughter of his former Cambridge tutor; in 1898, Fry married another man's long-term mistress. The latter was a most remarkable woman. In her teens, Beatrice Sumner had been a famous beauty, a brilliant huntress, and an object of the ardour of wealthy banker Charles Hoare, fifteen years her senior and already a father of five. Increasingly desperate efforts were made by their families to prevent a relationship, but on her twenty-first birthday, Beatie broke from her guardians, reunited with Hoare, and bore him a son, then a daughter. During the scandalous court case that followed, the judge described Beatie as having 'suffered a fall from which no woman could live to recover'. Yet by sheer willpower she clambered back into respectable circles, thanks to an old barque that Hoare turned into a boys' naval college at Hamble – and also to Fry.

On TS *Mercury*, the overpowering influence was Beatie, a wintry martinet whose religiosity was exacerbated by a passion for Wagner: Hoare built her a 300-seat theatre modelled on Bayreuth featuring a giant crucifix with a life-size Christ whom visitors were required to salute. In the fashion of Hornung's Lord Amersteth, Hoare also enjoyed hosting famous cricketers, and thirty-five-year-old Beatie diarised fatefully after one visit: 'Charles Fry came to play cricket today. I like Fry.' Fry's marriage to the woman he referred to as 'my madame' was immediately complicated by her bearing a third child who was probably Hoare's, but at least relieved him of the burdens of teaching. His lapidary turns of phrase began appearing in *Windsor Magazine*, *Lloyd's News*, *Westminster Gazette*, *Athletic News*, the *Daily Express*, and the popular boys' magazine *The Captain*. As Fry's first biographer recalled: 'Very often if you broke into his hotel at ten o'clock, when other players were at the play or the cardtable, C. B. Fry, in a loose flannel suit with the sleeves turned up, would be found in his bedroom turning out copy.' From such bedrooms soon emerged something peculiarly his own.

Fry's *The Book of Cricket* (1899), a collection of pen portraits of his contemporaries, was less comprehensive than the *Jubilee Book* but rather breezier, even humorous when the author limned himself in the third person:

> In his earlier days Mr Fry was a stiff, ungainly bat . . . Mr Fry
> is aware that from the moment he had the privilege of playing with
> Kumar Shri Ranjitsinhji he began to improve his game – a fact
> which, when the absolute diversity of their styles is remembered,
> emphasises the value of observing the methods of a great
> player . . . He is no cutter, and a very intermittent off-driver.

He plays chiefly with his shoulders and fore-arms; not enough wrist. He has confidence in his back play which is not altogether justified. He would do better with more patience, and with a little more judgement in hitting. He prefers not to refer to such bowling as he once did. He is generally fond of fielding, and is ready to go anywhere. He is thought by his friends to be slightly too theoretical.

The middle of the same page contained a vivid image: as Fry leaned into an on-drive, a ball hurtled towards the camera. The *Jubilee Book* had relied on demonstration poses by leading cricketers of the day, profuse but static and barely distinguishable from postcard portraits; *The Book of Cricket* was about action. A blurred ball energised Billy Murdoch's lusty square cut, Pelham Warner's firm punch, Archie MacLaren's on-side prod, the defensive shots of Bobby Abel and Arthur Shrewsbury; speed smudged the arms of Hugh Trumble and Monty Noble; Jim Kelly caught an unseen batsman at the wicket; Harry Wood stumped a genuflecting Fry.

Photographer William Rouch normally specialised in blood-stock; the impetus was assuredly Fry's. Back in April 1892 when Fry had broken the British long-jump record at Queen's Club, his leap had been captured by a member of Stearn Brothers, a family-run photographic firm from Cambridge. Fry loved the image, in which he appeared almost to be hovering as a top-hatted official looked on – it would take pride of place in his autobiography. In *The Book of Cricket*, he was seeking a similar vigour, enhancing the narrative vitality of the images with zesty captions. Albert Trott walked back with a knowing look ('Now for that fast one'), rolled his arm over vigorously ('Whizz!') and cupped a return catch ('That's what I bowl for'). Lancashire's captain George Bardswell was shown cogitating about whether to use his fastest bowler, Arthur Mold ('Shall I put

Man of action: C. B. Fry meets the camera.

on Mold?'); Mold himself then adjusted his field ('Third man back
for Mr Ranji'). If it did not match the *Jubilee Book* for sales, *The Book
of Cricket* attracted praise just as lavish: to a *Daily Mail* reviewer,
it was no less than 'the most remarkable record of cricket ever put
between two covers'. Beneath the headline 'What the Umpire Does
Not See', the reviewer made a far-sighted prophecy about future
relations between the 'patient, long-suffering, begowned' umpire
and the 'infallible' camera: 'When the machine has been perfected
so as to reproduce the picture instantaneously, it may supersede
the umpire altogether.' In the camera, Fry sensed different possibilities. What, for example, might a close study of his entrancing
friend Ranji reveal? If only he could locate a collaborator with parallel obsessions.

•

To account for his late blooming as a cricketer, George Beldam
explained that perhaps he thought too much. His favourite lines of
verse were the epistemic musings of Robert Louis Stevenson ('the
reason o' the cause, an' the wherefore o' the why') and Robbie Burns
('O wad some Power the giftie gie us/To see oursels as ithers see us!/
It wad frae mony a blunder free us,/An' foolish notion'). Such fascinations, he thought, bred a certain 'overanxiety' in his performances.
He fiddled compulsively with his technique. He developed a range
of unusual mannerisms, like measuring the crease with his bat after
taking guard, and fingering his bat face after hitting the ball. But he
also burned to improve, and had the wherewithal to fund his dedication. Aged thirty, in a final push to make a serious go at the game,
Beldam had two pitches of red marl laid at his home, Boston Lodge,
in Ealing: a winter pitch protected from the elements by canvas

blinds, and a summer pitch enclosed by stout netting. With younger brother Cyril as a practice partner, it paid off. After making 2200 runs in fifty club innings in 1899, he finally took his first tentative steps in first-class cricket, turning out for London County CC, an all-amateur club run by the Crystal Palace Company and led by W. G. Grace. When Middlesex then promoted him to their first XI, he joined the gilded circle of English amateurism: such personages as Archie MacLaren, Pelham Warner, F. S. Jackson, Gilbert Jessop, and, most charismatic of all, Fry and Ranji.

Beldam was by his account 'thirsty for knowledge'. Perhaps, he speculated, there was some secret means by which the best made the game look easy. By talking to them, he felt confident of learning the 'open sesame which opens out the golden way'. From conversations with Grace he left disappointed: 'The dear old man, like all the best, was unconscious of his methods; his only principle was to keep the eye on the ball and time it.' Fry and Ranji, the game's taste masters, were more willing to counsel a new boy prepared to sit at their feet, and Beldam hung on their advices, such as a tip from Fry to 'face the bowler a little more' that he followed successfully. When Beldam finished the 1901 season with 1158 runs at 38.6, *Cricket* judged him 'risen to the front rank of cricketers'.

Yet advice, Beldam grew convinced, could only take one so far. In the pages of *Amateur Photography*, he had followed developments in the capturing of images in ever-finer slices of time, made possible by new-generation gelatine emulsions, rendering perceptible such phenomena as bullets in flight and splashes of water. To pursue his own fascinations he invested in a new top-of-the-range reflex camera, the Videx, manufactured by Adams & Co. of Charing Cross Road, featuring a Zeiss lens and a focal-plane shutter adjustable by turning a knob on the revolving plate that went all the way

to one-1000th of a second. It was this camera that he took to The
Oval in August 1902, where he took those two snaps of a far-off
Trumper at the crease. Fossickings among Beldam's surviving plates
by the cricket-book dealer Michael Down have recently exposed a
little more: six never-before-seen Beldam photographs of Trumper
in the nets. The print of a seventh photograph evidently in the same
sequence is contained in a scrapbook in the possession of the prodigious collector Roger Mann, itself extracted from a scrapbook kept
by former Middlesex wicketkeeper Cecil Headlam – such are the
feint trails that Beldam left by never cataloguing or annotating his
own work. But if Headlam's caption on that seventh photograph can
be believed, the practice session in question, at which Beldam also
photographed Trumper's colleague Hugh Trumble, was at Lord's
preparatory to Australia v Middlesex, a fortnight after The Oval Test.

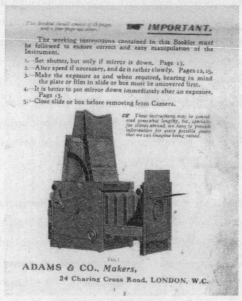

'Important': from the Adams Videx manual.

These are images Beldam never troubled to publish because, again, they're pretty poor. They suggest a photographer still growing accustomed to his apparatus, and to the challenges of composition, exposure and timing. In one photograph, Trumper plays an attractive shot off the hip; in another he is bowled. The photograph of Trumble shows his arm at an intermediate point between release and follow-through. The light is murky. The backdrop is messy. The plates have been damaged by inadequate storage. At this point, then, Beldam was not really a photographer; rather was he an amateur cricketer who owned a camera, a novelty presence, if an engaging one.

In the most appealing of the Lord's sequence, Trumper shapes to play a stroke while looking directly at the camera with a winsome smile, as though engaged by the fun of it all, and perhaps also by Beldam's busy, inquisitive personality. Though not long in the game, Beldam already had a reputation. One of his London County teammates that summer was Leslie Poidevin, a gifted all-round sportsman from Sydney who having represented New South Wales at cricket and tennis had just settled in Manchester to further his medical studies. He also sent off weekly tidbits of interest to J. C. Davis at *The Referee*, and was evidently rather taken by Beldam's slant on the game, his interesting hobby, and his obvious appreciation of Australia's finest cricketer:

> Beldam is one of those thoughtful players – a theorist many people might say, but I prefer to name him a genuine enthusiast – with a fine collection of blades and photographs, and a singularly pleasant, engaging disposition. He is at all times critically observant, ever-ready to pick up something that he may be able to adapt to his own use. He carefully studies the methods of other players, and he is not

content to see and admire Trumper; he must know how it is done, even if he has to ask the brilliant young Paddingtonian himself.

He must know how it is done: and this, with Beldam, amounted almost to an obsession.

•

Notwithstanding his experiments at The Oval and at Lord's, Beldam's first real photographic success would be in another sport. In addition to his cricket, he was also a scratch golfer, who introduced a number of cricket teammates to the game, including a quickly enthralled W.G.: 'It ought not to be difficult to hit that little ball lying so still . . . If it were rolled up towards me, I could guarantee to hit it a good distance and in any given direction, but as it lies staring me in the face invitingly, I feel a perfect fool.' Among his friends at Royal Mid-Surrey was the pro, John Henry Taylor, who with Harry Vardon and James Braid formed the game's 'Great Triumvirate'. Beldam struck Taylor in much the same way as he struck Poidevin:

> During my professional life I have come into contact with scores of theorists, those eager and almost demented seekers after truth, who have endeavoured to prove that if such and such a thing was done, something else was bound to happen, a something that would reveal the most vital secrets hidden from others who had not the courage or desire to probe for them. Mr Beldam was the champion theorist. The placing of the fingers on the grip of the club to within a fractional part of an inch, the question whether the toes of the feet were turned inwards or out was considered of sufficient interest

to set him off on a hunt for information and confirmation; and in the search for what he considered the truth he demonstrated so convincingly that the most hardened sceptic would be forced to acknowledge the rightness of the claim. In addition to this endless quest for rock-bottom divination that became a mania, Mr Beldam was an amateur photographer of genius.

Golf was an excellent photographic subject: distance was no impediment, the ball started from a stationary position, the action was concentrated in a small area. There were already a range of instructional books in which golfers held stiff poses for the purposes of tuition. But what might the camera discern that the human eye could not? With Taylor as adviser and ambassador, Beldam began assembling the bulging portfolio of 'Action-Photographs' of Britain's leading golfers that would compose *Great Golfers: Their Methods at a Glance* (1904).

'Action-Photographs': the very formulation was uncertain, provisional. After all, 'action' implied motion, 'photography' stillness. Beldam abandoned the inverted commas after a while, then gradually dispensed with the hyphen, but remained partial to the capitals, distinguishing the uniqueness of his vision. For in what he was attempting there were no guides, no mentors, not even rivals. The American Charles Conlon, a newspaper proofreader, was just starting out as an amateur photographer of baseball at New York's Polo Grounds, home of the Giants, but his snapshot souvenirs were not nearly so technically ambitious as Beldam's painstaking inquiries into the mysteries of the golf swing.

The trick of it, Beldam established by trial and error, was concentrating on the wrists rather than the club head. In order to compensate for the difference between 'the eye seeing and hand pressing', he also learned to press the Videx's button 'just before I wanted to'. His twenty-four subjects were patient because they were also fascinated. They were not, it turned out, reliable narrators of their own game. Beldam cited the case of Horace Hutchinson, twice Britain's amateur champion, and a celebrated golf critic. Hutchinson swore he had a short swing; 'Action-Photography' proved emphatically otherwise. Often Beldam would ask his subjects to demonstrate a point by striking a pose, only to find that the same point in an actual stroke looked quite different in motion. The conclusion was devastating to prior golf books with their emphasis on static illustration. 'Photographs taken "en pose" are not only worthless from the golfer's point of view, but are very misleading,' concluded Beldam. 'If an amateur champion, and a no less brilliant writer, were led astray, and allowed his years of close observation to be over-ruled – what chance would an ordinary man have?'

Great Golfers was an immediate success. 'There will be, I think, a general consensus of opinion as to the extreme excellence of the photographs throughout the book,' opined *Illustrated Sporting and Dramatic News*. 'If this study does not lead to improved form at the links, I for one shall be vastly astonished.' Reviewers were particularly taken with the quasi-scientific air that Beldam introduced to the photographs by posing his subjects on a grid 4 feet × 4 feet (1.2 metres × 1.2 metres) divided by painted lines into sixty-four squares. Beldam's patented linoleum mat, marked in the same fashion so that readers could mimic the greats more exactly, was presently paid the tribute of parody by *Golf Illustrated*'s cartoonist E. W. Mitchell, who transformed it into a griddle in the hands of chef 'Mons Georges Belledame': 'Golfers Grilled at a Glance.'

The most gushing testimonial for *Great Golfers* – 'Not only the book of the month but the best book on golf instruction yet produced' – came in a new publication. *C. B. Fry's Magazine of Action and Outdoor Life*, which commenced publication in April 1904, ran the full gamut of recreations: cricket, football, rugby, tennis, rowing, racing, wrestling, hunting, fishing and motoring. It was the brainchild of the proprietor of *The Captain*. 'Sir George Newnes . . . explained that a monthly magazine is the easiest production imaginable,' recalled Fry. 'I should sit in a comfortable chair with my mind at ease, and select some seven or eight excellent articles sent in for consideration by clever young men such as barristers waiting for briefs.' Beldam became one of those clever young men. To *Fry's* he provided numerous golf and cricket images, previewed the British Open and British Amateur titles, and undertook with Taylor a four-part guide to 'Golf Faults Illustrated', which became the basis of another book.

In addition, Beldam took on a further bold project. He had been approached by Percy Vaile, a flamboyant Auckland lawyer turned 'wanderer on the face of the earth', seeking 'instantaneous photographs' for an instructional book he had dashed off 'in a few days'. And after providing twenty-seven images for Vaile's *Modern Lawn Tennis* (1904), Beldam comprehensively photographed June 1904's All-England Championships for a larger follow-up entitled *Great Lawn Tennis Players: Their Methods Illustrated* (1905).

Despite its 229 images of thirty players, *Great Lawn Tennis Players* proved a less easy temperamental mix than *Great Golfers*. Unlike J. H. Taylor, Vaile was not a champion, even if this diminished the confidence of the views he expressed in London sporting journals, notably *The Field*, not a whit:

> Many players on whose judgement and integrity I would stake
> my – tennis – reputation have assured me that if I had started

much younger, and played a better game, I might even now be a
champion; and I know, without being told, that if I could play it
as well as I know and love it, I might even now be a champion, if
it were not for a trifling want of wind, and no want of that sort of
condition that tennis players are not glad to be without.

The divergence in the collaborators' approaches was reflected in
their prefaces: while Beldam gently cautioned that 'this work is not
to take the place of books on the game written by champions and
experts', Vaile unblushingly declared that 'the true science which
underlies the game of lawn tennis has not yet begun to be realised by
the players of the United Kingdom'. Reviewers, in fact, distinguished
carefully between the contributions of photographer and writer:
even Vaile's own employer, *The Field,* while judging the photographs a 'conspicuous success', dismissed the text as 'very florid',
'very unsound' and in places 'obviously absurd'.

Tennis was in any case merely a passing fancy. Beldam wanted
above all to contribute to cricket. Cricketers, he found, were as
kinaesthetically naive as golfers. One day, he and W.G. were part of a
group playing golf conversing about 'follow-through'. The Champion
scoffed. 'Follow-through'? Who'd ever heard of such a thing? It was
'all bunkum'. 'I could not believe he was in earnest but found that
he was,' Beldam recalled. 'I then told him I would prove by Action
Photographs that he had a follow-through.' They arranged to photograph W.G.'s swings for cricket and golf. The results were conclusive:
'When he [Grace] saw the photographs he had to own that they sur-
prised him, and he must have some kind of follow-through though
he could never have shown anyone what it was.'

What might this imply, Beldam wondered, about prior works of
cricket instruction, even by thinkers as advanced as Fry and Ranji?

The *Jubilee Book* had stressed the efficacy of stationary demonstration: 'The making of nearly all strokes in cricket requires the man to put himself in certain positions if the strokes are to be properly made.' Yet in real life a stroke was not a succession of 'certain positions' into which one 'put' one's self; it was a continuous motion. Surely it had to be illustrated as such. What if you could? What then? The open sesame? The golden way?

Fry was intrigued. *The Book of Cricket* had after all gestured in the same direction. But he was also not quite convinced. His classicist's interests spanned the aesthetic and antiquarian as well as the athletic. For the first issue of *Fry's Magazine* he had visited the octogenarian G. F. Watts, in the last year of the spirited artistic life that had begun with those little cricket sketches for Felix and was now culminating in his colossal equestrian statue 'Physical Energy'. Fry's profile, 'Physical Energy and Mr G. F. Watts, R.A., O.M.', read as a kind of proclamation, extolling art's power to infuse its viewers with 'a fresher-fountained energy', even when they were 'jaded by the cares and earth-ridden by the anxieties of our common day'. The statue, Fry argued, 'typifies the pause, the arrest, the interval between one act of supreme energy and the coming moment of continued action'. He dismissed carpings by some critics that the horse's pose was impossible. Art, argued Fry, was not a literal transcription of nature: 'Physical Energy' was 'a Watts horse and a Watts man, true to the mind and the hand of the maker'.

It was an esoteric diversion for an outdoor sport magazine. Newnes, Fry recalled, detested the piece: 'He smoothed his brown beard and kept repeating through it, "But Mr Fry, why Physical Energy? Why Physical Energy?" Like many other friends of mine who ought to have known better, he could not see any subject properly subscribed to my name except cricket or football.' Fry was unrepentant. In any case, there *was* a point to be made about cricket, or at least its visual representation, because of Watts' own enthusiasm for the game: 'And did not this same painter, taking his friend Felix, batsman and author of *Felix on the Bat,* make pencil studies of the art of cricket? Little studies which to this day, despite the progress of the game, remain, from the technical point of cricket, more perfect in showing correctness of poise and movement – the gist of style in cricket – than any instantaneous photograph, however aptly taken.'

Any instantaneous photograph, however aptly taken: of Beldam, perhaps, a subtle admonition. After all, Beldam fancied he knew a bit about art: his watercolours had by now been exhibited at the Brentwood and Dudley galleries; he counted two of England's leading realist painters, Henry Scott Tuke and Albert Chevallier Tayler, among his friends; and if his photographic purposes were chiefly pedagogic, he was not insensitive to beauties incidentally revealed. So rapt was he in one image of a drive by Harry Vardon that he had a friend, the cartoonist Hal Ludlow, render it in clay and in bronze: the clay model was displayed on a revolving pedestal in the Jermyn Street gallery of the collector A. Baird-Carter, who sold the bronzes for £25 each. Yet Fry's complaint was not an uncommon one: the greater the ubiquity of the camera, the deeper such quibbling. While Bernard Shaw was insisting that the camera had 'hopelessly beaten the pencil and paintbrush as an instrument of artistic representation', others weren't so sure: in a long editorial lamentation of the decline of racing illustration, for example, *The Field* deplored a public taste 'satisfied with photographic views', which were 'at the best cold-looking, uncompromising'.

When Beldam began photographing cricket systematically is unrecorded. But during his peregrinations for Middlesex that summer of 1904, around London, north to Sheffield, Nottingham and Manchester, south to Bournemouth, Brighton and Hastings and west to Taunton and Bristol, he packed his Adams Videx and Adams Extra Rapid photographic plates, sometimes in the trunk of his new De Dion-Bouton. From time to time newspapers would report his activities, at practice and during intervals. Before Middlesex hosted Yorkshire at Lord's in June, for example, the *Nottingham Evening Post* noted him photographing F. S. Jackson and L. J. Moon batting, J. T. Hearne bowling and Gregor MacGregor wicketkeeping. 'When these operations had been duly recorded on the plate, A. E. Trott turned out to be photographed as he took a catch in slips,' recounted the newspaper. 'All was in readiness, and Hearne threw the ball to the fieldsman. Just as it reached him Beldam pressed the button and – Trott missed the catch!'

Beldam photographed members of the visiting South African team, against whom he played for an England XI. He photographed Charles Ollivierre of Derbyshire via Trinidad – the earliest photographs of a black cricketer in action. With many subjects, Beldam had multiple sessions, including at least four with Grace, one of them on Beldam's home pitch at Boston Lodge, where he also hosted Archie MacLaren and the respected Surrey professional Tom Hayward. His arrivals at Newnes' offices in the Strand bearing sheafs of prints incited frenzies of analysis, especially of the differences between golf and cricket. Fry's young deputy Wallis Myers recalled one such:

> Suddenly Beldam whipped off his overcoat and seized the poker.
> I dropped my pipe in momentary alarm. But he was only giving us
> a practical illustration of Taylor. Then Mr Fry took the poker, stood
> at an imaginary wicket, and knocked George Hirst with terrific
> force past mid-on. A discourse followed on the subtleties

of wristwork, stance and follow-through. It lasted quite a long time, and I do not think we did any more planning that day.

Wristwork: this was an insight on which Beldam and Fry agreed – the involvement of the wrists relative to the arms. A powerful stroke had always been identified with a hearty armswing. What Beldam and Fry discerned among the best players were arms relatively compact and close to the body, and hands that remained in roughly the same space; from what they called a 'secondary position', reached at the top of the backlift, it appeared to be the wrists that imparted force and governed placement. The thesis awaited, as it were, the acid test – Fry's own batting ideal.

•

When George Beldam arrived in Brighton to represent Middlesex against Sussex on 25 August 1904, he first kept an appointment – in retrospect an ironic one. Following what had been standard practice among county cricketers for nearly twenty years, he took up his stance and gazed levelly into a Hawkins & Co. camera. To be turned into a cabinet card was a mark of some distinction, a confirmation of the progress he had made in his late cricket flowering. Three days later, Beldam took up the challenge of rendering such images redundant.

Middlesex had the better of the game, Beldam hitting the winning runs. Then he really got to work, returning to the centre of the empty county ground at Hove dressed in his cap, blazer and flannels, spreading his camera gear and erecting his tripod. Ranji put on his pads and assumed his stance; Fry returned from kicking a football with some of the Sussex professionals to bowl a ball; and Beldam started taking photographs, of off-side shots from short mid-wicket,

Frozen: Hawkins's Beldam.

of leg-side shots from short cover. As the report from his bat echoed, Ranji ran through his full repertoire. Boys fetched. Hours passed. Beldam's holder began bulging with 5-inch × 4-inch (13 cm × 10 cm) plates. Fry broke off at one point to take his own photograph of Beldam in action; he also took away, as becomes apparent reading the commentaries he later wrote about each image, a mind's-eye impression of each shot ('It was a good length, medium-pace ball outside the off-stump'; 'The ball rose rather high at the batsman's body' etc.).

Fry would preface these commentaries by quietly reiterating his original objection to 'instantaneous photography'. He had, he wrote, expected to see a 'very remarkable degree of difference' between Ranji and 'what other batsmen do': the still image could not quite do justice to Ranji's capacity for moving 'as if he had no bones'. Otherwise he confessed to being impressed: Beldam showed how economically Ranji's arms moved; how coolly Ranji rolled his wrists when cutting; how daintily Ranji crossed his legs in glancing. By one image Fry was exhilarated: his friend 'jumping out to drive', prancing like a warhorse, front foot high off the ground, back toe just grounded, eyes flashing.

Arguably, it was the least natural and most staged of all the strokes – eighty years later, it would be rather deliciously spoofed by the cartoonist Willie Rushton in his book *Marylebone versus the World* (1987). But perhaps it struck Fry as akin to 'Physical Action', capturing the feeling of Ranji at the crease rather than a mere instant, and somehow truer than fact: certainly, as that champion of Valentine Blanchard's had long ago pointed out, there was something uniquely compelling about photography's ability to capture the foot in space, the step in time, the texture of action beyond perception. Whatever the case, alongside a memoir of the day, Fry allocated this 'excellent specimen' of Beldam's 'swift-action photography' a full page in the next edition of *Fry's Magazine*. And he decided, with uncharacteristic restraint, that to the image he had little to add: 'The picture, more or less, speaks for itself.'

•

Beldam's mission at Hove nodded to another dimension of photography – its capacity to preserve for all time. Ranji was shortly to board a ship for India, determined to wrest back his princely inheritance in Nawanagar; his Test career was over; he would not play again for four years, and only one half-hearted season thereafter. Beldam had an eye to posterity, too. Having documented Grace, he also photographed Grace's erstwhile rival Fred Spofforth, now settled in England as manager of the Star Tea Company. Donning his creams at Hampstead CC, the fifty-one-year-old attested the vigour of his retirement regime. 'For my own part, I am still a believer in practice; and scarcely a day passes in the winter that I do not go through the delivery of at least twelve balls,' Spofforth explained. 'By this I mean that without any ball in my hand I bowl at least 72 balls a week with all the power I have, at some imaginary crack batsman.' As Beldam's shutter clicked, Spofforth bowled to eternity with an energetic fluency.

By now, Beldam's survey was all-consuming: the diary of his painter friend Henry Tuke includes a reference to a winter salon at Boston Lodge attended by Fry, Hal Ludlow and Chevallier Tayler at which there was 'great talk on the artistic aspects of cricket figures in action'. Beldam already seems to have had in mind a batting *and* a bowling book, as he commissioned Tuke to paint both W. G. Grace and Spofforth for frontispieces. The batting book would come first, the structure a hybrid of *Great Golfers* and *Great Lawn Tennis Players*: a joint preface about batting bookended by a Beldam epilogue about photography; between them a section dedicated to particular strokes ('Strokes Illustrated'), and a section concentrated on a batting elite ('Individualities'). Among these there would be the past master Grace, the Test stars Fry, Ranji, MacLaren, Jessop and Jackson, the professional stalwarts Hayward and Hirst alongside amateur stylists Lionel Palairet and R. E. Foster; and there would be – there would have to be – Victor Trumper.

5

'SOME DAY SOMEONE WILL PAINT HIS PORTRAIT'

'In Victor Trumper we have seen the very poetry and heard
the deep and wonderful music of batsmanship. Not the structures of a great
mentality, not the argument of logic, but a sweet and simple strain of beauty,
the gift of the gods alone. Stylish in the highest sense, orthodox,
yet breaking all canons of style, Trumper is just himself.'
– ALBERT KNIGHT, *The Complete Cricketer* (1906)

As they would outline in their introduction to *Great Batsmen: Their Methods at a Glance* (1905), George Beldam and C. B. Fry had two related purposes. First was to decode technique, to slow time down so that the action might be better understood:

It has often been said that more may be learnt by watching a good batsman actually playing than by reading all the books that have been written about cricket. But it is impossible to see the details of a stroke as the batsman plays it in real life: the eye cannot follow the rapid and complicated movements of arms, hands and bat. Here Action-Photography is of value since it shows in full detail the various stages in a stroke, and thus betrays secrets which the human eye cannot detect ... We hazard the prophecy that no one who studies the pictures in this book carefully will fail to acknowledge that they show him a great many points which he never suspected.

The second purpose was subtler but barely less pressing: they aspired to art, or at least to revealing cricket's artistic beauties, to make of batting's physical action something like Watts' 'Physical Action':

It has been said that the results of instantaneous photography, however true to nature, are generally inartistic in effect: 'very true but very ugly'. Possibly such an opinion may be revised in the light of a study of these pictures of live cricket. Some of the attitudes may seem strange and unfamiliar to those who have never studied great batsmen in action with very close attention. But some of them go to prove how beautiful a game is cricket, and to suggest that the sculptor of modern times might possibly achieve statues of athletic perfection in no wise inferior to those of ancient Greece in the days of the athletic prizemen. Apart from the purely technical aspect of the art of batsmanship in these pages, we hope that the pictures have caught something at any rate of the glow and glory of 'the game with the beautiful name'.

It was clear why Trumper should be foremost among their subjects. Since 1902 he had enhanced his reputation further by top-scoring in the Ashes series of 1903–04. 'The finest batsman in the world,' thought England's captain Pelham Warner. 'Undoubtedly the greatest batsman living and above criticism,' believed Warner's own star batsman R. E. Foster. Perhaps the most resonant summary was that of wicketkeeper Dick Lilley, who stood behind Trumper throughout the batsman's undefeated 185 at the SCG: 'Had he remained to double his score, I should never have tired of watching him.' Trumper's batting transcended national allegiance. Watching him was as exciting to English followers of the game as to Australians – an aesthetic experience to savour, to wonder at, to want to know more of.

No player, not even Grace, not even Ranji, was exciting responses of such widespread lyricism. All manner of interpreters aimed to penetrate the heart of his appeal, the secrets of his success. Even Fry's formidable wife, Beatie, made an attempt, with an unblushing paean in the London periodical *Voice of the Century*:

> There is something peculiarly satisfactory in his having such a suitable name. Victor Trumper, with a real healthy, fresh, pink skin, a long muscular neck, and small, keen, bright eyes. Nothing sad about those eyes, not for one moment. A pair of very fine arms, splendid forearms, wrists, and hands; the whole together makes up a very perfect telephonic communication between his eye and bat. Rather sturdy legs, which never are between the wickets or on the edge of a very wide boundary, but try all day.
>
> When Trumper, chasing the ball, comes towards you, the air seems to divide; he wakes a buzz of power, something like you associate with a very first-rate motor-car. When he bats, if you are fond of cricket in the right sort of way, to you then will Trumper's batting be like reading Robert Louis Stevenson's description of some great granite rocks.

'There they stand, for all the world like their neighbours ashore; only the salt water sobbing between them instead of the quiet earth, and clots of sea-pink blooming on their sides instead of heather; and the great sea-conger to wreathe about the base of them instead of the poisonous viper of the land.'[*]

It is good and pleasant to watch cricket, with the same mind's eye that glories in a beautifully written description. His timing has the exactness, rhythm, and fit of the oceangoing ship's piston-rod – true. Quite naturally his bat hits the ball. Owing to the fibre of the hit a beautiful stroke is the outcome, and this to almost every ball which is bowled. He shifts his feet, steps across, over and back with infinite variety and ease; he can play any bowling on any wicket, not from any particular luck, but just sheer natural ability. He is a poet of cricket; he has a poet's extra sense, touch, and feeling.

Trumper can play, with his bat, a cricket ball as Paganini played his violin; to him it is alive; he plays his strokes by nature, in the easiest possible way, to do it well, and get all there is to be got out of that particular stroke, a note. Trumper is an artist. Some day someone will paint his portrait; it will be hung in a National Portrait Gallery; he will be dressed in white, with his splendid neck bared to the wind, standing on short green grass, against a blue sky; he will be waiting for the ball, the orchestra to strike up. Not even a bowler need go away regretfully from this healthy, strong picture – so easily imagined, a white flannelled knight.

This traverses extraordinary vistas of aesthetic territory – physical, literary, artistic, musical, mechanical. One might even have thought it a bit rich for Australian taste, except that it struck an immediate chord on the other side of the world, being reprinted not only in

---

[*]   These lines are from Stevenson's 1882 short story 'The Merry Men'.

Sydney newspapers but in titles as diverse as the *Singleton Argus*, the *Richmond River Express and Tweed Advertiser*, and the *Albury Banner and Wodonga Express*. Farmers in rocking chairs who might never visit a gallery or hear Paganini learned that one of their country-men was scaling similar artistic heights. The Irish-Australian lyric poet Victor Daley, a *Bulletin* favourite, responded with a poem, 'The Great Trumper' (1904), using the penultimate sentence of Beatrice Fry's article as an epigraph:

> 'Trumper is an artist. Some day someone will paint his portrait; it will be hung in a National Portrait Gallery; he will be dressed in white, with his splendid neck bared to the wind, standing on short green grass against a blue sky; he will be waiting for the ball, the orchestra to strike up.' – *Mrs. C. B. Fry in an English periodical.*

> Ho Statesmen, Patriots, Bards make way!
> Your fame has sunk to zero:
> For Victor Trumper is to-day
> Our one Australian Hero.
> High purpose glitters in his eye,
> He scorns the filthy dollar;
> His splendid neck, says Mrs. Fry,
> Is innocent of collar.
> He stands upon the short green grass,
> Superb, and seems to be now
> A nobler young Leonidas
> At our Thermopylae now.
> Is there not, haply, in the land
> Some native-born Murillo
> To paint, in colours rich and grand.

This Wielder of the Willow?
Nay, rather let a statue be
Erected his renown to,
That future citizens might see
The gods their sires bowed down to.
Happy the man who while alive
Obtains his meed of glory!
His name for seasons will survive
In fable, song and story.
Evoe Trumper! As for me
It all ends with the moral
That Fame grows on the Willow Tree
And no more on the Laurel.

Daley's mock grandiloquence reveals his satiric purpose – anticipating decades of complaints from Australian artists and writers that all their countrymen care about is sport. There were other poems too, simpler doggerel like Oriel's 'A Bumper to Trumper' (1904) in *The Argus* and E. H. Garnsey's 'Trumper' (1905) in *Athletic News*[*]; in Trumper's honour, Thomas Spencer penned 'The Prerogative of Piper's Flat' (1902), a sequel to his famous comic ballad 'How MacDougall Topped the Score' (1896). Perhaps most ambitiously, Trumper appeared in what would now be regarded as a multimedia project. At the 'Sydney Opera House', then a theatre at the corner of York and King streets, a fine young baritone, George Warsaw, sang a new marching song in

---

[*] Trumper offered the versifier rather limited rhyming possibilities. From Oriel: 'Long life to Victor Trumper,/That record-breaker fine!/I drink it in a bumper/Of clear Australian wine.' From Garnsey: 'The pluck of a hero, a veteran's head,/And modest withal, though his fame it has spread/To the limits of Empire. A bumper!/We'll call it, and take the goodwill for the deed./(He drinks not, nor smokes, let us follow his lead)/Here's health to you, Vic – Victor Trumper.' A couple of years later came Guy Eden's bush ballad 'Victor Trumper'.

praise of 'Australia', whose arrangement featured the use of a bioscope, a form of projector, to display the images of prominent celebrities on a screen. To convey the message of national parity, images of Teddy Roosevelt, Lord Roberts and Lord Kitchener were interspersed with

'Australia now can hold her own': Joe Slater's tribute.

those of Melba, her singing rivals Amy Castles and Ada Crossley, actress Nellie Stewart, artist Phil May, swimmer Barney Kieran, and Victor Trumper, against whom cricket-loving composer Joe Slater had played for Leichhardt. When its words appeared on the screen, crowds sang along with the rollicking, patriotic chorus: 'Australia, Australia, she has her champions too/With old John Bull and Uncle Sam, they've shown what they can do;/In ev'ry land, in ev'ry clime, they kept their flag unfurled,/And Australia now can hold her own, with the wide, wide world.' For 15 shillings, the sheet music and slides could be purchased from the Haymarket.

The bulk of the appreciation of Trumper still ran in mainstream cricket circles, but it, too, was of a tone and intimacy unexampled elsewhere. The most startling passages were penned by Albert Knight, a dour professional batsman from unfashionable Leicestershire who played three Tests for England against Trumper in 1903–04. Knight was a Methodist lay preacher who prefaced each innings with a quiet prayer after taking guard, and a cricket writer in a uniquely abstruse vein – the historian Benny Green once joked that some passages in Knight's *The Complete Cricketer* (1906) have yet to be translated. Certainly on the subject of 'the most perfect and accomplished batsman of all time', Knight achieves a pitch of erudition that anticipates Cardus. His description of Trumper at the crease in Sydney has the quality of a religious vision:

> A slender figure, wan and drawn of face, cadaverous, but
> spiritualized with the delicacy of ill health, glides to the wicket.
> Nor ornament nor colour marked his featureless attire, the
> personality was all-dominating. He took guard quickly, more quickly
> took a glance around the field, and received his first ball. 'Dreams
> of summer dawn in night of rain' presented no fresher vision that

this boy's play to that black sea which hid the blistered grass of the
Sydney hill. Not in his fascinating collection of strokes, nor in their
frank and open execution merely, lay the charm; it was a man playing
away a power which was himself rather than in him . . . Saint and
savage and critic alike 'wondered with a foolish face of praise'. It was
a rare and moving sight to look upon that crowd as it rose en masse
to watch the ball strike the fence; to see those people standing in
hushed expectation ere breaking into unrestrained delight.

There's more – much more. Knight could not write of Trumper
without rhapsodising of his spirit, 'so self-forgetful, so manly'. But
what's perhaps most noteworthy in the foregoing passage is the waft
of mortality into the evolving Trumper legend. Elsewhere Knight
would discern in Trumper's batting a 'shadowy gleam of haunting
beauty', and a hint of 'where the outlook is infinite'. And while none
of his biographers has been able to shed much light on the subject,
the visiting Englishmen seem to have been aware that their star
opponent was unwell: Warner reported rumours 'going the rounds
that Trumper was in bad health'; Foster described Trumper as 'very
seedy', and thought he 'did not look at all strong'.

The likeliest explanation is tuberculosis, which claimed a third
of Trumper's sisters, three-year-old Elma Claire, in December 1903.
After the series, Trumper spent several months 'recuperating' in the
Southern Tablelands, at the Bengarralong homestead of a Gundagai
pastoralist and racehorse owner, Frederick McEvoy, related by marriage to the journalist J. C. Davis. And while other journalists fussed
about the possibility that Trumper might not tour England in 1905,
Knight went still further, as though twenty-six-year-old Trumper
was as foredoomed as Adonaïs. 'Perchance the statistical expert
will yet have many pages to fill with the first-class records of Victor

Trumper,' he wrote. 'Probably not, for such eye and wrist, such lightning celerity, such risk is for youth alone. Perchance the cold winds
of ill-health have already swept across the stream on whose surface
lies the glory and the gleam.' And he was, of course, right.*

Cricket fans trying to appraise players of different eras dwell naturally on statistics and averages; historians occasionally introduce
considerations like the covering of pitches and the sizes of stumps, bats
and balls. Invariably overlooked are the basic circumstances of day-to-
day living – nutrition, medical care, life expectancy, general levels of
prosperity. Trumper is a case in point. Given his proximity to suffer-
ers of the disease, he probably carried the *Mycobacterium tuberculosis*
most of his life. A great many did. In colonial Australia, tuberculosis
had stood at the head of medical causes of death, its symptoms of
a chronic cough, fever, weight loss, night sweats and heavy urina-
tion familiar to every family. By the early twentieth century, health
authorities understood its incidence to be worsened by dense urban
living and poor sanitation, but remained in the dark about treating it.
In *A New Treatment of Consumption and Other Chronic Chest Diseases*
(1904), for example, Duncan Turner recommended lengthy and energetic twenty-minute whole-body massages using liberal quantities
of cod liver oil, based on an observation by a Scottish doctor of the
low incidence of consumption among woollen-mill workers ascribed
to their absorption of lanoline through the skin. The commonest
prescription was simply a nutritious diet, bed rest and graduated

---

* These passages by Knight were noted in Australia, for they were cited on Trumper's
death by an anonymous correspondent in the *Mirror of Australia* on 1 August 1915:
'Knight was a very observant writer, and his reference to Victor "playing away a
power" was prophetic. To the writer's mind – and Victor's father is of the same
opinion – the deterioration of our late, great batsman's health dated from 1902,
when, playing in the wettest season on record in England, Victor scored 2570
runs, and made eleven centuries. The exertions of that tour, followed by another
strenuous season in Australia, undermined his health, and he never fully recovered.'

exercise preferably in a country location, such as Trumper undertook.

The *Gundagai Times*, naturally, welcomed the celebrity convalescent, not least for confirming the local reputation for healthfulness: 'His decision to seek a restoration to good health here is a wise one, for the climate of Gundagai taken all round is not to be eclipsed in any part of the state, as our health record proves.' And despite his ailments, Trumper reciprocated the local hospitality by turning out for Gundagai against Gobarralong: a huge crowd converged to watch 'the champion batsman of the world' play a whirlwind innings before contributing to local folklore by getting out to a railway worker from Cootamundra, Jack Harrold. Twenty years later, the *Gundagai Times* was still introducing Harrold as 'the man who bowled Victor Trumper'. Forty years later, an aspiring writer working with the Australian Department of Information based a short story on his father's recollection of Trumper visiting Gundagai: 'When Trumper Went to Billabong' (1944) by Dal Stivens, whom we shall meet more fully in Chapter 10, appeared in the popular weekly *John O'London's*. And while nobody knows for sure, it's not unlikely that the cricket-loving Bradman family of Yeo Yeo named their first son for the visiting divinity: Victor Bradman, elder brother to Donald, was born later in 1904.

Here in Trumper's time may have lain another reason for Beldam and Fry to set out to document him – that there was a sense of Trumper passing before the world. None could have known that he had a meagre decade to live. But perhaps his chroniclers intuited a special urgency about capturing Trumper for visual posterity. The 'portrait' Beatie Fry thought necessary could not wait until 'some day': it was an instant necessity, best suited to an instantaneous medium.

•

Trumper returned to England midst great enthusiasm. He was introduced to the Prince of Wales; he was invited to pose for a wax likeness by Madame Tussauds; he contributed that lengthy article to *Fry's Magazine* described in Chapter 2; he agreed to write cricket columns for the *Daily Chronicle*. Then, mysteriously, he didn't.

The custom among English amateurs of supplementing their income by writing for the press, established by Ranji and Fry, was now well entrenched. The sheer volume of articles by the likes of Warner, MacLaren and Jessop were the subject of some jocularity, as in lines penned the previous year for the *Evening News*.

> Oh, what will become of our national cricket
> When every player devotes
> The time he would otherwise spend at the wicket
> To penning elaborate notes?
>
> To face a fast bowler is always exciting.
> But wouldn't it cause you distress,
> If between each two overs you had to be writing
> Your views on the game for the press!

Trumper, an Australian, would have made an exotic addition to these ranks: as the *Chronicle* introduced him in an excited promotion of his forthcoming appearance, he was 'admittedly the finest batsman to visit this country'. But Australians, thinking them a source of needless friction, had remained averse to such forays into journalism. By signing a contract with the *Chronicle*, in fact, Trumper had placed himself in breach of a tour agreement he knew well enough to have quoted to Worcestershire's Paul Foley three years earlier. 'No member of the team shall correspond for any newspaper by letter or cable or otherwise during the tour,' read the relevant section. 'A breach of this clause renders the culprit liable to a fine of £100.' Its application must have been promptly brought to Trumper's attention. The day after his first scheduled column failed to appear, the *Chronicle* explained its absence by a letter of apology from the man himself.

> Dear sir – I regret that owing to a prohibition put on all
> members of the Australian team – a restriction which,
> unfortunately, I misinterpreted – I am prevented from carrying
> out the contract I made with you last week to write daily cricket
> notes in your paper. Trusting that this explanation will be accepted
> by your readers and yourselves, and that you are satisfied with my
> good faith in the matter.

What exactly happened here? Did Trumper fancy taking advantage of the same opportunities as were dangled before English amateurs such as MacLaren, also a *Chronicle* contributor? Was he pushing commercial boundaries, on the timeless principle that careers are short but life is long? After all, by now he had opened his sports store with one teammate, Hanson Carter, and married the sister of another, Jim Kelly; she, Annie, was actually on the tour, pregnant with their daughter. The only hint is contained in a single paragraph deep in *An Australian Cricketer on Tour* (1905), the travelogue published by their player-manager, the 'inveterate snapshotter' Frank Laver. Decrying the writing on cricket by English amateurs as 'being questionable in the interests of the game for it to continue' and outlining the Australian fine system, Laver reported: 'The proprietors of one newspaper were so anxious to get articles on the game by one of our members that they offered to pay his amount [£100] if one fine would cover a series of articles by that member.' As that member was almost certainly Trumper, one must presume that the *Chronicle* offered to pay the fine if it was a one-off, then perhaps baulked at the idea of covering it every time he wrote.

Like his flirtations with English counties in 1902, Trumper's dalliance with the *Chronicle* in 1905 is one of those oddities his biographers have sidestepped, perhaps because it scarcely reconciles with his reputation for a saintly scorn of 'the filthy dollar'. But Trumper appears guilty of naivety at least, caught up in mass media manoeuverings for celebrity and sensation. With this he and his teammates had a further brush when they stepped forth for their first practice session in the Nursery at Lord's on the morning of 1 May, and were surrounded by no fewer than twenty-four photographers massed to take team photographs, plus a newsreel cameraman from Edison Kinetoscope to film them doing so. The Australians were caught slightly off guard as they gathered in their usual hearty manner – on seeing the newsreel later at the Palace Theatre, they were amused at the vigorous V-signs that Laver exchanged with fellow Victorian Warwick Armstrong, and by spinner Bill Howell rolling a ball off Trumper's capped head. They were less impressed by the importunings of the photographers, whom Laver regarded as 'a perfect nuisance.'

> We required from each a guarantee that he would give each member of the team a copy and would not use the photo in any form whatever for advertising purposes on postcards. Some avoided the latter condition rather cleverly, making cards the same size and shape as ordinary postcards and selling them. With all our care it did not prevent postcards from being issued. Some of these were faked and frightful productions, heads were stuck on bodies of other people &c. The pictures on one postcard did not in the

least degree look like us. The publishers did not even trouble to put moustaches on faces where moustaches should have been.

Now, it's arguable, Laver was being the naive one. The money in cricket no longer came and went only via the gate. It underpinned other commercial objectives, leveraged from feat, name and image: if the Australians declined to make it themselves, it would be made from them. Nor need this always be crass or exploitative, and other ends were achievable. The visitors probably felt a certain reassurance when out of the ruck of photographers at Lord's that day stepped a figure they knew, liked and trusted.

•

Uniquely among Beldam's numerous 'sittings', this session with his Australian subjects is actually dated, in the diary of his artist friend Henry Tuke, who with his other artist friend Albert Chevallier Tayler were helpmates in the work. Beldam turned thirty-seven that 1 May, and had plans to celebrate his birthday later at a Royal Academy dinner. First, though, his purpose was to obtain photographs of Trumper and two teammates, Clem Hill and Algy Gehrs. The spring weather threw down a damp and blustery challenge, but the painters patiently anchored the camera as Beldam showed off a new trick, evolved over the past year, of bowling the ball with his right hand and taking the photograph with his left by means of a pneumatic push connected to the Videx by a twenty-metre cord. There was none of the larkishness of the morning. Three years earlier, Trumper had smiled at the novelty of being photographed; now, having first stood still in his stance then allowed his grip to be closely examined, he produced hooks, pulls, cuts and drives on

A day at Lord's: Trumper at a glance.

request, as Beldam strove to facilitate with sympathetic deliveries. On at least one occasion, perhaps when the ball was unsuitable, he was bowled.

The Australians and Beldam were to see a great deal of each other in this summer. Three days later, as the tour commenced formally at Crystal Palace, the photographer turned back into a cricketer and bowled to them in an actual match, representing a Gentlemen of England XI led by Grace, and also including Fry, MacLaren, Warner, Jessop and Poidevin. Now Beldam actually hit Trumper's stumps for real, to the disappointment of an expectant crowd. Had he detected some semblance of weakness from his photographic studies? After all, by agreeing to be frozen in time, Beldam's subjects were revealing aspects of their game previously imperceptible; they were consenting to their demystification.

Yet the mutual intrigue must have been strong. Photographer and subject could regard themselves as involved in parallel pursuits. 'Shot', 'catch', 'timing': these were words as meaningful in the use of a camera as of a cricket bat. The secret of his success, Beldam thought, lay in his being a cricketer himself, which put him 'in touch with the mind and movements of the player'.

A foreign pupil once thought it was the 'leetle' brush which caused the master to do such beautiful water-colour work. The master gave him the brush, and he came back with the remark that it was not the 'leetle' brush but the hand behind it, and his master ventured to suggest that there might also be something behind the hand. So in Action-Photography, given the right kind of camera, everything must depend on the timing powers and perception of the artist; and these must be also combined with good knowledge of the principles of cricket, golf, lawn tennis, or any other game of which photographs are required.

The surroundings, possibly the crowd, everything which is likely to distract the attention of the operator must be obliterated, and a kind of telepathy must exist between the player and the camera artist.

When Beldam next photographed Trumper, there were just such surroundings, and a 'kind of telepathy' very much at work.

·

To continue his study, Beldam now pursued Trumper to The Oval. Exactly when went unrecorded, but it was almost certainly before play on a day of Australia's game against Surrey, which spanned 11–13 May 1905. We know Beldam was present because the *Illustrated Sporting and Dramatic News* the following week published a photograph of Beldam in street attire standing at cover with his camera while Clem Hill played to leg on a pitch marked at the eastern edge of the square – from this can be inferred the services of a bowler. We know also that the game had a noon start with no tea break, and the

The photographer photographed: Beldam at The Oval.

shortish shadows in the photographs Beldam took of Trumper are consistent with their being taken in late morning.

The Oval was a location pregnant with meaning: the venue where Australians had made a fortune in 1878, lost a great Test in 1880, and won a great Test in 1882; the home of one of the county clubs that had recently sought to recruit Trumper. It was also a vision of the future of cricket watching, served as it was by the world's first electric tube and a brand new tram line, surmounted by a superb pavilion hosting 400 000 visitors a year. Overshadowed by the gasholders of the South Metropolitan Gas Works, increasingly encircled by factories, foundries and breweries, The Oval's playing expanse now had a *rus in urbe* quality, a remnant of the days when Kennington had been open fields and market gardens.

With the King as patron and the Lord Chief Justice as president, Surrey County CC was at a zenith of self-estimation. Secretary Charles Alcock had just published a sumptuous history billing the county as 'the Cradle of Cricket', dismissing the traditional claims to that title of the village of Hambledon, and also subtly puncturing the pretensions of Marylebone. Socially exclusive Lord's might headquarter cricket's high councils, believed Alcock, but The Oval was the ground of the people, providing 'a great education for them in every possible way'. In a verse in *Fry's Magazine*, the Surrey amateur Digby Jephson saluted the diversity of Oval crowds:

> There are soldiers, sailors and postmen there,
> There are clerks from their high-backed stools.
> There are tinkers, tailors and booing brats,
> And swells of The City in silken hats
> And men from the clubs in immaculate spats
> But all of them know the rules.

Their own rules were an attendance to pleasure of utmost seriousness and decorum. In the *Jubilee Book*, Ranji had reported the astonishment of a German visiting a county match at The Oval at 'the extreme orderliness of the many thousands' in the presence of a mere 'five policemen' when 'abroad it would require at least 300 policemen to keep such a large crowd in order'. When Neville Cardus later argued for cricket as the 'national art' of a people 'prone to be ashamed of living the life aesthetic', he gestured not towards St John's Wood but Kennington: 'Go among the shilling crowd any fine day at The Oval and what do you hear? Little technical jargon, little talk of off-breaks and the position of the left funny bone in the late cut. Instead you will hear many delighted cries of "Beautiful stroke – Beautiful!"'

That day at The Oval, Beldam was pursuing his own 'beautiful stroke'. His photographs at Lord's had been of different shots from more or less similar angles, just either side of straight. Now he sought the perfect encapsulation of the perfect drive down the ground. Peering down through the grid of his viewfinder, he worked his way around a 180-degree arc, stopping to take pictures at five points between mid-on and second slip, in the process exposing a background panorama of the ground: low-level terraces fringed by distant houses; the exoskeleton of the gasometers; the silhouette of a solitary tree beside the pavilion's solemn bulk. The passage of time can be sensed from the lesser and greater concentrations of onlookers, presumably building up as game time approached. In some images, smudged figures appear on the outfield, including a woman with a parasol, perhaps Annie Trumper.

A recurrent detail is noticeable: Trumper's front foot poised in midair as the bat flourished at the top of its swing, inspired perhaps by Beldam's successful picture of Ranji the previous year, as if to stress the subject's balance and light-footedness, and also the instantaneity

A day at The Oval: Trumper's foot hovers.

of the medium. In no other photographic sequence of Beldam's would this prove such a motif – there is a sense of him exploring his camera's limits as he documented Trumper's. When Beldam moved to point, side-on to the action, he paused with special care. This time, he wanted Trumper to commence his stride from outside the crease, his back foot a metre ahead of the line, a preliminary step to this position assumed – the straight drive potentiated, attack sharpened to a fine point. To capture it, he planned a photograph of equivalent skill and nerve, tilting the plate holder at the back of the Videx so as to produce images of a landscape rather than a portrait shape. This was something he very seldom did. In the rest of his oeuvre there are only a handful of none-too-successful attempts to work in such a way. Such a photograph required the leaving of a space for an on-rushing cricketer to fill – it risked a wasted plate, which Beldam deplored. It was a gesture of confidence in his subject, that Trumper had the athleticism to match the conception. It's also possible Beldam looked at the background, for from his sideways vantage was visible a gulf in the skyline opened by the width of Clayton Street stretching away from the ground – defined on the left by a boarding house and on the right by the Clayton Arms Hotel, it was in its way the perfect frame, especially in a photograph now absent the orienting presence of stumps.

The publican of the Clayton Arms, one Frederick Brooke, had shown a shrewd understanding of the conspicuousness of his establishment and allowed advertisers to emblazon its facade: a big banner spruiked *Sporting Life* ('The Paper the Professionals Read'); smaller ones promoted Rosbach ('Empress of Table Waters'), Bovril ('Bovril Always Scores') and Claymore Whisky ('Tired Nature's Sweet Restorer'). But Beldam blurred these, and also the legend 'Refreshments' on the front of The Oval's bar, by widening his aperture and shrinking his depth of field. A crowd had collected square of the wicket – all those soldiers and sailors, tinkers and tailors, orderly and dark-clad. With the twiddling of a knob, they too became an indistinct mass. Trumper would be the image's entire foreground in a narrow strip of focus.

There survives no contact sheet or diary note chronicling the order or even the number of photographs Beldam took of Trumper's spring from this angle. All we know is that three images survive. One he would save for his later small book *Cricket Illustrated* (1908). It was almost but not quite right. Trumper was *just* short of occupying the Clayton Street gap; his left wrist was bent *just* a little awkwardly; his weight had not *quite* fully transferred; two dark figures, perhaps police constables, loitered in the middle distance.*

Variation on a theme: Trumper drives.

---

* In his personal copy of *Cricket Illustrated*, now owned by collector John Hawkins, Beldam annotated the image for comparison with a photo on the adjacent page of W. G. Grace, using his favoured technical jargon: 'Well marked left arm screw but wrist joint bent (how unfortunate!). Right hand relaxed (not revolved). Symptoms cf opposite page reversed, bat face looking backward and not straight at you (due to left wrist joint) etc etc.'

It has the hallmarks of a first attempt, after which Beldam moved ever so slightly left, so that Trumper's head in his normal stance would have reposed between the distant ogee-roofed towers of the board school on Kennington Road.

Beldam's method was almost always to collect an image of the stroke in completed form, so he had Trumper proceed all the way to the follow-through, the bat having described more than a full circle, shoulders now completely turned. This time the framing worked better, for Trumper stopped just short of the right side of the gulf, almost vertically upright, eyes seemingly fixed on the disappearing ball. Beldam would have withdrawn the plate with a feeling of confidence. But could he get Trumper at the extent of his spring?

For Beldam, photography was often a rush, a compromise, seeking opportune moments when subjects were willing and the climate was favourable. Photography remained so novel that few had a clear idea how long it took. Beldam enjoyed relating a story of seeking permission to photograph the players at a certain county club, and the secretary asking the duration of exposures. 'A thousandth of a second,' said Beldam. 'Oh well, then,' the secretary replied. 'You'll soon be through with our eleven – about one one-hundredth of a second for the whole team.'

The build-up of the crowd visible through his viewfinder would have told Beldam now that time was running out. One can imagine ground staff, officials and policemen looking at their watches wondering when all this palaver would be done; one can imagine spectators looking on from afar bemused by the stop-start action; one can imagine the ball leaving the bowler's hand, the batsman commencing to leap, and the photographer clicking to release the mirror, engage the shutter, expose the plate, and wonder ... *had he got it?*

6

'HE HAS NO STYLE,
YET HE IS ALL STYLE'

'London, an Edwardian summer's day. George Beldam,
cricket's photographic pioneer, captures the essence of Victor Trumper
in a picture that has become an Australian icon.'
– Caption in *Wisden Cricketers' Almanack*, 2000

On 1 August 1905, Swan Electric Engraving Company, a West End firm specialising in art prints, made available an unusual item: a limited edition India proof photogravure, 14½" × 16½ in" (37 cm × 42 cm), of a cricketer in the act of jumping out to drive. The cricketer with that look; the cricketer who had to be seen; the cricketer whose strokes, in Philip Trevor's words, were beyond 'the ordinary eye to follow'; now, at least in theory, the sight of Victor Trumper's batting was available to all. And it was merely a foretaste. Three weeks later, Macmillan & Co. formally released *Great Batsmen: Their Methods at a Glance*, its 716 pages featuring '600 Action-Photographs' by 'George W. Beldam' and a text by 'Charles B. Fry'.

For a decade, cricket's benchmark pictorial work had been Alcock's stately *Great Cricketers and Cricket Grounds*, with its portraits, poses and panoramas. Now Beldam offered imperious drives, rasping cuts, fearless hooks, scintillating glances, lavish backlifts, flourishing follow-throughs – the accent throughout was on attack, and off the front foot. All were adorned with Fry's mandarin prose, pronouncing voluminously on 'wristwork', 'armswing' and 'shoulder turn', insisting on 'correct bodily mechanism' and the 'left-shoulder-forward principle', distinguishing sharply between 'upward forward swing' and 'downward flicking turn', between 'wrist leverage' and 'finger manipulation'.

Fry had arrived at length on criteria of batting style – that of minimal effort to maximum effect, and that of a tasteful orthodoxy that nonetheless did not impinge on individuality. He had discerned these in Ranjitsinhji those years ago; now they appealed to him as ideals to aspire to, as an index of batting's refinement. The structure of *Great Batsmen* told a tale of progress. Grace, as ever, was accorded pride of place in the 'Individualities' section, with twenty-six photographs, although with a note of apology for his proconsular bulk, stiff arms and heavy boots. 'What a pity Action-Photography was not invented twenty years ago!' exclaimed the authors, as if to ward off complaints of awkwardness.

Second in line of descent came twenty photographs of Ranji, wrists as supple as Grace's were unyielding. Third came no fewer than thirty-three photographs of Trumper, more than for any other cricketer, perhaps because none so completely fulfilled the co-authors' twin purposes of providing instruction and also aesthetic example. His slim physique bent this way and that; his strokes streaked away to every degree of the field; in the photograph being marketed by Swan Engraving, which in *Great Batsmen* became 'Plate XXVII', Trumper managed both to surge towards the future and to hark back to models of antiquity, in his classical proportions, broad shoulders tapering to the waist, and taut, dynamic muscularity. The image's antecedents, in fact, were as sculptural as pictorial, specifically the classics of *contrapposto* – the posing of a figure with weight unevenly distributed, one leg 'engaged', the other leg 'free'. Impetus for *contrapposto* had come from the desire to capture ideal male athletic form. Here was a modern culmination of that exercise, loaded with asymmetries: one foot grounded, the other airborne; one hand gloved, the other bare; the shirt both loose and tight; the arms both gloriously free and tensed for action. For all Trumper's evident agility, his position had a curious aerodynamic stability, controlled by the level, unblinking eyes, fit for plinth as well as pitch. And against the murkily dark backdrop, the batsman's flannels had a marble whiteness; the folds could have been worked by a riffler.

Fry followed Trumper, with practised modesty, then a procession of style's various interpreters in subtle alternation, of Australians and Englishman, amateur and professional. It's when the 'Strokes Illustrated' section is added that the mix can be seen as appreciably skewed. Sixty-five amateurs are sprinkled with only nineteen professionals – batting's example, the co-authors clearly agreed, could only be set by cricket's aristocracy.

Among that cognoscenti, *Great Batsmen* was understood at once to be a landmark publication. Copies were presented to the King, to the Prince of Wales, and to Surrey CCC, among whose members advertising leaflets were circulated. *Cricket* offered a prospectus. Swan Engraving released two further photogravures, of prancing

Ranji and seigneurial F. S. Jackson, to complement the Trumper.*
Critical acclaim was unanimous. 'The best book about England's game

Icons in the making: yours for a guinea.

yet published': *Evening News*. 'The most precious gem that cricket literature has ever possessed': *Sporting Life*. Here, explained *The Graphic*,
was a whole new way of approaching the game. Hitherto it had been
impossible 'to see the details of a stroke, so momentary [was] every
movement'. At last, with this 'very large number of photographs of
famous batsmen in action', one could 'study at leisure the most minute
details of their methods'. For critics' abstractions had been substituted
the camera's artless truthfulness: 'Every one of the six hundred photographs is an actuality. If the proverb is true about an ounce of fact and a
pound of theory, the book ought to be invaluable.' Classical criteria of
beauty, moreover, had been met, claimed the *Illustrated London News*:

> Sometimes the pose in which the batsman has been caught is
> ungraceful, even awkward; on the other hand we are inclined

---

* Swan made available 500 India proofs – a fine, very smooth paper, designed to
show off every small detail – of each image at a guinea each. There was also an
unspecified number of plain prints at 10s 6d.

to think that had our national game been known to the ancient
Greeks, their sculptors must have discovered on the cricket-ground
suggestions for statues of athletes equal in grace and vigour to any
inspired by the Olympic Games.

Thank you, Victor Trumper.

•

Cricket and art: the intersection exercised Beldam ever more, so
much that he had been working secretly with another collaborator.
His friend Albert Chevallier Tayler was at peak renown as a portrait and genre painter, recently acclaimed for 'The Ceremony of the
Garter' (1901) and 'Five Kings' (1903); he was also a cricket devotee,
appearing regularly for the Artists XI (Hillyard Swinstead, Reginald
Blomfield, G. Spencer Watson) against the Authors XI (E. V. Lucas,
P. G. Wodehouse, Arthur Conan Doyle, E. W. Hornung). Now, just
as Hal Ludlow had turned Beldam's Harry Vardon into a statue,
Tayler agreed to produce pastel drawings of leading players based
on Beldam photographs. Over summer the forty-eight prints in
The Empire's Cricketers were exhibited in batches of four at the New
Bond Street Gallery, marketed as folio-size lithographs by the Fine
Art Society, and finally collected by Dawbarn & Ward in a cloth-
bound portfolio: thirty-seven Englishmen and eleven Australians,
pristine in white against grey-green backgrounds, splashed with colour by their caps and waistbands.

Art inspired by sport derived from photography? It was a doubly
bold notion, and the co-venturers seem to have known it, for Tayler's
catalogue downplayed his debt to the camera, merely acknowledg-
ing Beldam's 'information and assistance'. Nor was the response

better than lukewarm. The *Illustrated London News*'s reviewer, 'W.M.', thought that the 'complex excellence of this or that action' would be 'lost on those who are not keen followers of the game'. But those keen followers, increasingly accustomed by photography to exact likenesses and fine detail, weren't impressed either, troubled by touches like artistic blurrings and contoured hatching. *Cricket*'s perennial editor Charles Alcock, in this context an important arbiter of taste, regarded the drawings with particular disfavour. The average cricketer, he thought, 'may want to know why Dr Grace looks five feet high, and why he wears boots without laces; why Pelham Warner uses a bat which is not spliced, and why he is also without laces to his boots; why Rhodes has a deformed right hand and why he is bowling a ball which would be discarded, even in a preparatory school, as much too small'; not to mention 'why all the cricketers wear shirts with stripes running in all sorts of curious ways – he is hardly likely to be satisfied with being told that the stripes are really shadows, for he will say that he never sees a cricketer wear shadows in that way'. From photographs Alcock could accept angularities and oddities; from art he expected . . . well, art.*

Yet Alcock had a point. From Beldam's portfolio, possibly because he was straining to avoid too obvious a reliance on the photographs, Tayler chose rather less than compelling examples, muting the effect of his images: sales duly fell short of expectations, and a further forty-two drawings were never released. Where *The Empire's Cricketers* did enjoy a curious afterlife was in Melbourne the following year, local tobacco manufacturers Sniders & Abrahams reproducing forty of the drawings as cards for their 'Milo' cigarettes – unusual cigarette cards for not relying on regulation portraits, and a foretaste of the promiscuous uses to which Beldam photographs would later be put.

---

* If the co-venturers were disappointed, they might have consoled themselves with an idea they were ahead of their time: nine of the prints have since found their way into Britain's National Portrait Gallery, alongside only one other work by Tayler.

The Empire's cigarette: Tayler's Trumper as print and card.

Great Batsmen itself had by then made the journey to Australia, and been received as favourably as it had in England. 'Even in these days of marvellous productions and reproductions it is scarcely possible for the work of the photo-author-cricketers to be excelled': *The Argus.* 'No cricketer should fail to see it, while batsmen who aspire to distinction should study it': *The Queenslander.* 'Not all the theory in the world from the pen of the best writer could convey to the mind the full idea of how to make a stroke or bowl a ball in the same convincing manner as that supplied by the art of photography': the *Sydney Mail.* Which pointed up a subtle tension. 'Mr. Fry has very high praise for our own Victor Trumper's style,' reported *The Australasian,* 'and certainly the attitude and poise of the incomparable New South Wales batsman are so graceful in making certain strokes that they would serve admirably as a model for a cricket sculptor.' Yet in the presence of the finest image, it was noticeable that Fry had virtually nothing to say.

•

Trumper enthralled both collaborators, but on them he appears to have had quite different effects. Of no other individual batsman did Beldam include more images; to no images did Fry add less. Fry seems to have found the Australian slightly perplexing. 'Victor Trumper is, perhaps, the most difficult batsman in the world to reduce to words,' he began his succinct appreciation. 'He has no style, and yet he is all style. He has no fixed canonical method of play, he defies all the orthodox rules, yet every stroke he plays satisfies the ultimate criterion of style – minimum of effort, maximum of effect.' By this last observation Fry accommodated Trumper in his aesthetic convictions. But to Beldam's most exquisite image, he could add only a sixteen-word caption: 'Jumping out for a straight drive. Shoulders, arms, and wrists will all come into the stroke.'

This terseness stood out because Fry was otherwise so prolix, capable of spending whole pages on individual stances and grips, and of distinctions of an almost inconceivable fineness.* By now he was almost prepared to accept the visual as the preferable form of immediate testimony: 'The truth is that the action of any stroke is very complicated, and impossible to describe completely and accurately

---

* As an example, Fry explaining the difference between a 'drive' and a 'push':
　　'It is almost impossible to distinguish between a stroke which is a genuine outright drive and one which is played with a modified swing scarcely amounting to more than a forward push. If there is any swing at all in the stroke, as distinguished from thrust, the stroke immediately differs in kind from the genuine forward stroke played only with a thrusting action of the right arm, aided perhaps by the wrists. But as some players manage to play this push-stroke in a very lively manner, and as others drive with a very short and modified swing, and as the foot-work in both these strokes is often precisely similar, it is very difficult to distinguish between the two strokes. When a batsman either runs or jumps out to the ball, or when he moves his left foot to the ball with a very short step and hits with a pronounced swing, the custom is to call the stroke a drive. But when a player reaches out at the ball with one long stride of the left foot, just as in playing the push-stroke, and swings at the ball, the stroke is sometimes called a forward stroke and sometimes a drive . . .'

in words . . . The actual movements in a stroke can be portrayed only by a series of instantaneous photographs.' But the concession did not come easily, partly because any image that 'spoke for itself' left the critic such as Fry uneasily placed – as Walter Benjamin would observe, the circulation of mechanically reproduced images subverted the former circles of privileged interpretation by rendering every consumer a 'semi-expert'. It may not be coincidental that Fry's writing on cricket technique after *Great Batsmen*, mainly in disquisitions for his magazine, grew ever longer and more complicated, to the point where he confessed a fear of growing 'too abstruse to be intelligible' and of indulging in 'unblushing theoreticalness'. Abandoning references to 'the sculptor of modern times', he began exhorting batsmen to behave as 'a live machine, a system of levers whose action in each case must be perfectly adjusted in order to produce the perfect stroke': the images in Fry's solo treatise *Batsmanship* (1912) are staid and inert. Fry's 1939 autobiography then mysteriously omitted Beldam altogether, in favour of, among other things, an account of his 1934 meeting with Hitler and sympathy with Nazism.

Trumper's influence on Beldam was quite otherwise. He also had to 'reduce' the Australian, from a moving three-dimensional subject to a stationary two-dimensional object. But for the first time in sporting history he demonstrated how skilfully and memorably this could be done. At a time when sport and photography were barely acquainted, he integrated them like extensions of the other. 'Jumping Out' represents an incunabula, a first tracing, of the modern action photograph, anticipating its whole grammar of athletic motion and of mass spectacle. Aspects of its memorability go to the essence not just of cricket but of image making itself.

•

At the simplest level, 'Jumping Out' is black and white, with all the shades between: the pale cream of Trumper's attire standing out against the inkiness of the terraces, the dark line of the buildings against the grey luminosity of the sky. It is thereby rendered at once historic and classic, fitting into the tradition of serious photography that scorned colour film long after it became freely available – 'black and white *are* the colours of photography', decreed Robert Frank famously. 'Jumping Out' has been 'colourised' at various times since, but always at a cost to its sensitivity of detail and nuances of mood, its roundness, volume and depth. For where black-and-white tends to date cinema and television, we seem to read black-and-white photographs in a different way. As the noted British colorimetrist David Wright put it: 'You may get closer to reality with colour, but the closer you get the more obvious it becomes that the picture is not a real thing.'

Beldam also freshens a relatively familiar action by a novel vantage. The stroke is both instantly recognisable as the platonic ideal of a straight drive, returning the ball from whence it came, and uniquely Trumper's: this is the way to play it, yet only *this* batsman can play it *this* way. Trumper hurtles headlong across the frame, insouciantly out of his ground, taking what's implied is a second stride towards the ball, the safety of the crease far behind. There is no hedging, no half-measure – Trumper is daring all on the basis of his skill, eye, and also, in some measure, his amateur status, ambiguous and disputed as it sometimes was.

To Beldam's photograph, in fact, there is actually a curious counterpart. Two years earlier, Hurst and Blackett had published an instruction manual, *The Cricket of Abel, Hirst and Shrewsbury* (1903), featuring thirty-four photographs of the so-named professionals, Abel, Shrewsbury and George Hirst. The author, E. F. Benson,

The Governor of the Colony (Sir Henry Barkly) was present in his Pavn on the Stand, and the Game was staged in situ for the photograph, — but the Idiot Batt rub in an amicable moved just then !!! B.J.

icket Match at Melbourne, Australia. 1860. Between New South Wales & Victoria (Hot wind blowing.)

THE TYRANNY OF DISTANCE: Action and proximity were beyond Barrett Johnstone en he took Australia's oldest surviving cricket photograph at the MCG in 1860 p); artworks like 1887's 'The Imaginary Cricket Match' by Robert Ponsonby Staples d George Barrable (bottom) were better able to capture an instant, while still falling ort of intimacy.

1899 AND ALL THAT: In the earliest film footage of Australian cricketers, at Cheltenham (top right), the newsreel cameraman somehow captures Victor Trumper in characteristic attitude (top left). The twenty-one-year-old's first tour of England was also a pilgrimage to places weighted with imperial meaning, like Nelson's flagship HMS *Victory* (bottom).

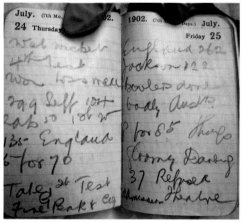

MAKING HIS MARK: In repose on his first tour, Victor Trumper stopped to carve his initials into a dressing-room balcony at Lord's (top); and to receive the tribute of a bat from the past master W. G. Grace (middle). Three years later, he kept a diary, briskly noting the first century before lunch on a Test's opening day: 'Self 104' (bottom).

FOCUS ON TRUMPER: Bewitched by the Trumper of 1902, amateur cricketer
and photographer George Beldam snapped him from afar during the Test at
The Oval (top) and in the nets at Lord's soon after (bottom). With three further
years' experience, Beldam would immortalise his subject at the same locations.

THE BATSMAN OF THE YEAR

K. S. Ranjitsinhji jumping out to drive. An action-photograph taken by G. W. Beldam at the County Ground, Hove, on the last day of the Sussex Cricket Season, 1904.

PIN-UP BOY: Prince Ranjitsinhji, most exotic of Edwardian cricketers, flashed before readers of *C. B. Fry's Magazine* in 1904 as an example of Beldam's art. 'The picture, more or less, speaks for itself,' wrote an appreciative Fry – a rare concession.

OVAL-SHAPED: In 1902, local hero Bobby Abel demonstrates 'running out to drive' on his home ground The Oval, static and earthbound (top); the background which George Beldam would reduce to a suggestive blur can also be seen in a 1906 view of the ground and its precincts (bottom), including the Clayton Arms loudly spruiking *Sporting Life*.

VICTOR TRUMPER

PLATE XXVII

Jumping out for a straight drive. Shoulders, arms, and wrists will all come into the stroke.

VICTOR TRUMPER

PLATE XXVIII

Finish of a stroke exactly the same as in Plate XXVII. These two pictures together show
Victor Trumper's drive to perfection.

STROKE OF GENIUS: Stages in the Trumper straight drive shown 'to perfection'
across a double page in 1905's *Great Batsmen* by Beldam and Fry.

THE SPORTSMAN'S LIBRARY.

(Our illustrations are reproduced from "Great Batsmen: Their Methods at a Glance," by George W. Beldam and Charles B. Fry, by permission of the publishers, Messrs. Macmillan and Co., Ltd.)

There is a delightful simplicity in the text, which is Mr. C. B. Fry's contribution. The writer clearly and forcibly explains each photograph in as few words as possible. His first subject is, of course, Dr. Grace, to whom the book is dedicated, and than whom, apart from his position in the cricket world, no finer model could have been selected. Next follow K. S. Ranjitsinhji, Victor Trumper, C. B. Fry, Clem Hill, F. S. Jackson, R. A. Duff, A. C. MacLaren, M. A. Noble, Tom Hayward, R. E. Foster, J. T. Tyldesley, George Hirst, L. C. H. Palairet, J. H. Sinclair, W. W. Armstrong, G. L. Jessop, and W. G. Quaife. Part II. of the book is entitled, "Strokes Illustrated," and the plates here include photographs of many more notable batsmen.

———

"THE LOSS OF THE MALPASIA." By J. St. A. Jewell. (Yachtsman Publishing Co.) A collection of real sea stories, told by one who has evidently served under the red ensign, and very well told, too, for the author has a fund of humour in him which mingles pleasantly with the flavour of the salt sea-spray which pervades most of the yarns. The first tale tells of the wreck of a mail-boat, which was run on to a rock, while the fourth officer, who should have been on the bridge in charge, was making love to a lady passenger elsewhere. "The Line of Burling's Drift" is one of the funny stories. It concerns the adventures of an old tub of a vessel which was anchored well to windward of a fleet of smart cutters, yawls, and motor-boats, in order to sell the first thing in the morning. In the middle of the night, however, a gale unexpectedly sprang up, and the old craft started drifting, smashing up all more delicate and expensive boats one by one until she fetched up alongside Southend Pier.

G. L. JESSOP.

"At first sight the batsman here appears to be beginning an ordinary forward stroke to a ball outside the off-stump. . . . But in point of fact we see here the beginning of a stroke which hits the ball to square leg from well outside the off-stump."

K. S. RANJITSINHJI.
"This is the famous so-called leg glance, which is perhaps the best known and most admired of Ranjitsinhji's strokes."

THE suggestion that a man learnt his game from a book is generally regarded as a reference of contempt. The inference was justified before the art of illustration had reached its present stage of perfection, and authors candidly admitted that oral instruction and instruction by example were absolutely necessary. But the enormous strides which have been made, during recent years, in rapid photography have almost worked a revolution. In such a volume as that issued by Messrs. Macmillan and bearing the above title, we have not a few plates to illustrate the meanings conveyed in the letterpress, but deductions drawn from no fewer than 600 photographs. A run through the pictures will surprise the reader. He will see

"ARCHERS OF THE LONGBOW." By Arthur Moore. (Constable, 6s.) This is properly described as an "exorbitant story, for a wilder plot never entered the head of modern writer, nor was more cleverly worked out into such a comedy of errors. A young fellow fresh from college is fascinated by a pretty girl, who, he discovers, resides with a Mr. Plinssl Drew, who carries on the business of "expert adviser." Consulting with a 'Varsity chum, they resolve to invent a case which will require expert advice, and so possibly obtain an introduction to the fair unknown. Accordingly an Anarchist plot with conspirators, an injured Olga and bombs, all complete, is promptly organised, and related to the adviser with such circumstantial detail that he is completely deceived. Not so the young lady, however, and she invents counterplots, and they get most horribly mixed up, but it is too good a story to spoil by entering into further particulars. It will pay for reading.

tainly opposed by birth and position, as their parents were the most bitter enemies. The girl's father was a vulgar, assertive man, a company promoter and financier, while the young man's parent was a member of the aristocracy who had been used by the other as a cat'l bird, so that it may be imagined that there was no love lost between the families. However, all comes right in the end.

"RHYMES OF THE EAST AND RE-COLLECTED VERSES." By Dum Dum. (Constable; 3s. 6d. net.) The majority of these verses have appeared at various times in the pages of *Punch*, but were well worth rescuing from that literary "blend" and given a chance to flourish on their own merits, which they certainly should do, for some of them are particularly clever, and most of them full of humour.

"STORIES AND ESSAYS." By Kate Scanlon. (Henry Drane; 3s. 6d.) This is an unfortunate mixture of fiction and fact, for the subjects do not amalgamate very well. "Pickles" is a pathetic little anecdote of a small boy's first love, which occurs on the voyage home from the Cape, but it is not of sufficient importance to take the leading place in a book of this sort. By the way, where was the corrector to the press when "Medical Men and their Bedside Manners" was being put into type?

VICTOR TRUMPER.
"The finish of a cut. The bat has been completely turned over by the wrists."

famous cricketers in positions in which he can never have remembered seeing them on the field, and positions which will seem to him to be exaggerated. But close inspection will reveal to him a certain grace in all the movements portrayed. Mr. G. L. Jessop has even less respect for style than most of us had imagined, whilst, for his photographs, R. E. Foster might almost have posed, so well does he conform to orthodox methods.

Percy White New edition. (Constable, 2s. 6d. net.) The fact that it has reached another edition speaks more loudly in a book's favour than a hundred reviewers; but this is really a very charming novel, including a prettily told love story, and flavoured with delicate satire and up-to-date cynicism. It is related by an old bachelor of sixty odd, who has been the *deus ex machina* to bring about the marriage between two young people who, however well they may have been fitted for each other by nature, were cer-

F. S. JACKSON.
Captain of England XI., 1905.

'THE MOST PRECIOUS GEM THAT CRICKET LITERATURE HAS EVER POSSESSED':
Great Batsmen enjoyed a rapturous critical reception exalting Beldam's images,
including this testimonial in *Illustrated Sporting and Dramatic News*.

THE MORTAL VICTOR TRUMPER: A newsreel camera records Trumper's 1915 funeral procession to Waverley Cemetery (top); Victorian cricketers paid their respects after the war in a very different Australia (bottom).

MR. J. C. DAVIS.

THE LEGEND LIVES ON: J. C. Davis,
Frank Iredale, Sir Neville Cardus and
Jack Fingleton (clockwise from top
left) kept fresh the Trumper story in
print. 'To change the old saying about
the strawberry,' Cardus wrote in 1929,
'God no doubt could create a better
batsman than Victor Trumper had He
wished but so far He hasn't.'

COVER POINT: As Bradman rewrote the statistics therein, the NSW
Cricket Association put Trumper on the cover of its yearbook (top left),
where he remained for twenty-five years. Perhaps no image has adorned
so many cricket book covers since.

WE CAN DO IT: Trumper goes colour for the Bicentenary Test (top left), likewise his emulators Dean Jones (top right) and Belinda Clark (bottom). Photographer Ian Kenins even posed Clark on Trumper's native heath, Moore Park.

TRUMPER THE SALESMAN: The icon sells a beer (top) and a band (left).

TRUMPER IN INDIA: In *Sport & Pastime* in 1952 (middle); by artist Balaji Venugopal in 2014 (bottom right).

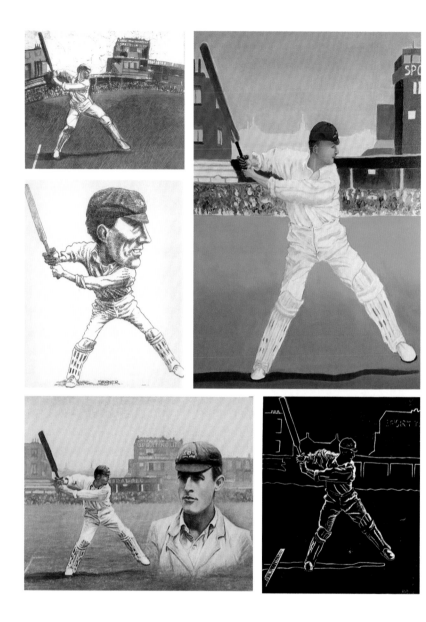

THE ART OF CRICKET: Beldam's Trumper reinterpreted by (clockwise from top left) Judith Dobie, Peter Young, Russell Ayres, Dave Thomas and John Spooner.

THE CRAFT OF CRICKET: Beldam's Trumper (clockwise from top left) in china, in chalk, in silver, in resin and in tapestry.

THE SPIRIT OF CRICKET: Beldam's Trumper revived by *The Age*'s Jim Pavlidis to celebrate Ashton Agar in 2013 (top); evoked by the *Daily Telegraph*'s John Tiedemann to mourn Philip Hughes in 2014 (bottom).

is remembered today for a sequence of comic novels, the Mapp and Lucia series, and for membership of a gifted family – an older sister was a trailblazing Egyptologist; an older brother wrote the words to 'Land of Hope and Glory'. His role as instructor in this case was based on the eccentric premise that as himself a poor cricketer he was better equipped as a teacher: 'On the principle of "Set a thief to catch a thief", a duffer has here been set to catch a duffer, while at the same time the whole teaching is, I hope, strictly according to the actual play of good players, as shown by observation, by photographs.'

Except that from Edgar Basebe's photographs could be deduced almost nothing: the subjects stood solemnly and stonily still. To illustrate 'running out to drive', Basebe positioned Abel in the same place at the same ground against the same backdrop as Beldam positioned Trumper for a more or less identical stroke. Yet the differences are so marked that the latter could almost be a comment on the former. Abel's sole semblance of animation is a slightly raised back heel; Trumper appears as if taking wing. Abel's hands are cautiously parted; Trumper's act in harmonious concert. Abel is anchored by the stumps and a heavily criss-crossed crease; Trumper is alone but for a fraction of a crease line falling irrelevantly away. There is nobody to watch Abel; Trumper is the cynosure of all eyes. Between them, the photographs form a world view. Abel, the archetypal professional, is ultimately a drudge with an eye to his livelihood; Trumper, an amateur at least for the sake of this argument, is the free spirit at play. Only one has the dash, the *élan*, to inspire and lead. It's worth noting, too, that Abel, despite having accumulated more than 20 000 first-class runs in the previous decade, was granted but a single small photograph in *Great Batsmen*; Arthur Shrewsbury, having gloomily taken his own life not long before in fear of a suspected illness, did not appear at all.

If that social demarcation is no longer significant to a modern audience, the sense of expansiveness, abandon and even innocence remains. The shot is all instinct, no calculation. The backlift is high, thrillingly high, and straight, pendulously straight; the high grip reveals most of the handle; the protective gear is light, the clothing unmarred by logos or brands. The contrast is now, perhaps, between Trumper's unsullied whiteness and the encroachments of commerce, symbolised in the brand names looming indistinctly in the background, in anticipation of the role of sponsors, broadcasters and other corporates in sport's diffusion. Trumper is holding aloof from them, his absorption in his task reinforced by the photograph's perspective. His face is in profile – physiognomically distinctive, inherently fleeting. The profile is the way we would see passers-by if we turned sideways in the street, the view we have when invisible to another person, the underpinning of the silhouette, the mug shot and the regal outline on coinage. Around the turn of the century it was also enjoying a quiet vogue. Aubrey Beardsley had turned languidly side-on to Frederic Evans; Rodin had stood out in relief against the backdrop of his alter ego, 'The Thinker', for Edward Steichen; Virginia Woolf had accentuated her melancholy beauty by looking away from G. C. Beresford. Trumper's spontaneous profile now seems differently expressive, enacting big sport's performative relations: as he is appraised, appreciated and consumed, he has eyes only for the ball.

Trumper's quickness, meanwhile, is conveyed by the picture's tiny tincture of imperfection. With only a thousandth of a second to play with, the Videx has done its best. Batspeed sometimes confounded Beldam: the nearer the bat to an approaching ball, the likelier it would be bowed or blurred on the print; from one Beldam photograph of Frank Ford, the bat is missing altogether. Not here: in the top left of 'Jumping Out', Trumper's bat is not only captured at the point of perfect stillness before commencing its downswing, but slightly tilted to pronounce its wandlike slimness. The background verticals of the three little chimney pots and the horizontals of The Oval terraces narrate the bat's imminent passage down and through the plane of the ball; the open sky in the top right suggests an exit point for the stroke. But in the lower right, Trumper's forward-flung front foot is ever-so-slightly blurred.

The effect is accidental: the cause is the focal-plane shutter's transit, exposing the right-hand side of the plate ever so slightly longer than the left. It's also predictive of the role distortion would play in the photographic documentation of sport, beginning with the very first outstanding vision of motor racing, Jacques-Henri Lartigue's 'Grand prix de l'ACF' (1912), in which the body of a Schneider automobile is sharply defined but its wheels cartoonishly elongated. Later on such effects would be deliberately sought after, most famously by *Sports Illustrated*'s John Zimmerman in his images of the basketballer Tiny Archibald (1958 and 1971), and the pitchers Vida Blue (1971) and Nolan Ryan (1973). In 'Jumping Out', it is more a case of nature defying technology: Trumper meets the machine, and transcends it.

Another effect in *Great Batsmen* seems perfectly deliberate: Beldam's placement, as Plate XXVIII, immediately following 'Jumping Out', of his photograph of Trumper's follow-through. By compelling their consecutive reading, he lends the images a cinematic quality. Since the Australians had filed past the British Mutoscope camera in 1899, there had been other gestures to recording cricket as a moving image. In 1901, Fry and Ranji had played half a dozen hasty strokes for a home motion-picture device called a Kinora; that same year, the newsreel makers Mitchell & Kenyon had filmed Lancashire's controversial fast bowler, Arthur Mold, in the nets at Old Trafford after he had been no-balled for throwing in a county match; from 1905 footage survives of the Australians in the field at Trent Bridge and going through stilted motions in the Nursery at Lord's. In juxtaposing the start and finish of a straight drive, Beldam foretells the precedence of the moving image in sport.

It was a mode in which Beldam continued experimenting. For *Great Bowlers and Fielders* (1906), he linked no fewer than seven plates of his Middlesex teammate J. T. Hearne for a complete 'pictorial analysis' of successive stages of his action; for Wallis Myers' *The Complete Lawn Tennis Player* (1908), he assembled two sequences of the Australian Norman Brookes demonstrating the American service; for *Fry's Magazine* in 1909 he put together a ten-shot 'cinematographoid' of Harry Vardon teeing off. Before motor drives, these were compositional exercises of supreme difficulty: Beldam had to have the action demonstrated as many times as it took to obtain adequate illustration of each stage. Not until the 1920s would he enjoy equipment equal to capturing all the phases of a single

Advantage Australia: Norman Brookes by Beldam.

action, when he applied a 250-frame-a-second Ultra Rapid Camera to the swings of half a dozen eminent golfers.[*] This was a way to which Trumper had pointed twenty years earlier.

Finally, consider the backdrop – because, first of all, it *is* a backdrop. Left behind are those classic representations of big cricket, from 'A Cricket Match between the Counties of Sussex and Kent, at Brighton' (1849) to 'An Imaginary Cricket Match: England v Australia' (1887), with their foregrounded crowds and recessed on-field activities. Beldam made the player into the centre of the action, extending a thousandth of a second for all time; the crowd was a blur, like a pictorialist print, or even one of Monet's recent canvases of the Houses of Parliament. Into cricket stepped the cricketer in the role of star, unselfconsciously showcasing the skills that made him so.

Superficially, the crowd, even indistinct, introduces a disjunction to 'Jumping Out', in the sense that it implies a game in progress, at the same time as the deserted outfield suggests otherwise – the result of it being taken, as described, during an intermission in a match. This was, of course, never Beldam's intention. He had as little interest in crowds as those previous artists had shown much. Congregations of spectators feature only occasionally, and incidentally, in his work. Most of his backgrounds are deserted – empty grounds, bare nets – with no attempt made to disguise the nature of

---

[*] With the Photochrom Company, Beldam published ten two-shilling pamphlets in the series, *The World's Champion Golfers: Their Art Disclosed by the Ultra-Rapid Camera* (1924): they feature strokes from Walter Hagen, Gene Sarazen, Arthur Havers, Abe Mitchell, Roger Wethered and Joyce Wethered, divided into photo sequences of thirty-six displayed in a fold-out section. The Ultra Rapid Camera had been developed by Cinechrome Instruments Company for the British Admiralty to study aircraft-carrier accidents, and it proved a prohibitively expensive venture, each second of film costing thirty shillings. But Beldam persisted, explaining his determination in the same terms as he had with his earlier books: 'The Ultra-Rapid Camera pictures give actual facts – not what the player thinks he does, but what he really does.'

the exercises. Yet as 'Jumping Out' was detached from its context as a plate in an instructional book of other similar plates, and became 'Beldam's Trumper', and finally just 'Trumper', confusion would arise. Was it an artefact of an actual game or was it not? Judges as august as Jack Fingleton and Richie Benaud were perplexed.

Fingleton was long transfixed by plates XXVII and XXVIII. 'Cold figures on paper are drab things when considered in the light of immortality that these two photographs throw upon the cricket world,' he wrote in *Cricket Crisis* (1946). 'Such photographs should be framed and hung in every pavilion in the world for players to see and pay homage to, and seek inspiration from, as they take the field. A coach is incomplete without them.' His faith was shaken, however, by a conversation he recounted in the manuscript for *The Immortal Victor Trumper* (1978):

> That astute man Richie Benaud first of all drew my attention to the master picture of all, Trumper jumping down the pitch to drive. It is a much-used photograph, but Benaud suggested to me that the picture was a fake because it pretended to be of Trumper in a match and it was nothing of the sort. The photographer had certainly taken the picture of Trumper batting but it was on a practice ground and superimposed on the background of a crowd on an English ground. It looks like a crowd at Bramall Lane, Sheffield, with a scoreboard. There is no other person in the picture, no fieldsman, no square-leg umpire, no one. I accept Benaud's opinion that it is a fake, though it greatly disappointed me because I had once written that the picture is so inspiring it should be hung in all the cricket dressing rooms of the world but no matter.[*]

---

[*] In the published version of the book, the third and fourth sentences of this rather obtuse passage were deleted, apparently on the advice of the historian David Frith, but the rest remains.

Both Fingleton and Benaud were misled, effectively, by pictorial cliché. By the time they were scrutinising 'Jumping Out', the huge, receptive, anonymous crowd had become ingrained in the depiction of big-time sport. They took its presence as indicating a match in progress . . . which then, of course, could *not* have been in progress, because of the absence of other figures.

Yet in 1905 this pictorial cliché had yet to emerge. It would be another three years before a significant sporting event was photographed effectually, and then only because at the Games of the IV Olympiad in White City Stadium it was possible to draw close to the athletes, including to the Italian Dorando Pietri as he was overenthusiastically assisted to a controversial marathon victory, overturned on protest. In the most famous image, disoriented Pietri crosses the line with a sturdy, moustachioed official at each elbow; the drama is further magnified by the background, thick with onlookers at what was then the world's largest arena. 'The crowd' as sporting scenery, also providing its imagined soundtrack of approving roar, today passes virtually unremarked; it is an absence of spectators that is likelier to occasion comment. In 'Jumping Out', the background effectively modernises the picture by foretelling the place of fans in future depictions of sport, the massed faces surrounded by murky visual clutter lending a disarmingly contemporary feel.

Does it matter that 'Jumping Out' was to a degree contrived? Arguably less than Fingleton and Benaud supposed. After all, photographs are by nature dissimulations. Time does not stand still. Instants are constantly superseded. Photographs lop life off at the edge of the frame, and yank a fraction of a second out of swiftly forgotten circumstances. Consider what some would regard as the finest sporting photograph of all, Muhammad Ali looming over supine Sonny Liston at Lewiston, Maine in 1965, as seen by Neil

Leifer. The clash looks titanic; in fact, the fight was a seven-round squib. The crowd looks immense: actually, it was the smallest to witness a heavyweight title fight in modern history. Ali seems to have landed a killer blow; rather, he had administered a featherlight touch that nobody saw connect. The victor is not braying defiance; he is admonishing a rival whom he thinks has taken a dive. But, to quote Leifer, none of this mattered: 'This photo became the way people wanted to see Ali, charismatic, tough, confident. The circumstances didn't end up mattering.' It supports the argument of documentary maker Errol Morris that photography reverses the old nostrum: 'It is often said that seeing is believing. But we do not form our beliefs on the basis of what we see; rather, what we see is often determined by our beliefs. Believing is seeing, not the other way round.'

The most important element of 'Jumping Out' is just this: the photograph is the perfect match for the legend, the complete corroboration of the claims, even an anticipation of words attributed to the subject. 'Spoil a bowler's length, and you've got him,' Noble would later quote Trumper as saying – it was 'one of his maxims'. Here he is seen doing just that, invading a space that a thousandth of a second earlier had been effectively conceded, demonstrating that length is not something the bowler sets alone, providing the batsman is quick enough. The picture takes on a hybrid identity as an action photograph that effectively serves as a portrait, in fulfilment of the idea that athletes are defined by their deeds.

All the foregoing facets lay encoded when 'Jumping Out' was published in *Great Batsmen*: the implied commentaries, the subversive blur, the invitations to consider the image as part of a continuous action in front of a reverential crowd, and to relate it to previously held convictions about the aesthetic superiority of Trumper's batting. In the near-term, it also evinced sport's unpredictability. The day Beldam studied him at The Oval, Trumper was at the peak of his fame; by the time it was available for public consumption, he was coming off the poorest series of his career.

•

'An ordinary batsman who makes nearly 1400 runs before the middle of August is usually heartily patted on the back,' reported *Cricket* as the Tests of 1905 ended. 'But Trumper is not an ordinary batsman.' And of those first-class runs only a meagre 125 in seven completed innings had come against England, preluding a succession of bold but brittle Australian batting performances in a 2–0 defeat. 'There is too much attack about our batting,' complained Leslie Poidevin in *The Referee*. 'It is all very fine for the spectators, but one is not so sure that it is very fine for the team.'

Such criticism reversed that of just a few years earlier. Australian batting had then been too stodgy; now it was too stimulating. It marred the transformation for which the Australians had recently been commended. At the outset of the 1905 tour, *The Field* acclaimed Trumper and his teammates for having 'thrown off the stiffness which characterised the play of some of their precursors' with a 'very exceptional amount of daring', blessed by 'the "eye" which enables Ranji to execute his marvellous *tours de force*'. By the end, *The Field* was tut-tutting in similar terms: 'It may be doubted whether the plan of making a *tour de force* of every stroke and trusting almost entirely to the "eye", of which Trumper is so brilliant an exponent, can be recommended for long wear.'

It's this, perhaps, that has led to the regular misdating of 'Jumping Out' as being from '1902' – the desire to link the photograph to that great pageant of success rather than its muted follow-up. Though

Victor Trumper perhaps *should* have been immortalised in 1902, Beldam was not equipped to do so. There exists a gulf in proficiency between the photographs Beldam was obtaining while Trumper set new batting standards and while he was subtly disappointing them three years later. 'Jumping Out' captures Trumper not at the peak of his powers, but during a diminuendo in his form as his scores and perhaps also his health wavered. He is a man with a decade to live. The photograph might even be thought a hint of this in its resemblance to the genre of the photo finish, automatically generated in horseracing and athletics: Trumper is racing against mortality's encroachments, time's ravages, memory's fading.

The opposite is true of the only surviving newsreel footage of Trumper in a match – also the oldest of a Test in Australia. In December 1910, a *Pathé Animated Gazette* cameraman was present for the opening day of the Sydney Test between Australia and South Africa. He got one glimpse of Trumper – being run out by a direct hit from point on the impetuous call of his opening partner, Warren Bardsley. Trumper was just beginning an extraordinary late-career efflorescence: this thwarted cameo of 27 from thirty-eight balls commenced a ten-innings sequence of 774 runs at 96.75. Yet against Beldam's frozen thousandth of a second, this fifteen seconds of motion has never stood any chance of being remembered. Who cares about a batsman sprawling, picking himself up and walking off, even if he is about to compile a great quantity of runs? In the dawning competition between image and achievement, then, image opened up an early lead – an inference of the fame of 'Jumping Out' is that an image memorable enough will tend over time to draw achievement towards it.

Although not quite yet. For there is a concluding irony to the creation of cricket's first great image. Beldam's photograph was cordially received but not rapturously. The gravure did not sell out; nor did the others. Despite the critical acclaim they enjoyed, *Great Batsmen* and its sequel were too expensively priced to sell in great quantities. We are accustomed now to the idea of content 'going viral', electrifying the world in an instant. A hundred years ago there was neither the telecommunications nor the reprographic technology for this to happen. Wire transmission of images was still a dream; even in illustrated weeklies, such as *Illustrated Sporting and Dramatic News* in England and *The Australasian*, the quality of halftone reproduction was indifferent. The legend of the inaugural cricketer of the visual age would be established in other ways before returning to the image for, as it were, verification.

7

'I FELL IN LOVE WITH HIM AT ONCE'

'You want me to talk about Victor Trumper? Well, I warn you that if I start
you won't be able to stop me and that it will be with tears in my eyes.'
– ALBERT VINCENT, player with Redfern CC and captain of North Sydney
CC 1909–33, quoted in *Captains Outrageous?*, R. S. Whitington (1971)

At 2.15 p.m. on 31 January 1903, Victor Trumper took his partner Dan
Gee with him to open the batting for Paddington against Redfern.
It was the first time he had been seen in grade cricket since returning
from his triumphs in England, and the crowd at Redfern Oval was
swelling. Shortly the onlookers would be ducking for cover. Fifty
was on the board in twenty minutes, Gee's share of it 5. The hundred
was raised in forty-five minutes, 200 in seventy-five minutes, 300

in a hundred minutes, 400 in just over two hours. Spectators kept arriving, including cab drivers, hawkers and tradesmen who abandoned their vehicles in Chalmers and Phillip streets; some ascended trees for a better view. The total was put at 8000. Uncomprehending Chinese shopkeepers pulled down their shutters, interpreting the crowd's roars as preluding a riot. Lawn bowlers on the nearby green curtailed their game, fearful of the risk from Trumper's hitting.

Gee was out for 175 with the score on 517; twenty minutes later Trumper fell for 335 out of 558, stumped off the wicketkeeper who had desperately shed the gloves to bowl, having hit thirty-nine fours and twenty-two fives – the 1903 version of the six, which entailed the batsmen changing ends. The crowd immediately began dispersing, traffic to recirculate outside the ground, reporters to compose dispatches that would be printed in every state, in newspapers as far afield as Rockhampton and Kalgoorlie. *The Referee* went to the extent of transcribing Trumper's innings from the scorebook, and rapping it out like a numerical cipher:

442441451444441442141412124145141251141142 5
215314152541451154441452544424444141112151111
211125525254511155414445254 14

They could barely do better. 'To try and describe Vic's innings on paper would mean failure,' acknowledged *The Sportsman*. 'It required to be seen to be fully realised and appreciated, and it will be sufficient to say that it was a marvellous and masterful display.' Well, perhaps not quite sufficient – over ensuing years an inventive means was found of preserving the occasion.

Redfern's biggest industry was then footwear, and its biggest building the six-storey factory owned by John Hunter, who had arrived from the goldfields twenty-five years earlier and now dominated the trade. His 450 employees churned out 100 000 boots a month, each pair proudly labelled 'Made in Sydney'. That balmy afternoon in Redfern, one of Trumper's fives cleared Chalmers Street and broke a second-floor window in the factory, the ball apparently being discovered among shattered glass on Monday morning. The shrewd Hunter paid Trumper the tribute of decreeing that the window should never be repaired: one could look through the hole left by the ball and wonder at the 140 metres it had soared from the centre of Redfern Oval. Hunter's son reiterated the instruction when the old man died after the war, and an explanatory plaque was added.

In time, the feat grew in memory. In a column in *Truth*, the sempiternal barracker S. H. Gascoigne ('Yabba') sent the blow soaring higher: 'One of Vic's hits I shall never forget. It landed on top of John Hunter's boot factory.' In reminiscences in *The Sportsman*, the renowned bookmaker Andy Kerr ('The Coogee Bunyip') turned the blow into a barrage: 'He broke every window in John Hunter's boot factory, and the club members returning to Glebe were worried as they reckoned up how much the damage would cost. But old John Hunter, one of our best sportsmen, refused to take a shilling.' Forty-five years after the game, *Sydney Morning Herald* sports columnist Ken Hardy solicited the memories of spectators and was overwhelmed by the response: 'Our telephones rang all day. At one time, three people were on different phones. I have a sheaf of letters.' Prime Minister Ben Chifley and Governor-General William McKell both revealed that they had been in the crowd. Hardy urged that the ground's new pavilion be named in Trumper's honour, although a new tenant, the South Sydney Rabbitohs, was by then making Redfern Oval into a football stronghold, and would shortly acquire the now-dormant factory to extend its leagues club.

At the time, the window apparently remained sacredly broken, for the *Sun-Herald* revisited 'The Redfern Hit of 1903' sixty years after the event, and reported a decision to 'mount the window in a place of honour in the club'. After all, what more appropriate symbol could there be of a player identified with the cricket of Sydney's streets and lanes than a shattered window? Ninety years after the hit soared, it was still being recalled by locals at the Bat and Ball Hotel in Redfern's Cleveland Street, one of whom described it to a young barman, Brad Diebert. Then an aspiring artist, Diebert was inspired to mock up a frame containing a broken pane of glass, which he entitled 'Six and Out' and sold during the first of cartoonist Reg Lynch's Crickart exhibitions at the Bat and Ball in December 1997. Now a filmmaker, he remembers not being paid for it.

Hits and memories: *Sun-Herald*, 6 October 1963.

What in the meantime had happened to the real window? By then, it was all a little misty. Seeking information at the leagues club, the South Sydney Heritage Society was told that the window had indeed been removed and displayed then lost. When music journalist

Mark Mordue took up the threads of an abiding interest in Trumper in 2010, his inquiries convinced him that the promised preservation had been thwarted by a site manager during the leagues-club take-over who in unthinking zeal had the window repaired. In a fragment prepared for a sort-of novella of Trumper, Mordue had the scene witnessed by an elderly cleaner:

> An even older fellow arrived late that afternoon, a former Hunter's Boot Factory employee who had been given a part-time job on the site, a little cash earner on the side to supplement his pension. He had a broom in his hand and was moving steadily across the floor when he saw the window no longer broken. The cleaner stood and stopped and, much like the site manager a day before, he looked out to the sporting oval. Workers nearby were surprised to see this old and somewhat reticent figure then begin to cry.

Asked about it, Mordue can't quite remember if this was something he was told, or something he imagined. More than a century after Trumper's death, a little urban legend goes on accumulating.

•

Victor Trumper made 3163 Test runs at an average of 39.04, 16 939 first-class runs at 44.57, 9244 first-grade runs at 62.04. For the time, it was an imposing record. It is also almost exactly comparable with that of his South Australian contemporary Clem Hill. Yet nobody wrote of or responded to Hill as they did Trumper – not even Hill, as one who played with both, the cricket writer and broadcaster Johnny Moyes, was to note: 'To Clem Hill, there was no one like Trumper, either as a batsman or a man.' All of which can make Trumper an awkward figure in this rational, quantifying age. About him there often seems more folklore than fact. Did he really not care about records? As we have seen, records seem to have excited him in 1902. Did he really gift his wicket to deserving bowlers after scoring hundreds? After all, his career is scattered with large scores. And there are so many anecdotes, mostly long separated from their original sources, fortified by their repetition, yet often the quotation of quotations of quotations.

This has troubled a few chroniclers. Some of the stories must be apocryphal, but which? Even worshipful Jack Fingleton felt his scepticism hardening on occasions. For example, he ran across a yarn from Trumper's first tour that involved W. G. Grace, recently retired from Test cricket aged fifty-one, visiting the Australians in their dressing-room. The Champion asked Trumper for a bat in return for one of his own, which he handed over with words to the effect of: 'From yesterday's champion to tomorrow's champion.' Fingleton dismissed the tale as too good to be true: 'It is a pretty story, but on checking the scores in Irving Rosenwater and Ralph Barker's splendid book, *England v Australia*, I find that Grace had been dropped for the Lord's Test match in an English home Test series for the first time, so the alleged facts must be dubious.' In fact, Fingleton had looked only cursorily: Grace played four further first-class matches against the Australians, including for an eponymous XI at Crystal Palace, in 1899. And what do you know? Tenderly stored at Canberra's National Museum is a heavily used Stuart Surridge Patent Rapid Driver on whose oil-darkened shoulder is unmistakably inscribed: 'To V. Trumper from W. G. Grace'. In its unique entwining of two cricket legends, it may be the most valuable bat of its kind.

If other stories must have been exaggerated or distorted by multiple retellings, their context should also be recalled. The number of people who watched Trumper each time he batted represented only the minutest fraction of the interested public – the proportion of his countrymen who saw Trumper establish himself as the world's best batsman in 1902 was vanishingly small. Critics often stressed the importance of seeing Trumper in the flesh. In January 1905, 'Gulliver' of *The Arrow* cast it as a veritable duty: 'If you have seen Trumper play a big innings you have seen something to remember; something you have never seen from anyone else. If you have not seen Trumper bat, and you live in Sydney, you deserve not to have seen him.' But an overwhelming majority would never share that experience. In his whole career, Trumper played three first-class games in Brisbane, one in Hobart, none in Perth. He had to be cultivated in the mind, carolled by contemporaries, even sacralised by object. Quaint as it may seem in this age of instant news and plentiful image, leaving a window broken was a way of capturing Trumper, of memorialising and honouring him.

More often, of course, the medium was print – to record, to persuade, to move. A later afternoon at Redfern Oval yielded the prime example. Arthur Mailey's autobiography, *10 for 66 and All That* (1958), contains probably the single best-known piece of writing about Trumper, and what the historian Gerald Walsh has called 'one of the most touching vignettes in the literature of cricket'. It has generally been left at that, as simply a charming yarn. In fact, it is based on a real game, on 1 April 1911, between Mailey's Redfern and Trumper's Gordon. It is also a fascinating evocation of pre-modern connectedness.

A carpenter's son, Mailey left school aged thirteen for a series of dead-end jobs. At first he came no nearer to Trumper than a photograph – 'the only picture I had in my room' at his family's draughty hessian-lined cottage in Waterloo. 'When the wind blew,'

'My particular hero': Mailey's Trumper.

Mailey recalls, 'Vic appeared to go through his whole repertoire of strokes.' In a complementary cartoon, Mailey has Trumper's bat protrude invitingly from the corner of the 'pin-up', as if beckoning him towards a fantasy life beyond the ignominy of pressing trouser seams – a job he proves unable to keep anyway:

My boss, the meanest man I ever knew, caught me leaning over the pressing board *thinking*. What was I thinking? About Victor Trumper as usual, I fancy. I couldn't imagine he had ever had to press seams or be cooped up in a factory and ridiculed by his workmates. Perhaps he was living in a castle or a palace somewhere listening to lovely music while he was served with the tastiest food. Perhaps sitting on the deck of one of those wonderful Orient ships on his way to England. England? Gosh, I'd never even spoken to anybody who'd been to England. What chance did I ever have of getting there? [...]

'What's up with you – are you sick or something?' It was the boss's voice and at that moment it was like a fast ball in the teeth. 'Why aren't you working? Come on, tell me.'

'I'm sorry,' I said. 'I must have been dreaming.'

'Well, you're not paid to dream. Get your coat and get off the premises.'

Mailey's 'dream', it turns out, is to be fulfilled by cricket. An unnamed benefactor in Waterloo Park shares with him the secret of the googly – or, as Mailey calls it, the 'bosie', in honour of the Englishman B. J. T. Bosanquet, who had first bowled the double-dealing delivery in Australia. Soon Mailey is carrying a cricket ball everywhere, bowling it wherever he can, including at Redfern Oval, at first badly, then ever better. His communion with his idol intensifies when he is gifted an old bat of Trumper's in lieu of payment for painting a house: 'The fantastic, legendary Trumper, my particular hero. A hundred pounds could not have given me more pleasure.' In the next moment, when Mailey is picked to play against Trumper, the great man himself seems to step down from his photograph on the wall.

At this point, Mailey makes a disarmingly candid admission: he has never actually seen Trumper play. He has built Trumper into an 'ethereal and godlike figure' simply by staring at the picture, reading about and hearing of him; perhaps he has also gazed up in wonder at the broken window in the neighbourhood boot factory.

On the morning of the match he slips into a reverie wondering what Trumper is doing, as giddy as a commoner preparing to meet royalty:

> Bet he's not ironing his flannels. Sends them to the laundry, I suppose. He's probably got two sets of flannels anyway. Perhaps he's at breakfast, perhaps he's eating bacon and eggs. Wonder if he knows I'm playing against him? Don't suppose he's ever heard of me. Wouldn't worry him anyhow, I shouldn't think. Gosh, what a long morning! Think I'll dig the garden. No, I won't – I want to keep fresh. Think I'll lie down for a bit . . . better not, I might fall off to sleep and be late.
>
> The morning did not pass this way. Time just stopped. I couldn't bring myself to doing anything in particular and yet I couldn't settle to the thought of not doing anything. I was bowling to Trumper and I was not bowling to Trumper. I was early and I was late. In fact, I think I was slightly out of my mind.

Trumper lives up to Mailey's imaginings. He emerges in his 'creamy, loose-fitting but well-tailored flannels', walking his 'springy athletic walk', and taking guard 'like a panther ready to spring'. Reluctant at first to bowl him, Mailey's captain then changes his mind and decides 'to put me out of my misery'. Trumper takes toll of his first two deliveries, despite the second being what should have been a perfect leg break, 'singing sweetly like a humming top':

> Down came his left foot to within a foot of the ball. The bat, swung from well over his shoulders, met the ball just as it fizzed off the pitch, and the next sound I heard was a rapping on the off-side fence. It was the most beautiful shot I have ever seen.

The immortal Yabba made some attempt to say something but his voice faded away to the soft gurgle one hears at the end of a kookaburra's song. The only person on the ground who didn't watch the course of the ball was Victor Trumper. The moment he played it he turned his back, smacked down a few tufts of grass and prodded his way back to the crease. He knew where the ball was going.

Here the abiding tension in sport between the contest and the spectacle spreads from the crowd across the field. The bowler is almost as much a spectator as Yabba. Like the English keeper Lilley, who would have been happy for Trumper to bat twice as long, Mailey is caught up in his appreciation of the game. Then the tension breaks. After 'one or two other reasonably good balls', Mailey deploys the 'bosie', which deceives the advancing Trumper, who is stumped by metres and courteously retires:

> Vic made no attempt to scramble back. He knew the ball had beaten him and was prepared to pay the penalty, and although he had little chance of regaining his crease on this occasion I think he would have acted similarly if his back foot had been only an inch from safety.
>
> As he walked past me he smiled, patted the back of his bat and said, 'It was too good for me.'
>
> There was no triumph in me as I watched the receding figure. I felt like a boy who had killed a dove.

As forty-five years elapsed between the match and the writing of *10 for 66*, it's not surprising that Mailey's retelling is somewhat enriched. He had actually played against Trumper at least once before. During the match he described, furthermore, he actually took the new ball, and was treated respectfully by Trumper and partner Frank Iredale for three-quarters of an hour before the incidence of 'Trumper st Hayes b Mailey 34'. Yet the point is not Mailey's deviance from literal truth *per se*. It is the purpose that deviance expressed – people who could not see him, might never see him, and by the time Mailey was writing would never see him, had to be persuaded of Trumper's unforgettability as a figure.

His unforgettability, although not his infallibility. In 'Opposing My Hero', the hero falls, yet remains a hero by bearing his defeat chivalrously, in the knightly tradition; the victor attains a similar nobility by disclaiming the spoils. A little gilt is peeled from 'Jumping Out': sometimes the boldness and beauty availed Trumper not. But that gilt is reapplied more thickly: what is batting without risk? In this sense, the story sits at an angle to much Australian cricket folklore, full of big hitting, fast bowling, laconic victors, hard drinkers and Bradman's mighty inevitability. *Like a boy who had killed a dove*: it is an arresting image, considering the dove's associations with femininity and with spirituality, as well as acting as an analog for the brevity of Trumper's life, given the funerary custom of a dove's ceremonial release. Which is why, perhaps, the piece has been so widely anthologised and endlessly quoted. For example, so forcefully did it strike Melbourne guitarist Marty Donald while reading one of his father's cricket anthologies in 1993, that he incorporated it into a song for his band, the Lucksmiths. 'Victor Trumper' concludes:

I am bowling to Victor Trumper
And he dances down the wicket
And he is stumped and I am stunned
[spoken] I feel like a boy who has killed a dove.

But perhaps the symbolism of the line is less significant than that it was attempted at all. Mailey was a droll, whimsical, often entertaining writer on cricket; not, though, especially ambitious or ornate. And there is a sense more generally in Australian writings about Trumper, contemporaneous and posthumous, of a need to find a particular note of lyricism, to sustain a special emotional pitch. Australian cricketers have incited frenzies of adoration, waves of awe, gulps of fear. But no player, we might think, has touched admirers so tenderly as Trumper; arguably no athlete in our history has been so simply loved.

In part this was to do with Trumper's seeming accessibility. Mailey's strange sense of connectedness to an athlete he had never seen bears out the relative smallness of the urban sporting community of which Trumper was part. Albert Knight noted the deeply personal affinity of Australians for their paragon: 'Every member of the great crowd which darkens the Sydney mound knows "Our Vic". If one hasn't been to school with him, he knows someone who has or he knows the champion's father, or touched the fringes of his garments somewhere. Trumper's batting moves them as neither victory nor defeat quite touch them.'

Trumper was also possessed, it seems, of an acute personal magnetism – a magnetism that somehow complemented his cricket. Tall, slim, broad-shouldered, fresh-faced, he looked the part of a sporting saviour, and acted it: modest, reticent, unselfish, unostentatious, from the first. *The Australasian*'s veteran cricket correspondent Tom Horan introduced Trumper to readers in December 1898 by his charm as player and gentleman: 'He is a singularly nice young fellow, to whom I have cottoned amazingly, and his style as a batsman is just as good as his style and winsome ways as a man.' About that charm, there was also a reassurance, of a goodness in the world, of a rightness of things. While a guest of Ipswich Grammar in December 1899, Trumper caught the imagination of fourteen-year-old Vance Palmer. The school had recently been scandalized by the homosexual indiscretions of a master with members of the choir. For Palmer, Trumper was nothing less than an agent of redemption: 'For myself I carried Trumper's remembered figure around with me, as an image of some kind of human perfection. It didn't belong to the cricket-field alone: it could easily be transferred to other areas of life, such as scholarship or adventure . . . Trumper's figure acted as a foil to that of the sinister [teacher], for the question of what evil was and where it came from was never far from my mind.' In Palmer's sometimes primly moral fiction, his biographer Harry Heseltine detected a frequent opposition between a 'Trumper-like figure' as a 'positive epitome and dashing vindication of all that is decent and good' and a darker background presence pressing against sexual rectitude. In *The Swayne Family* (1932), Palmer would even grant George Swayne a moment of Trumperian triumph in an interstate match:

> Every vestige of self-distrust had fallen from him: every movement of his compact, vigorous body expressed power and mastery. Taking full charge of the bowling he cut and drove, finding the open space in the field, sending the ball skimming to the fence again and again. He was changing the whole aspect of the game. The barrackers in the outer ring had taken him to their hearts and were making the ground echo with his name.
>
> 'That's floggin''em!. . . Is he any good?. . . Oh, you beauty, Swayne!'

Wandering into the Trumper & Carter sports depot in 1905, a contributor to New Zealand's *Young Man's Magazine* warmed immediately to the owner's cordiality and humility:

Trumper is without doubt the most popular cricketer in Australia today, and is generally recognised to be the best batsman in the world. Twenty-six years of age, well proportioned, standing over six feet [183 cm] in his socks, with square shoulders, well-made limbs, and a bright open face, he strikes one as being a fine type of the young colonial. I fell in love with him at once. The most striking thing about him, however, is his manner. Cordial, frank, and absolutely unaffected, he charms you and commands your friendship at once. He put me at ease straight away with his warm handshake and entire absence of 'side'. '. . . the proudest moment of your cricket career?' I enquired. 'Oh, I don't know,' he replied evasively, 'I know I've felt jolly wild when I've got out for a duck when I should have made a score, but I don't remember ever feeling too pleased with myself.'

The modesty also struck Beldam, when he wrote of Trumper for Chevallier Tayler's *The Empire's Cricketers*: 'Rapid as has been his rise to fame, he has been slow to expand in other ways. He is still the same genial, charming fellow, unspoilt by all the worship of the cricket world. Long indeed may he live to charm cricketers by his skill, and his friends by his delightful companionship.' When Trumper did not, tributes extolled his perfect balance of sporting and personal excellence. 'As clean in mind as he was generous in spirit,' believed Monty Noble. 'As modest as he was magnificent,' thought Pelham Warner. 'Trumper's batsmanship was in keeping with his beautiful character,' maintained Victorian wicketkeeper Elliot Monfries. *Sporting Life*'s H. J. Henley thought Trumper a creature of nature itself:

Quite unassuming, he was a man who found delight in the touch of the sun, the green of the turf, the scents and sounds of the open-air life. Had you asked him to decline Mensa, or to explain the first proposition of the first book of Euclid, you would probably have stumped him first ball, as it were. But he knew all about birds and the way to grow things. Something of this happy, open-air spirit, the laughing joy of being alive, came out in his cricket. Batting was to him a matter to be taken light-heartedly, and every innings was a new adventure.

His era's moral expectations of sportsmen Trumper shouldered effortlessly. As an upstanding abstainer, he was claimed by the Sons & Daughters of Temperance and the No-Licence League. A Methodist evangelist, Rev. Raymond Preston, proclaimed him 'one of the cleanest, straightest, most upright men I have ever known'. In his only surviving letter to a young fan, Trumper preached 'a good healthy life' as a prerequisite of success: 'Dr W. G. Grace is still a non-smoker. Avoid alcohol for it will tell on a player's constitution sooner or later . . . Don't let sport worry you. If it does give it up.' And around no cricketer have accumulated so many stories of spontaneous kindness: his scattering threepenny bits among boys outside the SCG so they could get into the Shilling Stand; his letting a pickpocket go at Marrickville Oval rather than await the police; his liberality with bats as tokens of affection and encouragement. The veteran Derbyshire amateur Levi Wright, for example, recalled Trumper's solicitude when he played the Australians for the last time in 1909:

> I was caught in the first innings by Victor Trumper for 1. He scored a brilliant 113 and I still see the stroke he made to square leg off the first ball he received. Before we commenced our second attempt Victor came to me and had a little chat. He noticed that I was a little downhearted when I told him I had about finished.

He laughed in a happy light-hearted way and said, 'Nothing of the sort. Wait a minute I will fetch you one of my bats and I hope it will bring you luck.' I used that bat, which shewed many marks of good usage, but without much success and I now believe it is in the possession of the Derby club to whom I gave it.*

Mixed in with this side of Trumper's personality, his admirers would claim, was a certain unworldliness, a seeming uninterest in temporal concerns. 'Victor was not the sort of man to succeed in commercial pursuits,' said Noble loyally. 'He was too soft-hearted, too gener-ous.' Some contemporaries appear to have been almost discomfited by his altruism. Bookmaker Sam Vandenburg grew afraid of walk-ing into the shop: 'I used to take him a gift to try to do something for the most generous man I ever knew. But I always found myself leaving the store with something more valuable than the present I had brought him.' When Trumper worked as a mercer towards the end of his life, according to Johnny Moyes, former comrades actu-ally avoided him: 'Cricketers visiting Sydney, who used to make his shop their first port-of-call out of love for the man, had to give it up, because he always wanted to fit the team out with neckties.'

It's doubtful whether this is all there is to tell of Trumper's var-ious financial misadventures. The Sydney sporting-goods business, overshadowed by bigger emporia, was highly competitive. Players as well known as Charlie Turner and Syd Gregory had gone broke

---

* Wright's cherishing of the gift is corroborated by the Derby *Daily Telegraph*, 28 April 1931: 'At the lecture theatre of the Central School, Abbey Street, last night, Mr L. G. Wright, who was introduced by Mr T. S. Sephton, delivered a most instructive and interesting lecture to Derby elementary school boys on cricket. The speaker exhibited a bat presented to him by the great Victor Trumper, and asked the boys to wish for some achievement in cricket for themselves as they stood facing the uplifted bat.' The following February, the *Telegraph* reported that Wright had presented the bat, now bearing a silver inscription, to Derbyshire.

in the trade before Trumper. His partners – Hanson Carter, James Giltinan, Leonard Dodge and Dudley King – came and went. A study of the available evidence by insolvency practitioner Ron Cardwell has suggested that Trumper was a serially overextended businessman, seriously indebted even at his death, fortunes having slipped through his fingers. His tours of England were lucrative; likewise a private tour he organised of North Queensland. In 1902, in recognition of his triumphs abroad, the NSWCA presented him with more than £100, a small fortune; in 1913, in appreciation of his career, the NSWCA voted him a testimonial that raised nearly £3000, a sizeable fortune; two years later he left an estate worth £5. And as we have seen, Trumper was not so callow that he did not countenance forsaking Test cricket for county cricket, not so unambitious he did not explore writing for a newspaper in spite of relevant prohibitions.

It was hard for admirers to know what to say about this. So, at least in permanent form, they elected to say nothing. The next chapter will explore some parts of Trumper's life for which the legend found no place; suffice to say for the moment that he was a more complicated figure than hagiography allowed.

•

There remained the daily challenge of describing a batsman who, in the words of *The Sportsman*, 'required to be seen'. 'When [Trumper] came forth into the cricket firmament, and played his game, no one knew what to think,' said his long-time teammate Frank Iredale – that included those charged with reporting the game. If the torrentially eloquent C. B. Fry found Trumper difficult to 'reduce to words', what chance anyone else? Sometimes it seemed as though cricket needed a new vocabulary. In a 1912 column, 'Arawa' of the *Daily Telegraph* described being ticked off at the SCG for using merely the word 'fine' while describing Trumper's batting against South Africa:

> One of those uniquely Trumperian efforts had dazed me – it was all wriggle and wrist, and the ball shot away as if it had been belched forth by a 9.2 [a naval gun]. I just murmured in a kind of spellbound reverie, 'What a fine batsman Trumper is.'
>
> 'Fine?' shrieked an aged historian near me. 'Where did you ever see the like?'
>
> I hadn't. I said so, and made up my mind that I would consult Crabb for the right word next time.[*Crabb's English Synonyms Explained in Alphabetical Order*, a popular thesaurus].

When contemporaries *did* try reaching further, they had recourse to a rather lofty term. Trumper was deemed a 'genius' even before he represented Australia. Having known the boy, *The Referee*'s J. C. Davis felt entitled to a certain grandiloquence about the man scoring a double century for Paddington against Waverley in February 1899: 'Trumper does not belong to the ordinary class of batsmen; he is above them, for he is a genius.' Davis repeated himself in like terms at intervals up to the end of Trumper's life when he concluded with a quiet insistence: 'The word genius may often be misapplied to men who achieve wonders in sport and art, but Trumper was an absolute genius in cricket.'

Tom Horan of *The Australasian* agreed that Trumper approached strokes as 'only a batting genius could do'. Albert Knight, as ever, allowed himself free rein: 'With luxuriant masterfulness, yet with the unlaboured easy naturalness of a falling tear, or rather of showers from the sunny lips of summer, he diverted the ball in every conceivable direction which his genius willed.' In January 1911, the

Sincerely, Victor Trumper: postcard likenesses.

Sydney Morning Herald thought Trumper superior to all before: 'The batting genius of Trumper is best to be focussed perhaps by consideration of a simple matter of fact. There is no record in the history of cricket of any batsman of his versatility, or his complete command of the bowling attack, and though he has played representative cricket for many years now there is no batsman who is within range of rivalry of him in those respects.' In February 1913, the *Herald* thought Trumper superior to those foreseeable: 'There is not likely to be such another batting genius for many years to come.' Noble set the seal on its usage with the subtitle to his autobiography-cum-manifesto *The Game's the Thing* (1926): 'With special chapters on the Genius of Victor Trumper'. Noble further explained Trumper's uniqueness by reference to the general inadequacy of words: 'In many ways he reminded me of a great orator. You follow the discourse, even anticipate correctly the words he is going to use – it all seems so natural and so easy – yet, if you try to do it yourself you fail miserably.'

In Robert Musil's *The Man Without Qualities* (1930), Ulrich famously renounces all ambitions in protest against overindulgence in the word 'genius': 'The time had come when people were starting to speak of genius on the soccer field or in the boxing ring . . . If a racehorse can be a "genius", what then?' But the Victorian age experienced no such taboo, and the idea that 'genius' might be obtainable in popular pursuits like sport enjoyed widening appeal. When Francis Galton had popularised the subject in *Hereditary Genius* (1869), his survey had included rowers and wrestlers alongside artists, scientists, writers and jurists. Some asserted preconditions of genius did not suit Trumper: in his popular *Study of British Genius* (1904), for example, Havelock Ellis argued that geniuses tended to come from large families with elderly parents, to be feeble in youth but live long lives involving late or sexless marriages. Other qualities, however, fitted the cricketer well: the idea that geniuses were untutored, ungovernable, and unconscious of their prowess. Besides, celebrating a 'genius' in cricket's midst was fun, a licence to think and write expansively. As Cardus would stipulate: 'Whoever would not be spendthrift of language about Trumper, let him not write on him at all.'

About genius, too, there was and remains something ineffable – genius, in Thomas Carlyle's famous *mot*, is 'ever a secret to itself'. It's possible that bestowing the mantle on Trumper also became a means of dealing with his enigmatic qualities, such as his extremes of reticence and beneficence, and the ticklish issue of his ever-precarious finances. These no longer needed exploration or accounting for; they could merely be observed. In this context it is worth citing one of the original and most fulsome tributes to 'Australia's greatest genius with the bat', by the aforementioned Frank Iredale.

Teammates in England in 1899, Trumper and Iredale also became clubmates at Gordon; they socialised extensively, even travelled in

Europe with their wives en route home from England in 1905. The chapter concerning Trumper in Iredale's autobiography *33 Years of Cricket* (1920) approaches his remoteness with quiet frankness:

> When I take up my pen in an endeavour to put in words what I knew and felt of the life of Victor Trumper, I know only too well how futile anything I might say would do justice to the memory of one whom all the world loved and respected.
>
> Through many years of connection with him, which I am proud to say was never clouded by any misunderstanding, I felt how greatly our country was honoured by his presence as a sportsman in the highest sense. To be near him always, as it were, seemed to me to be an honour . . .
>
> In all my cricket years, and association with cricketers, I never knew a man who practised self-effacement so much as he. He loved the game and he respected those who played it. In victory and defeat he was just the same – his demeanour never changed. If by any chance a player coveted a bat he used, he gave it to him. His unselfish nature was of such breadth that it at times became embarrassing to his many friends who had to avoid his favours.
>
> I never knew a cricketer who showed his emotions as little as he did. No one could read his mind, therefore he was never understood. Everything he did was seemingly taken for granted. It was never necessary to ask him to do anything in a match because everyone felt that before the words were out of one's mouth they were conscious that he knew what you were going to say.
>
> No work was too hard for him, and if he did more than his share, no word ever passed his lips which would convey the thought that he knew. If there was a bad seat on the train, he was in it; if the sleeping compartment happened to be over the wheels, one always

felt sure that Victor had changed his seat from somewhere else and had taken the worst one.

On the steamer going perhaps to England, he was always helping someone, no matter who. If the steward offered an apology for the food he would say it really didn't matter as he was not a bit hungry. He never sought publicity, and shunned any attempt of anyone else to put him forward.

Even in his everyday life, going to and fro to his business, he would always be found round the back of the steamer or at the end of the train where no one could see him. His nature was just as hard to describe as his cricket, because one cannot recall, in one's acquaintance with men, a nature such as he had.

While typically affectionate and laudatory, the tribute betrays Iredale's sense that there remained aspects of Trumper beyond his understanding. At the outset, too, Iredale refers to 'many years of connection with him, which I am proud to say was never clouded by any misunderstanding'. It is an instance of protesting too much: as a few contemporary readers would have known, Iredale and Trumper had undergone a protracted estrangement. Mentioning this, however, would have been tactless in the extreme. For what had ended it was Trumper's fatal illness.

8

'WHO SHALL RULE THE GAME OF CRICKET?'

'The members of the board can plume themselves on their wonderful work.
They have at least succeeded in putting Mr. Victor Trumper out of the
Australian Eleven. They should feel very happy about that.'
– CLEM HILL in the *Daily Herald,* Adelaide, 24 February 1912

The men march in step, in jackets, ties and hats, the uniform of masculine respectability; the presence of a solitary female onlooker by the roadside accentuates that this is otherwise an exclusively male affair. A cart as it passes in the opposite direction reveals the length of the columns that stretch out of frame. Presently, there emerges a horse-drawn hearse, so laden with floral tributes it resembles a mobile flowerbed. Flanking it are cricket eminences including

Monty Noble, Frank Iredale, Charlie Macartney and Hanson Carter; another wagon also piled high with flowers follows. In the last of the clip's fifty seconds, a motorist streaks past, an unanticipated flicker of modernity. So ends 'The Last Innings of Victor Trumper, Champion of Champions' as recorded by *Australasian Gazette* newsreel on 30 June 1915, two days after Trumper's death, aged thirty-seven.

It is a brief glimpse of a long day. No bridge then linked Sydney's halves. From his home in Help Street, Chatswood, Trumper's casket proceeded by road to Milsons Point, by water to Fort Macquarie, then through the neighbourhoods of his childhood, columns four and five wide stretching more than 5 kilometres. As many as 20 000 were involved at some stage in the cortege. Lastly, special trams provided transport from Paddington to Charing Cross for the interment at Waverley Cemetery. This did not make it the biggest funeral of its kind: many more had attended the ceremonies for sculler Henry Searle in 1889. But twenty-three-year-old Searle's death from typhoid had had little news to compete with. In 1915 the daily newspapers were beginning to fill with wartime woe, even if the toll of the distant conflict in the Dardanelles was still to be fully felt. One of Trumper's mourners was his former boss Tom Garrett, whose son had just hours before been shot by a Turkish sniper at Pope's Hill, although Garrett would not receive word for another fortnight. The senior government representative at the funeral, assistant defence minister 'Jupp' Gardiner, had been assailed in Parliament that week about conscription, which he opposed.

Trumper had not died a martial death. His kidneys had been overwhelmed by Bright's disease.[*] Yet the mourners probably sensed in it a

---

[*] Bright's Disease is a kidney disorder brought about by an excess of protein in the urine, typically accompanied by edema, hypertension and excrutiating pain. A hundred years ago there was no treatment. For a useful primer, see 'Victor Trumper and Richard Bright' by Professor David Tiller AO in *The Life and Times of Victor Trumper* (2015).

greater cessation – of sunnier days and of simpler pleasures. They may even have felt a curious gratitude, that Trumper's memory would now remain fresh and green. The past? Maybe some parts were best let lie.

.

To understand these aspects of Trumper's life and death, it's useful to go back a decade – back, in fact, to 'Jumping Out'. It marked a zenith not only in Trumper's fame, but in the affairs of his teammates. From the pioneering 1870s, when Tom Garrett's contemporaries had formed part of that first trailblazing XI, through the unruly 1880s and reinvigorating 1890s, Australian cricketers had built a formidable franchise. In this they had gone more or less alone, assisted by their *entente* with the Melbourne CC, keeping the colonial associations at arms length, and scorning efforts to establish an overarching administrative body. The 1905 Australians enjoyed an unprecedented autonomy. They chose themselves – the selectors were Joe Darling, Monty Noble and Melbourne CC's Bob McLeod. They ran themselves – they elected Darling captain and Frank Laver manager. Some took their wives – not just Trumper but Clem Hill and deputy keeper Philip Newland. They undertook a leisurely journey to England via New Zealand and Fiji, then traversed North America by train. And, of course, in going their separate ways, they split half the gate – £5650, an increase of almost a third on the tour three years earlier. Yet, not surprisingly, covetous eyes were being cast on such windfall gains, reflecting an Australian strain of that abiding English belief in amateurism. While there was not the same class-based split among Australian cricketers, among Australian cricket administrators, almost entirely honorary, there were strong leanings against commercialisation that stressed the need to 'keep the game clean', to 'curb the curse of gate money', and at bottom to have their way.

Skirmishings resumed during the preparations for the 1905 tour, when the NSW and Victorian cricket associations abruptly tried to usurp Melbourne's role as provider of the team's initial outlays and role as first-ranked creditor, and to nominate a manager from outside. The players brushed these off. 'It is a matter for the players and I don't see that it concerns the associations at all,' countered Joe Darling. 'The England trip is a financial speculation on the part of the players who entrust the manager with their business and hold him responsible for all accounts . . . The players have as much right to appoint their own manager as I have to appoint a manager of my business.' Between Beldam's photographic sessions with Trumper at Lord's and at The Oval, however, took place the inaugural meeting of the 'Australian Board of Control for International Cricket'. Though barely more evolved than the late, unlamented Australasian Cricket Council, its ranks contained individuals of grittier fibre, notably a Sydney commercial solicitor, thirty-four-year-old William McElhone from East Sydney CC, and a Melbourne public servant, thirty-eight-year-old Ernest Bean from North Melbourne CC. These were not the gerontocrats who later predominated in Australian cricket's governance, but able and ambitious young men resolved to seize the management and finances of Australian cricket for their amateur administrative caste. It was easy at the time to dismiss their pretensions – two relatively junior delegates from two small clubs. 'Billy Mac' and Ernie Bean sounded more suited to the Tivoli stage. But then, how representative were the players?

At issue, in a sense, was proprietorship of what Trumper wears in 'Jumping Out': the national cap, inaugurated by Darling's team of 1899, signifying a tight-knit elite. Like a good many cricketers,

Trumper was superstitiously attached to his headgear: his team-mate Hill recalled that 'there was a row if one of the humourists of the team took his cap and hid it'. But behind the Australian green and gold, McElhone and Bean detected the red, white and blue of Melbourne, which they feared and envied as the land's biggest and wealthiest club. In this they had significant allies, including some who, for Trumper, cut across old loyalties, such as *The Referee*'s J. C. Davis, perhaps his greatest booster, and NSWCA board representative Frank Iredale, one of his oldest friends.

The board's fight to form would last three bitter years, and its fight to secure absolute control of Australian tours of England a further three. By the end of the campaign, the players had been more or less disenfranchised – reduced from semi-independent contractors in a free market to completely dependent hirelings in a monopoly, their only eventual recourse being to withdraw their labour.

'Billy Mac': W. P. McElhone.

The process revealed in Trumper an unsuspected obduracy: in the course of six seasons, he represented New South Wales in only six of a possible twenty-four Sheffield Shield matches. Sometimes vague reasons were given for his unavailability, such as 'business' or 'illness', and his tubercular constitution, further weakened by scarlet fever in 1908, was certainly frail. Yet in the same period he hardly missed a tour, trial or testimonial match, and some thought, not surprisingly, that he wished to make a quiet point of his sufferance of the regime – because on occasion, it was not so quiet.

•

A chronology of Australian cricket administration between the turn of the century and World War I reads back rather like a history of the Balkans: endless noisy wranglings, temporary alliances, and fights within fights. At the time the board was mooted, for instance, Melbourne's secretary, Ben Wardill, was working to thwart the Victorian Cricket Association's advancement of 'electoral cricket' – the kind that had democratised the competition between premier clubs in Sydney ten years earlier, but that south of the border was complicated by his club being larger than the rest put together. Publicly agnostic about the new body, privately he derided it. How could it claim to be representative when New South Wales and Victoria had won to their side only the impecunious Queensland Cricket Association? For the players, meanwhile, the missing feature of the new board was them. Where was the recognition of their status, as the men who had won the fame?

These factors drew the Melbourne CC and the players ever more tightly together. When Wardill revealed in May 1906 his plan for a new governing body in Victoria, it also emerged that he had secretly recruited the eleven biggest stars of Sydney cricket, including Trumper and Noble, to play against an English team in 1906–07. Needless to say, cricketers in cahoots with the hated Melbourne caused gouts of indignation, and the NSWCA resolved to fight back. 'What are we to do?' exclaimed secretary Percy Bowden. 'If such actions are permitted it would strike right at the root of the sport. You see, it's either the Association or eleven players who are going to run this show.'

Trumper himself was actually in Townsville when the story broke. He and an old cricket friend, James Giltinan, had assembled a private team, including two other Melbourne CC signatories, Bert Hopkins and Tibby Cotter, for a five-week tour of North Queensland. Trumper's relations with his association were already uneasy: he was disgruntled, for example, about the business Bowden sent Trumper & Carter's way, which he thought paltry. But he would have been taken aback at how decisively and unsentimentally the authorities moved, and the support with which they did so. From his bully pulpit as 'Not Out' in *The Referee*, Davis referred to the need for 'the powers-that-be in this State' to protect 'the honour of the great game . . . even though it means the cricket ostracism of friends and comrades of years'. When the players were indefinitely suspended, Davis toppled over into martial imagery even more florid:

This is the saddest business one has ever known in Australian cricket. However, just as nations succeed only after war, bloodshed and trampling over their dead comrades, the leading cricket associations of Australia must now trample over some of those who are among the ablest exponents of the game . . . in their efforts to put Australian cricket on a sound basis.

They did. 'The Great Cricket Split' roiled for months, full of acrimony and intrigue. It was finally resolved by the South Australian Cricket Association joining the board in return for undertakings about players' entitlements, including no trammelling of their tour profits and no infringement of their right to choose team management – undertakings, it would turn out, worth little. For McElhone and Bean it was a triumph: McElhone now enjoyed complete dominion in his state; Bean successfully forced 'electoral cricket' through in Melbourne. The peace, furthermore, contained punitive terms: it was none other than Iredale who seconded a motion requiring 'a personal letter containing an admission of error' from players as a condition of the removal of their suspension. Perhaps it was this encounter with one sporting monopoly that roused Trumper against another.

•

Accounts of Australian rugby league's break from rugby union vary in how deeply they incise Victor Trumper. It's unlikely the professional code could have taken its initial steps in August 1907 without him. It was Trumper who led the crucial recruitment of Dally Messenger, himself known in some circles as 'the Victor Trumper of rugby'. It was Trumper who recited to Messenger's mother the hard-luck stories of Bluey Burdon and Harold Judd, left uncompensated when rendered unable to work by injuries, which won her crucial support. Yet it was Trumper's confrere Giltinan who was more truly the impresario, burning the midnight oil at Trumper & Carter to arrange a visit by New Zealand's 'All Golds' to Australia, and a tour by the new 'Kangaroos' to the British Isles. Trumper seems more to have put his reputation at Giltinan's disposal – it was not enhanced.

The reaction of the New South Wales Rugby Union to the

creation of the NSW Rugby League, with Giltinan as secretary and Trumper as treasurer, was reminiscent of cricket's atmosphere of reprisal the previous year: life bans were imposed on defectors to the league's new clubs; Messenger's records were expunged for 100 years. Again, Trumper found himself on the other side of the barricades to Davis, who as 'Censor' in *The Referee* redoubled his injunctions against professionalism. 'There is a large section of the rugby-loving world who do not want, and will not have, football "on commercial principles",' insisted Davis. 'Once a sport becomes professionalised and free from control by amateurs, the sporting gives way to the business instinct, and in national sports that must tend to debasement.' This 'debasement' Davis used to restate the case for cricket's Board of Control: 'Fortunately in Australian cricket the reins of government are held by men who have no financial interest in the game. Hence the strong support given those in power by the public and the Press in the recent crisis.'

The venture soured quickly. Perhaps cricket profits had blinded Giltinan and Trumper to the risks of long sporting sojourns in the northern hemisphere. Whatever the case, the failure of the Kangaroos abroad sowed restlessness, coinciding as it did with financial stresses at several of the newly established NSWRL clubs. The result was a putsch against the league's executive – and although Giltinan would return as a club president, Trumper and the league never reconciled.

The relevance of the advent of rugby league to Trumper's life, however, is perhaps more in terms of what did not happen in cricket. There were years of division, rather than a convulsive, irrevocable split. There had in Australia been no equivalent of the rigid hierarchical distinctions between amateur and professional; rather had the game's financial arrangements taken many pragmatic shades, the

Australian 'amateur' being neither fish nor fowl. In that spirit, despite deep and abiding distrust, the players and administrators were able to work through a series of temporary compromises. Each had a different definition of compromise in mind: ultimately McElhone and Bean would accept from the cricketers nothing but total fealty. But once the Melbourne Cricket Club exited the field, the parties more or less acknowledged that they were stuck with one another.

The 1909 Australian tour of England was just such a compromise. The board had assumed Melbourne's former mantle as up-front financier in return for a guaranteed portion of the proceeds. The players maintained one remnant of independence, protected at the SACA's insistence by Rule 9 of the board's constitution: the team exchequer was still vested in the player-appointed manager Laver. To infiltrate those tightly guarded finances, McElhone and Bean made an instrument of Victoria's captain Peter McAlister, who nursed a seething grievance about his omission from the previous Ashes tour. When the board provocatively elected him Australian selector, McAlister wasted no time voting himself into the team, with the assistance of Iredale, whereupon the board appointed him as Noble's vice-captain and as Laver's treasurer.

Friend, manager, martyr: Frank Laver.

The fury of the players, who by convention had elected their own executive, was channelled into passive resistance. They formalised Noble's appointment by holding their own election anyway, then more or less ostracised McAlister, who not only failed as a player but somehow omitted to discharge his treasurer's responsibilities.[*] Laver, meanwhile, became something of a hero of the tour. Having expected in his fortieth year to play only as an emergency, he topped the bowling averages with his pawky medium pace.

The board obtained little satisfaction from the Australian team's victory; on the contrary, their resolve to curb overmighty players was stiffened. Trumper was a particular target. Aware Noble was to retire, Trumper hurried home from England in the expectation of succeeding to the captaincy of New South Wales, only to find that the NSWCA had emulated the board and made an appointment to the role rather than allow a player vote. Austin Diamond was a sound batsman and a likeable man, but only peripherally a team member. Trumper resumed his self-imposed exile, fuming in a letter to Bowden of the 'injustice' done him.

By now, Trumper was fully at loggerheads not only with McElhone and Bowden but with old friends like Iredale and Davis. Iredale had contributed outspoken articles favourable to the board to London's *Daily Mail*. In *The Referee*, Davis worded his support for Diamond tactfully but unambiguously: 'Wonderful cricketer that Victor Trumper has been and is, the history of our cricket during the past ten years or so proves that, however keen he may be

---

[*] Laver's recollection, from his May 1912 pamphlet, 'The Cricket Dispute: A Reply to the VCA', is worth quoting: 'It was not until the end of the tour that he [McAlister] asked me [about the finances], when by a chance remark he appeared to realise, for the first time that he had been neglecting his duties. He mentioned something about the balance sheet, as if he took it for granted I was going to prepare it, but to his unconcealed astonishment, I informed him I wasn't going to prepare a balance sheet for the board, as that was his duty.'

when on the field of play, he has not evinced the keenness of other noted players . . . to enhance its prestige and preserve for it the State championship.' Davis was at least more emollient than the correspondent of *The Sportsman*: 'It is a matter for regret that Mr Trumper and a few other excellent cricketers will not realise that the "old order changeth," and a new era of method and management has arrived; that while he and a noisy minority are apparently determined to resist reform, they stand almost isolated from the great body of cricketers and supporters of the game.' The question was clear: 'Who shall rule the game of cricket? Shall it be Trumper and Co. or the NSW Cricket Association? And to this there can be but one answer. The Association.'

When Diamond was a failure, Davis adjusted his *pince-nez*, forgot all about the evincing of keenness, and consented that Trumper 'must be captain'. By now confident enough of their authority, McElhone, Bowden and Iredale agreed, and New South Wales regained the Sheffield Shield in 1910–11 under its foremost player. Over the next year, in fact, the NSWCA drew Trumper a little closer. He was elected a state selector; he became Gordon's delegate to the association; his store was awarded a sizeable contract to supply caps and blazers. But old animosities welled quickly in December 1911 when, unilaterally overriding Rule 9, the board insisted on an appointed 'representative' accompanying the Australian team on its scheduled visit to England the following year to 'keep books of account relating to the tour and generally to supervise all matters', which it advised would render a manager 'unnecessary'. The board was transparently out to 'get' Laver. McElhone, doubtless urged on by McAlister, deemed him untrustworthy. It was not a provocation to be lightly borne.

•

In the summer of 1911–12, Clem Hill's Australian team was defending both the Ashes and the last vestige of the birthright it had inherited from the teams of the era of Billy Murdoch and Fred Spofforth. It failed in both tasks. The final confrontation was as violent as its cause was trivial. In the telegram traffic among selectors Hill, McAlister and Iredale ahead of the Third Test at Adelaide Oval, at which point the series was poised one-all, Hill confirmed the fitness of Charlie Macartney and his preference for leg spinner Jimmy Matthews over all-rounder Roy Minnett. McAlister's reply was pure coat-trailing: 'My team as forwarded yesterday. Still oppose Macartney's inclusion. If Iredale agrees with you, favour yourself standing down, not Minnett.' The policy of pinpricks had become personal. When six players signed a letter to the board demanding the reinstatement of Rule 9 a few days later, it involved more than a constitutional nicety. Protesting their disenfranchisement were the best of Australia's best: Hill, Trumper, his state colleagues Hanson Carter and Tibby Cotter, and Melbourne's Warwick Armstrong and Vernon Ransford.

The flurry of telegrams would continue for months, culminating in a *papierkrieg* of pamphlets – by the board, the NSWCA, the VCA, Laver, the Melbourne CC. But the key incidents condensed to two meetings at Bull's Chambers in Sydney's Martin Place a fortnight hence. The first was a board meeting making it clear that it regarded the players' letter as an ultimatum and would 'not permit any number of Cricketers to dictate the terms and conditions on which a visit is made'. The second, the next night, was a selection meeting at which Hill and McAlister met for the first time since their trading telegrams and traded blows instead.

Hill walked into a room he would have regarded as full of board sympathisers: not just McAlister and Iredale, but J. C. Davis and the zealous new secretary, Syd Smith. Bickering broke out immediately about the merits of individual players: Laver, Minnett, Macartney, Matthews. After Davis withdrew, McAlister threw down a gauntlet by coolly denigrating Trumper and Armstrong. 'Fancy you comparing yourself to men like Trumper and Armstrong,' retorted Hill. 'At all events, I reckon I am a better skipper than either Trumper, Armstrong or yourself,' McAlister claimed. The volatile Hill rebelled. 'You've been looking for a punch in the jaw all night,' he said, and administered it. Did the ensuing brawl last ten minutes? Did it last twenty? Testimonies differed. Agreed only is that Iredale and Smith had at one stage to prevent Hill defenestrating McAlister via a third-floor window, and that the meeting room was left a shambles. Australian cricket was in much the same state.[*]

So it remained, despite endless private councils, public debates, newspaper fusillades, talk of High Court injunctions and of pirate XIs, not to mention interventions by optimistic would-be go-betweens, including England's captain Pelham Warner, Marylebone CC president Lord Desborough, and the governor and the premier of NSW. The letter's six signatories – as they became known, 'the Big Six' – forfeited the tour rather than accept the board's dominion. None were aware that 'Trumper c Woolley b Barnes 50' at the SCG on 28 February 1912 would prove Trumper's final Test innings. But his reported remark to a correspondent of *The Leader* suggests that he might have sensed it: 'What are we to do? Go down on our knees and ask the Board to let us go to England on any terms they like? No, they have got the thing down to bedrock, and it can stay there as far as I am concerned.' There

---

[*] For a detailed retelling from the point of view of the players, see my book *The Big Ship: Warwick Armstrong and the Making of Modern Cricket* (1999); for an account from the point of view of the board, see the first two chapters of *Inside Story: Unlocking Australian Cricket's Archives* (2007) by myself and David Frith.

was a final showdown at Bull's Chambers two weeks later, when Trumper, as delegate of Gordon, voted unsuccessfully in support of a motion from Burwood's Frank McMullen 'that the delegates representing New South Wales on the Australian Board of Control have by their attitude during the recent cricket crisis forfeited the confidence of this association'. But soon after, the board's minutes record him making an ironic, practical accommodation with his predicament: he and his new business partner, Leonard Dodge, invoiced £43 for providing the Australian team for England, severely depleted and doomed to defeat, with caps, blazers and mufflers. Having lost his 'ownership' of the Australian cap, Trumper was reduced to selling them.

Coincidentally or not, Trumper subsequently gave his own cap away, to a Sydney High School boy, Victor Hyde, whom he saw playing on Moore Park. Hyde had been born in 1902, and named for Trumper, as he presumably explained, although the gesture only came to light ninety years later when the cap was auctioned by Hyde's

'V. Trumper': signatory to a failed 'no confidence' motion.

grandson. It echoes W. G. Grace's exchange of bats with Trumper fifteen years earlier, even if any prophecy went unfulfilled, for Hyde himself went on to be a baseballer. But perhaps it also reflected the players' loss of control over the symbol they had originated. If it was no longer theirs to bestow, they could at least hand it on.

•

What do we learn of Trumper through Australian cricket's pre-war quarrels? Like his contemporaries, he was heavily invested in the men who did the deeds earning the rewards. He was adamant, immoveable, and, in Sydney, an identified troublemaker. In a discussion of 'disaffected players' at the NSWCA in November 1910, McElhone laid it on the line: 'There were certainly some in the last team who would never agree with any principle laid down by the association. It was just as well to be perfectly plain about the matter – he referred to Trumper and Carter.'

In the climactic confrontation over Laver, there was no obvious ringleader. Publicly the refuseniks spoke with the voice of their captain; between them there was not a chink of light to be seen. After events they gave their loyalty material form, presenting their friend with a handsome five-drawer document cabinet, now in the collection of the Melbourne Cricket Club, bearing the inscription on a sterling silver plaque: 'To F. Laver from "The Six".' No need for names: they knew who they were. Of them all, however, it was Trumper who probably sacrificed most. In bloodying McAlister, Hill had almost certainly disqualified himself from leading Australia to England, whatever transpired. The Australian captaincy, then, lay within Trumper's reach. But if he was tempted to breach solidarity, it never showed.

Trumper was also putting a high price on his sense of the commonweal – because, quite frankly, he could have done with the money. Around this time, Trumper's financial straits seem to have been relatively common knowledge. His short-lived venture with Dodge was petering out; his wife had made an unsuccessful foray into millinery, deepening the family's debts. Even on the reduced terms the Board was offering, the proceeds of a tour would have represented a timely infusion of funds, and what he was giving up would need to be made good. What happened next allows another observation to be made of Trumper: that he possessed a streak of pragmatism.

•

The players of 1912 enjoyed more public sympathy than those of 1906: David Frith has observed that had the Board of Control been a democratically elected government during its wranglings with 'the Six', it would almost certainly have fallen. As it was a sporting monopoly, and monopsony, it emerged stronger. Yet it still needed some measure of popular support. The weakly led, cobbled-together team that toured England that year endeared itself to nobody. How to rally a cynical, disillusioned public? McElhone now did something typically shrewd: he exalted Victor Trumper. Six months after being more or less hounded from Test cricket, Trumper led his state throughout the Sheffield Shield, batting with renewed surety of touch. That was in large part because the NSWCA had also approved a Trumper testimonial, organised by a citizens' committee with Tom Garrett as secretary, NSW Legislative Council president Sir Francis Suttor as chairman and governor Lord Chelmsford as patron.

It was a coup of public relations and private diplomacy. Everyone could agree on Trumper's greatness, and magnanimity showed the NSWCA in a favourable light. 'If there is any cricket proposal that should meet with enthusiastic and universal approval, here it is,' said the *Daily Telegraph*'s 'Arawa'. Iredale in the *Sydney Mail* acclaimed 'the daring and multiplicity' of Trumper's strokes and the 'frank and manly' nature of his character; Davis in *The Referee* praised the recognition of 'the greatest batsman of the age, and the greatest Australian of any age'. Subscription lists opened in all capital cities and several country centres. The NSWCA made a handsome donation of £105. The VCA stationed collecting tins round the MCG. Even the Victorian Ladies' Cricket Association held a fundraising match. A surviving ledger, now among the Fingleton Papers in the Mitchell Library, lists contributions from eminences like Hill, Noble, Laver, Macartney and Warner alongside contributions of the 'Income Tax Department', 'a few clerks of Winchcombe Carson', 'a few admirers Walgett', 'Pupils of St Stanislaus College' and 'King of the Nuts'.

For some, it *was* all rather soon. The acerbic correspondent of Sydney's *The Sportsman*, for example, felt unable to modify his enmity for 'the Snivelling, Striking Six' who had 'crucified the interests of Australian cricket on a cross of cash', and deprecated the testimonial as 'equivalent to subsidizing disloyalty'. The NSW Rugby League also voted against contributing. And when it came to staging a celebratory game at the SCG, the NSWCA baulked at Garrett's suggestion that Trumper lead a select XI against the Australian team recently tried and found wanting in England – the comparison might not have been flattering. Their insistence that Trumper lead New South Wales against 'the Rest of Australia' may partly explain a sentiment ascribed to the beneficiary by a member of the citizens' committee, Thomas Houghton, who awarded himself a handsome credit on the 3d scorecard, then the following year sued Trumper for non-payment of services rendered. Although a jury dismissed the claim, Houghton said Trumper had confided in him that 'the match would be a failure if left to the cricket association', and that Bowden in particular would 'do his best to make it a failure'.

Trumper need not have worried. The match could hardly have been more successful. So lusty was the three minutes' cheering as he walked out to bat that it drowned out the band's rendition of 'For He's a Jolly Good Fellow'. Trumper batted breezily for 126 not out and 61, playfully demonstrating strokes as they were suggested by the slip fielders. The association vested the £2950 in a trust controlled by McElhone and two other association office holders, who acquired six rental cottages at Petersham for the income – a paternalistic step but perhaps not ill-advised given the beneficiary's fluctuating fortunes and importunate creditors. In doing so, of course, Trumper became beholden to his former tormentors – needs must when the devil drives.

The testimonial match was lavishly reported. On the first morning, *Australian Town and Country Journal* presented 'Victor Trumper, Wizard of the Willow' on a double-page spread, the eleven action photographs of him involving the most detailed study since Beldam's. The strokes are not so dynamic as eight years earlier. Trumper is older, more austere and stately. There's a touch of Greg Chappell's later controlled splendour. The buff pants and bare hands suggest something improvised at short notice; the purpose is promotional rather than instructional. But certain signatures remain: the low-tugged cap; the sleeves folded just so; the originality of a deflection behind square leg from under a raised back foot, a 'Trumperian masterpiece . . . captured by the art of our photographer'. There's a haunting quality, too. They form the first photographic sequence of Trumper on his own soil, and also the last: within eighteen months, their subject would be too ill to take the field.

No meaningful image survives of Trumper's final tour, as a member of a private team to New Zealand captained by Arthur Sims, a meat-packing magnate, and including Armstrong, Laver and Arthur Mailey. In ten minutes over three hours at Lancaster Park on 28 February 1914, Trumper and Sims added 433 for the eighth wicket – a world record that still stands. To describe Trumper's 293, cricket writers strained one last time. 'The cricket scribe's vocabulary is quite inadequate to describe Trumper's innings,' conceded *Christchurch Press*. The enigma of the man also persisted, to his final recorded public utterance – an announcement, just before Australian selectors met to choose a team to visit South Africa, that he would not be going:

> 'I am not available,' he said.
> What does that mean?
> 'Simply that I want to save the selectors trouble,' he replied, 'and
> I make the announcement early. I don't want any misconstruction
> put on my words. I am not available.' No amount of questioning
> or coaxing would get more from Trumper.

'Trumper is within his rights in refusing to go out to South Africa, and he needn't give his reasons to the Board of Control particularly,' complained *Table Talk*. 'But he might let the local public who admire him so much into the little secret of his reasons for refusing to represent his country in an international tour.' Nothing further was heard, and there would in any case be no tour – no big cricket, in fact, for six bleak years.

'Wizard of the Willow': *Town and Country Journal*, 29 January 1913.

With the outbreak of war, Trumper appeared briefly in a couple of patriotic causes, but dropped from view as his illness worsened, retiring to his home, then to St Vincent's Hospital. Various stories circulated of his declining months. In a 1930 biography of Rev. Raymond Preston, Trumper was quoted as telling the Methodist evangelist that he had offered himself to Christ: 'I began to pray and asked God to save me, and He did, and I know it's all right, and if the worst comes, I shall go to the better place, where there is no suffering, and I shall be there when you come, to welcome you.' Making peace was the theme of another story narrated later by Bert Shortland concerning their Gordon clubmate Iredale, who had by then succeeded Bowden as NSWCA secretary:

> When Victor was practically dying I saw him and told him Frank had given a message for him, and Vic said: 'Tell Frank I am having my final knock out. The Greatest Umpire of all will shortly give his decision, and *I know it will be "Out"*, but I have always tried to play the game, and I am not afraid. Tell Frank to let bygones be bygones.' When Frank received this message, he was overcome, and said: 'Victor is the finest sport of all.'

Doubtless this was the sentiment at Waverley Cemetery on that June day of milky sunshine. Members of the NSWCA mourned alongside players they had suspended in 1906, members of the board alongside players they had essentially exiled in 1912; representatives of the NSW Rugby League stood graveside with representatives of the NSW Rugby Union, having been irreconcilable since the split in their game. A wreath from the Melbourne CC reposed among floral tributes from those who had sought its annihilation; it received less attention than a wreath in the colours of the German flag, which turned out to be from the Somerset County Cricket Club. Confusion about Trumper's origins remained unexamined to the end: he was reported as variously thirty-six, thirty-seven and thirty-eight.

It was the epilogue to an era that the participants were unaware had already ended: with a winding-down of the game's administration, first-class cricket would not resume the following summer. Two years later, a bigger and angrier Sydney funeral, that of the boxer Les Darcy, would involve an instant addition to Australian martyrology. The development of the Trumper legend would be a slower-forming affair, partly influenced by sentiments Davis cited in his reporting of the funeral. For this he pulled down his copy of Beldam's *Great Batsmen* and reproduced Fry's verdict: 'Victor Trumper is, perhaps, the most difficult batsman in the world to reduce to words.'

9

'SEE HIM AND MARVEL!'

'Gather round me, you fellows of the younger cricketing generation,
and I'll try and give you a pen-picture of the Immortal of the Bat – Victor
Trumper. I saw kings of the willow before him, and I have seen all the
giants since the Grim Reaper said, "Out," to the Peerless One, but no
batsman before or after him, in my generation, so truly revealed the
soul of cricket to me as did Trumper, the Imperishable.'
– *Northern Star* (Lismore), 5 November 1927

Not everyone at Victor Trumper's funeral was a hardened veteran of
the decade of administrative strife. Among younger mourners was a
gifted twenty-year-old law student, secretary of the cricket club in
whose second XI he played. Herbert Vere Evatt probably accompanied University CC elder Tom Garrett. He was destined for a
brilliant career; but first, like his country, he would have to outlast
a bitter war.

Australia was about to receive a gruelling initiation in the griev-
ing of life cut short. Within a couple of years, Evatt would lose both
brothers and suffer the desolating sense that had he gone to war he
could have saved them. 'Oh! Dear God, I yearn/For those dear boys
who never shall return,' he wrote in a self-lacerating sonnet. Eleven
University CC players likewise failed to come back; so did two
youthful mourners at Trumper's funeral, his state teammates Tibby
Cotter and Norman Callaway.

In the course of war, in fact, funerals of the size of Trumper's
would slip from fashion. Historians regard World War I, a wave of
random violent mass fatality that left the bereaved without bodies to
mourn over, as a watershed in rituals of death and modes of conso-
lation. In Australia, one in five of those who left did not return, and
every second household experienced loss. Grief grew more intense,
more private, less ostentatious. Much tends to be made of attendance at Trumper's funeral, of Australians turning aside from war to
honour a great sportsman; more properly the funeral was a last gasp
of former customs. *

What *was* a match for the times was Trumper's life – bold, vital
and cut short after service to greater glory. Leslie Poidevin's obituary
in the *Sydney Morning Herald* made the martial connection explicit:
'The hero of many of the most historic battles of the greensward, and
withal the most modest of men, having "played the game" all his life,
he has at last bravely answered the final call all too soon.' Trumper's
death would be noted in *Wisden* in the distinguished company of

---

* Typical in this respect, Jack Pollard's *The Turbulent Years of Australian Cricket*
(1987) ('Despite the importance of the war news, Trumper's death, at the age
of only 37, was splashed across the front pages of Australia's newspapers') and
Peter FitzSimons' *Great Australian Sports Champions* (2006) ('It took a lot for
anything other than the news of the war to dominate newspaper billboards at that
time – when so many of our own were fighting for their lives on Gallipoli – but
the death of Victor Trumper accomplished that easily, and not just in Australia').

W. G. Grace, who perished to a heart attack in October 1915, but was somehow closer in nature to the obituaries in the same edition for the nearly 200 young cricketing men killed on duty. Certainly a young major in the 60th Rifles serving in France thought so. As a schoolboy, H. S. Altham had seen Trumper's maiden Test hundred; as a schoolteacher, he would later write cricket's first significant synoptic history. 'I can remember . . . feeling no real sorrow for W.G. passing Homeric and legendary into Elysian fields,' he recalled, 'but an almost personal pain that Trumper's gallant spirit and matchless grace should have been called so early from the world it enriched.' *Called so early*: it was not a term that Altham, recipient of the Distinguished Service Order and Military Cross, would have used lightly.

Elsewhere in the same lists of what has become its most famously poignant number, *Wisden* reported the death of Sub-Lieutenant Rupert Brooke, who left a corner of an Aegean field forever England by succumbing to sunstroke on Lemnos in April 1915. The almanack scrupulously documented his 1906 Rugby School season of nineteen wickets at 14 before noting his having 'gained considerable reputation as a poet'. It was a time, in fact, when poetry often seemed the only adequate form of expression and source of solace – not necessarily the poetry being written, deepeningly bleak, but the stocks of verse already dedicated to premature death, such as Milton's 'Lycidas', Tennyson's 'In Memoriam', Shelley's 'Adonaïs', Kipling's 'Recessional', Housman's 'A Shropshire Lad'. C. J. Dennis grumbled about all this high-falutin' stuff when he farewelled his protagonist at Gallipoli in *The Moods of Ginger Mick* (1916): "E found a game 'e knoo, an' played it well;/An' now 'e's gone. Wot more is there to tell?' But the space of special honour that sport reserved for its dead took particular comfort in Housman's *fin-de-siècle* words:

Now in Maytime to the wicket
Out I march with bat and pad:
See the son of grief at cricket
Trying to be glad . . .
Smart lad, to slip betimes away
From field where glory does not stay
And early though the laurel grows
It withers quicker than the rose.
Eyes the shady night has shut
Cannot see the record cut,
And silence sounds no worse than cheers
After earth has stopped the ears:
Now you will not swell the rout
Of lads that wore their honours out,
Runners whom renown outran
And the name died before the man.

This eventuality would now not befall Trumper. In a sense, all athletes die twice, the first time with the end of their competitive span. For Trumper the twilight was brief and the darkness descended swiftly. The tragedy that befell his family when he left a widow with a nine-year-old daughter and an eighteen-month-old son also relieved his image of the toll of decline. 'I have one great satisfaction regarding Victor Trumper,' wrote Charlie Macartney, a Gordon teammate and protégé. 'I never saw him grow old as a cricketer.' As J. C. Davis concluded in his eulogy in *The Referee*: 'Those whom the gods love die young.'

•

A corollary of this is that gods can seem ambivalent about those to whom they grant longer life. This is also evident in the Trumper story. As war wound on, the sun set on a whole sporting world. The leisure society of which C. B. Fry and George Beldam had been gifted members would reconvene afterwards in reduced circumstances and darker hues.

Fry's gilded youth and exhilarating maturity, noted his contemporary Lord Birkenhead, petered out 'into a somewhat desultory and disappointed career'. He dabbled in diplomacy, advising Ranji at the League of Nations. He detoured into politics, thrice running unsuccessfully as a Liberal. He fantasised of a movie career, making several trips to Hollywood. Most of the time he wandered the TS *Mercury* in a uniform that purportedly made him 'look every inch like six admirals', while remaining a clear subordinate to his mirthless and tyrannical wife, whose boy cadets endured a regime heavy on deprivation, sadism and surveillance – they answered to numbers rather than their names, had their bowel movements documented and their genitalia examined daily. Thanks to Charles Hoare's will, Fry enjoyed a twenty-five-room mansion on spacious grounds with a butler, servants and a Rolls-Royce – but not much else. In the late 1920s he suffered an acute mental breakdown.

Six years' convalescence later, Fry found a niche with an idiosyncratic column in the *Evening Standard*, 'C. B. Fry Says' – even if what Fry said, like his flirtation with fascism, did not always show him in a flattering light. Beatie's death in 1946 seemed to cheer him. His biographer Denzil Batchelor recalled Fry's eccentric greeting at her memorial service. 'Look!' Fry exclaimed. 'I'll show you an infallible way to play a googly.' When the chapel bell rang while he was demonstrating, he said: 'Never mind, we'll finish afterwards . . .' But at seventy-four it was too late to act on any of his periodic enthusiasms. On one occasion, Fry professed boredom with cricket and said he would go into racing. 'What as?' Batchelor asked. 'Trainer – jockey – or horse?' So in declining years, Fry would lie awake on the *Mercury* reciting aloud the details of cricket matches he had played. It was not the end anyone had foretold for this most omnicompetent Englishman.

Multiple enthusiasms stretched Beldam thin, too. Having provided the illustrations for no fewer than eight sizeable sporting books within three years, including a pioneering textbook on jujutsu, he also suffered a breakdown, ascribed to overwork. Forty in May 1908, he forsook flannels at Lord's for Savile Row suits in the City, although he maintained his old contacts: he diversified Beldam Packing & Rubber into sporting goods, including partnering J. H. Taylor in the marketing of a 'JH' golf ball, and formed the G. W. Beldam Tyre Syndicate, whose shareholders included his brother Cyril, Ranji and Archie MacLaren. Beldam Packing insulated the boilers of the *Titanic*; four Beldam anti-skid tyres were beneath Lawrence of Arabia's Rolls-Royce during his desert campaigns.

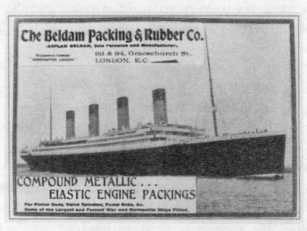

Back to business: Beldam insulates the *Titanic*.

After World War I, George Beldam's life look a racier turn. First he abandoned his wife Gertrude for Margaret Frew Underwood, an old schoolfriend of his daughter, whom he married in June 1921. She bore him a son and a daughter, but their relations were volatile, and they parted. Then he fell in love with his children's twenty-year-old nurse, Christina Thompson, and eloped with her to Biarritz. After a while they took up residence in a village in Surrey where Beldam lived under an assumed name, and Christina bore a daughter. Margaret, however, would not consent to a divorce until just before Christina gave birth to twins, a boy and girl, in June 1930.

The couple finally settled on 24 acres (8 hectares) near an old market town, Farnham, where Beldam took pleasure in growing rhododendrons and driving a twelve-cylinder Packard with fold-out seats for his third family. A certain bohemianism may even have been in the blood. In November 1937, brother Cyril was involved in a scandalous breach-of-promise case that became a tabloid sensation: the inamorata was an artist's model with two sisters. 'I am not going to put Mr Beldam before you as a man of morals,' admitted his defence counsel, former attorney-general Sir Patrick Hastings. 'He has behaved extraordinarily badly. But this is not a court of morals. These three sisters have put their heads together to rob Mr Beldam.' No sooner had the court agreed than George suffered a fatal coronary, leaving his young widow with three children – again, not perhaps the end one would have prophesied for this cultured and eclectic English gent.

On the other side of the world, Sydney's *Referee* recalled Beldam's legacy of *Great Batsmen* and *Great Bowlers and Fielders*: 'These books hand down to two generations in picture and prose the beauties and the methods of masters who have passed on. These include several Australians. The man closes his chapter. The book never.' With that, at least, Beldam might have rested content.

·

Of sport as well as of society, postwar rebuilding would never be quite complete. By the time cricket resumed, only Warwick Armstrong and Hanson Carter remained of the recalcitrant six, and briefly. Administrators found their younger players, many of them having served, more tractable, happy enough to be playing at all – some had undergone acute hardships, such as all-rounder Charles Kelleway, four times wounded, and keeper Bert Oldfield, five months in hospital with shell shock after being blown up at Polygon Wood. In England's hobbled economy, cricket made faltering progress. Amateurism was a social luxury hard to afford. In the 1920s the proportion of amateurs in county cricket halved, and their quality was thinner. England's foremost cricket hero, Jack Hobbs, hardly resembled Jovian Grace, versatile Fry or vivid Ranji: a professional, the son of a Cambridge groundsman, he personified in his batting and bearing the scaled-down ambitions of English suburbia – dedicated, unassuming, thrifty, abstemious, a proud tradesman who nonetheless deferred to amateur inferiors. And although the distinction between gentlemen and players would survive another world war, England's foremost cricket personalities through that time would file chiefly through the professional gate: Woolley, Hammond, Hendren, Sutcliffe, Larwood, Hutton, Compton.

The scene was also psychically bleaker. Worcestershire's Fred Root, who opened England's bowling ten years after he was told war wounds in France would prevent him playing again, recalled rolls of honour in every county pavilion, and memories everywhere: 'Village shrines, the larger war memorials of the towns and cities, and all things which are built "for ever to acknowledge those great sacrifices" bear names associated with the game of cricket. And we who were spared – *remember* –.' In his travelogue *England Over* (1927), *Times* journalist Dudley Carew watched the Eton v Harrow match with a dignified black-clad woman for whom it was the annual pilgrimage in honour of her lost Harrovian son: 'The things he was going to do! He loved cricket so.' It is a stage without an end: '"There are years to come," she said slowly. "Years and years, years and years."' Carew's other two cricket books, *The Son of Grief* (1936), a cheerless novel of professional cricket, and *To the Wicket* (1946), a set of pensive essays, both nod to Housman in their titles.

In *Cricket in Firelight* (1935), a memoir of *Observer* journalist Richard Binns, pre-war cricket lay preserved as if in amber, the relic of an irrecoverable comfort and innocence. Before joining up, Binns and his 'cheery, happy-go-lucky friend' Jerry Murgatroyd had been busy cricketers and fans who rejoiced in cricket talk: of village matches, of Test and Roses matches, of Grace ('The Champion'), of Ranjitsinhji ('the shining star from the East') and of Trumper ('the greatest batsman of all time . . . a lion whom no bowler and no pitch could tame'). Returning maimed from 'the Last Great Match of All', they spent 'many days of sickness and disability' consoling themselves with their cricket memories until Murgatroyd's death, and the toll on Binns of 'a wartime legacy of broken health'. The book, popular enough to be reprinted twenty years later, is Binns' attempt to recreate their chats: 'In the lowering firelight the enlarging shadows grew more vaguely grotesque and moved more slowly on the walls as Jerry Murgatroyd called back one after another these grey spirits of cricket past, noble shadows that even in the ghostliness of memory still bore themselves as proudly as in the full panoply of hot action on the field.' Trumper, whom the pair saw as boys in 1902, is evoked in all his vitality as 'a young athletic god trailing clouds of glory about him as he moved', then mourned in his premature mortality: 'It is hard to think that such graciousness as Victor Trumper brought to cricket and to life should be foredoomed to travel the dusty way of common mortality and decay. Victor Trumper died in 1915, after a painful illness, in his thirty-eighth year.' The implicit parallel is with the dimming of Jerry's once brilliant light. The question was now how best to remember, in a fashion that did not become its own form of torment.

•

Shortly after World War I ended, a man visiting his brother's grave in Waverley Cemetery was approached by a woman asking directions to Victor Trumper's final resting place. The man, he recalled in a letter to *The Referee*, asked if she was a relative. No, she said, nor even a friend. 'I belong to the country, and when visiting Sydney I have seen him play cricket on several occasions,' she said. 'He struck me as being such a fine sportsman that I have come out this afternoon just to see the place where he is laid to rest.' It wasn't surprising that she was having trouble: the only marking on the tomb was 'VIC' incised in the freestone railing. Crown Street School had opened a fund to erect a memorial, but as of three and a half years after Trumper's death he had no headstone.

Like Australia itself, cricket was in straitened circumstances. The NSWCA had a bank balance of £9 11s. A suspended plan for a memorial drinking fountain in Trumper's honour was revived, and subscriptions invited. 'To many of the present-day players, Vic Trumper is little more than a name,' commented 'Point' in the *Newcastle Sun*. 'I am afraid many of them do not know their cricket history as they should . . . Let the memorial be worthy of him.' But barely had the lists opened than the association learned that Trumper's widow was in financial hardship: it pragmatically gave her the bulk of £229 raised, retaining just enough to pay for a plaque at the rear of the Sheridan Stand.

Trumper's memory remained up for claiming. In January 1919, Victorian cricketers made a pilgrimage to Waverley Cemetery and laid a wreath blessed by Rev. E. H. Sugden, the venerable master of Melbourne's Queen's College. Victor Trumper, said Sugden, had been the personification of amateurism: 'Had the German nation been imbued with the same sporting spirit, the war, involving so much bloodshed, may never have occurred.' The *Sydney Morning Herald* dedicated a lengthy editorial to the Victorians' 'graceful and appropriate' gesture hoping that cricket would revert to being played in 'Trumper's spirit', forgetfully opining that it was 'never so popular or so free from disputes as when both players and officials remembered that it was a game'. Trumper's memory affirmed imperial ties, too. When MCC visited six years later, their well-liked captain Arthur Gilligan enhanced his popularity by laying a wreath at the SCG plaque in honour of 'the greatest batsman the world has ever seen'. Trumper, Gilligan explained to widespread approval, had been his 'one idol on the cricket field', too.

Agreement on a more substantial monument remained elusive. In August 1923, perhaps inspired by the recent example of the Grace Gates installed at Lord's, Paddington Council announced their intention to rename Hampden Oval in honour of the greatest player it had hosted. At the last moment, however, they were unexpectedly thwarted by Lands Minister Walter Wearne, who was unpersuaded of the case for a rededication. Viscount Hampden had been an inoffensive state governor in the 1890s; Trumper's 'success in the cricket field', the minister felt, was 'not sufficient reason why the name should be changed'. Needless to say, Wearne courted considerable disagreement, even in his own ranks. At a public meeting, the speaker of the Legislative Assembly, Daniel Levy, distanced himself from his fellow Nationalist and advertised his support for the campaign. Other speakers joined in. What was an English governor compared to Trumper? How much fame for Australia had been won by 'all the Joe Cooks and high commissioners'? Wearne remained unmoved. Yet there was emerging a way to recapture Trumper without the rigmarole of public collections and ministerial petitionings – and it had been around twenty years.

In an era when the simplest image can be proliferated and distributed so easily, it can be hard to imagine the scarcities and restrictions of the past. *Great Batsmen* had been an expensive book; the few copies of the gravure of 'Jumping Out' that had made it to Australia were in private hands.* One hung inside the door of the NSWCA's premises at George Street, where Leslie Poidevin described it for the *Sunday Times* in November 1922: 'It is a near perfect illustration of the essential features in the correct execution of the off-drive. The swing of the bat, the poise of the body, the positions of the left leg and foot in the air ready to go forward and come down, with the bat to meet the ball – it is a classic photograph, to my view, and I commend its study to *anyone having the opportunity to view it*.' [my italics] Because the quality of halftone illustration on Australian newsprint was insufficient to do the image justice, the reader had to take Poidevin's word for it.

---

* In Ceylon on his way to Australia in 1936, Fry mentioned that he had recently been asked for a copy of *Great Batsmen* by Princess Mary, learned that the book was 'not to be had anywhere', and at last obtained a copy for fifteen guineas. Clem Hill attested both volumes' rarity in a 1940 letter to a correspondent in Surrey: 'The two great books *Batsmen* & *Bowlers* written by C.B.Fry & pictures taken by Beldam was [sic] wonderful – Don't know whether [you] can get it now – but if procurable get it.'

In England, Beldam's work enjoyed continued cachet: his Trumper photographs featured in the new edition of *The Badminton Book of Cricket* (1920), Pelham Warner's *Book of Cricket* (1920) and Gilbert Jessop's *Cricket and How to Play It* (1925); 'Jumping Out' took pride of place on the office wall at Fleet Street's Cricket Reporting Agency, *Wisden*'s inner sanctum. As it should, thought H. S. Altham in his ongoing 'History of Cricket' series in *Cricketer*: 'To try to reduce to words the art of this consummate batsman is almost an impertinence, but to those who never saw him at his best I would suggest that they should study the glorious series of photographs of Trumper in action contained in Beldam and Fry's *Great Batsmen*. From these they will catch at least a reflection of the ease, the balance, the perfect naturalness that made him surely the most fascinating batsman to watch in the history of the game.' But when Noble published *The Game's the Thing* (1926), with its lengthy and lyrical evocation of Trumper, he omitted 'Jumping Out', as though his friend should linger chiefly in the mind's eye.

Then, in October 1927, the *Sydney Mail* took a chance. The fifty-page Sydney weekly had been redesigned to lead the market in illustration, using a new Hoe Fine Art Rotary Web Press, and printing exclusively on art paper. Its circulation had surged during the war, and its pictorial ambitions grown, not least in cricket. English-born staff photographer Herbert Fishwick persuaded the paper's owners to indulge him with an English-made accessory, a 43-inch (109 cm) Ross & Co. lens, for his Graflex camera. Such lenses had been developed for photography from aeroplanes and balloons, but they also proved a superb means of bridging the distances involved in photographing cricket, of which Fishwick made a speciality, his signature being the use of diagonal angles from vantages backward of point.

It's likely that Fishwick had a hand when the *Mail* dedicated half a page to a reproduction of the NSWCA's copy of 'Jumping Out'. The context of its Australian rediscovery was a tribute, 'The Standard Set by Victor Trumper', by former Crown Street classmate and Gordon clubmate Bert Shortland. The standard Shortland had in mind was less Trumper's batting than his sportsmanship and good nature: 'There are many modest players, but was ever such modesty blended with such capacity for great achievement? He was well named Victor, and his memory shall endure, a standard for cricketers for ever.' The unadorned grave was now of a piece with these qualities: 'At Waverley by the sea – there he rests! No great headstone covers his resting-place; those who seek may find. Just three magic letters mark the spot, and they are "V I C." Nothing more – as in life, so in death – Modesty.' As far as the batting genius was concerned, Shortland could allow the photograph to do the work, with a little help from the complementary caption:

> To look at this picture (kindly lent by the N.S.W. Cricket Association) is to see Victor Trumper as we used to see him from the pavilions. See him and marvel! It does not show his face clearly, but as an action picture it is wonderful. No hesitancy here. He is stepping out to meet the ball. Strength, grace, and balance, combine to reveal joyous and youthful sense of mastery. What was the secret of this joyous freedom? Simply the beautiful character of Victor. All young players should know all that can be told of him, whose other name was Modesty.

Here was a blissful solution to the challenges of remembrance. No need to worry about monuments; no need to strain for the words and phrases that had always felt inadequate; reproducing 'Jumping Out'

Victor !

To look at this picture (kindly lent by the N.S.W. Cricket Association) is to see Victor Trumper as we used to see him from the pavilions. See him and marvel! It does not show his pace exactly, but as an action picture it is wonderful. No wondering here. He is stepping out to meet the ball: strength, grace, and balance, combine to reveal power and wonderful sense of mastery. What was the secret of this famous freedom? Simply the beautiful character of Victor. All young players should know all that can be told of him, whose other name was Modesty.

The Standard Set by Victor Trumper

By H. S.

With the cricket season opening we commend to all players these references to the late Victor Trumper. There is more in cricket than skill in batting, bowling, or fielding. Not only for his wonderful batting will Trumper never be forgotten. His name will always be to cricketers a synonym for sportsmanship, and especially for one phase of sportsmanship—Modesty. There are many modest players, but was ever such modesty blended with such capacity for great achievement? He was well named Victor, and his memory shall endure, a standard for cricketers for ever.

LAST season the standard of umpiring was often discussed, and some of the "wise-acres" had their qualifications challenged by disappointed players. Whether the criticisms were justified is doubtful. An umpire may—and occasionally does—give a wrong decision, not the standard here is probably as good as is possible. I am inclined to question not the umpires, but the good taste of the players when umpires are attacked, and it may be timely to give a few examples of Victor Trumper's attitude in respect of such ethics.

I went to school with Victor, and played with him, off and on, right up to the end. On one occasion a school match. Vic was about out in a match which was an absolute hump ball, and his team (mine was very exasperated. Victor's only remorse when he came in was: "Never mind; we will do it next time." And sure enough he did: for he scored 204 not out.

Getting a fast ball on the leg side in a match played by Gordon, Vic tried to glance, and in doing so the ball just reached the buckle of the pad. Someone in the pavilion appealed, and the umpire gave him out. I was batting with him, and told him it was a bad decision. Vic asked me to walk with him to the pavilion, and on the way he gave me a little lesson about doubting the umpire. When walking into the pavilion a barracker asked him if he was out. Vic's reply was: "I had a splendid knock" (he scored 125); "it was about time I was out."

ONCE, when playing Gordon, playing "Yabba," who was really a very amusing barracker, exasperated me, and I suggested to Vic that the only man might be spoken to by the groundsman. Vic's reply was: "What! He is one of the Globe team, and is the best member in it." He would not hear of "Yabba" being stopped.

He regarded "Yabba" as a "character," and took no notice of his comments in the right spirit.

Another time when playing in a minor match I umpired for Vic, and the batsman was given out by the umpire. Our opponents were patients in a mental hospital. Vic, strolling up to me one moment said that it was up to me to give the poor fellows as much pleasure as possible, and not to appeal in the slightest—why, by the way, were also patients. Vic agreed to my suggestion that all Vic's sportsmanship. Playing through one day two centuries. I have never seen those quoted when reference is made to doubtful umpiring. I happened to be batting with him each time when he reached his 100, and in both knocks he purposely gave his wicket to "Mackie" podium, as he reckoned that he took wickets the hardest and he always had a kindly feeling for him.

Finally, Vic, and Frank Iredale were as bigger-block, over the board of Control trouble. When Victor was practically aloud I saw him and told him Frank had given me a message for him, and Vic said: "Tell Frank I am having my first knock out. The Greatest Umpire of all will shortly give his decision, and I know it will be 'Out,' but I have always lived to play the game, and I can say about. Tell Frank to let Iredale know I am beaten. When Frank received this message he was overcome, and said: "Victor is the finest sport of all." Poor old Frank has since joined him.

ONE more incident before closing to show the kindly spirit of this greatest of all players. Gordon was the premiership in 1911, and after a keen struggle it came to the final match. Gordon v Paddington. I happened to be a newsletter, with Victor on the team. On the Thursday before the match I received a ring from him to go down to his sports shop, and on comparing our teams we differed by one player.

He had included Dan Campbell, father of the present interstate cricketer. Now, that was really not in the first grade in those days. The standard was high. He had, however, been a wonderful worker for the game at his life, and he had the ambition to play in a first-grade match before retiring. Victor knew this, and enabled the match. The match earned a great deal of interest at the time in Sydney, and 15,000 people went out to Rushcutter and the gate money, after a keen struggle, although Gordon had to catch only 173 runs to win the bowling period so doubtly and they failed by 37 runs. Victor always tried to give pleasure to others. He was far from well, but at 6 o'clock the Gordon barrackers would not leave the ground until he batted. I tried to persuade him not to go in, but he replied: "I like to please the crowd," and he went in dressed in his ordinary clothes, except that he wore his cricketing boots. He hit a sweet sing, scoring 14 in 16 minutes. This includes 10 fours and five "sixers." Iredale said he had never seen such batting. Arthur Mailey should remember this, as Arthur bowled Victor cheaply in the first innings; but in the second—well—on the Wednesday I received a message from Mr. McQueen, then President to call at his office. When I arrived there Mr. McQueen, Victor, Frank Iredale, and others were present. Vic then handed me the belt used in the final match. Together should so it reads: "From Vic Trumper to ——." He remains premiership 1910-11." Here again he showed his great sportsmanship.

CRICKETERS and all sports, you cannot all be champions; but you can all try to emulate his spirit. One quality of sportsmanship is modesty. At Waverley, by the sea—there be rests! No wind footsteps covers his resting place; those who seek may find. Just three magic letters mark the spot, and they are "V.T." Nothing more—so in life, so in death—Modesty.

(Continued on Next Page.)

'The Standard Set by Victor Trumper': vertiginous.

225

was the equivalent of expressing an artist by his work, or quoting a public man in his own words. It was also to modernise Trumper, to bring him into the pictorial economy of the *Mail*'s well-to-do readership, interested in sport, fashion, travel and a growing Australia. His leap had the optimism of Sydney's stretching across its mighty harbour, the Bridge's progress being one of the *Mail*'s illustrative staples.

Following up Trumper, the *Mail* published another indelible cricket image. Fishwick's subject in November 1928, busily compiling 225 for MCC against New South Wales, was the Englishman Walter Hammond playing a sumptuous cover drive, with keeper Bert Oldfield in seemingly sympathetic attendance, as alert as a gun dog. 'A Vigorous Drive by Hammond' was accorded vigorous

'A Vigorous Drive': Fishwick's Hammond.

treatment, occupying the entirety of the *Mail*'s page five, with a distinguished afterlife ahead.* It was at the very least a technical breakthrough. Never able to draw the action toward him, Beldam had had to contrive to meet it halfway; Fishwick's lens now did the work unassisted.

So it was that virtually a quarter of a century after it was taken, 'Jumping Out' began at last to reach a popular audience, and it would become a common sentiment that no Australian cricket location was quite complete without it. It hung in the members stands at the SCG and the MCG. In October 1931, when the government relented and agreed to rechristen Hampden Oval as Trumper Park, Monty Noble unveiled a handsome print in the clubrooms at the tea-break of a charity match. Visitors to the chambers of Bill Dovey, later Gough Whitlam's father-in-law, were impressed by his gravure. Visitors to Bert Oldfield's sports store in Sydney's Hunter Street saw both Beldam's Trumper and Fishwick's Hammond, forming a kind of aesthetic continuum. Hanging on the wall at Crown Street Superior School, 'Jumping Out' was drummed into the next generation. 'You got so used to seeing that picture that after you had been at the school a month you would wake up in the morning and see it in every detail on your bedroom wall,' recalled Colin McCool, then a tiny opening batsman on the fringe of the school XI but destined to play fourteen postwar Tests for Australia. 'Once at Crown Street School, I found my life dominated by the picture and the memory of Trumper. His name was in every conversation, every move we made on the cricket field.'

Personal copies also reappeared. Clem Hill's adorned his cricket reminiscences; Hugh Trumble's was displayed in the window of the

---

* Scyld Berry argues for it in *Cricket: The Game of Life* (2015) as 'the most beautifully composed photograph of the most beautiful cricket stroke'.

Orient Line office in Collins Street; Joe Darling's was shown off to federal cabinet when they visited his home in Claremont, Tasmania, in February 1939. Interviewed by journalists, Darling gestured to the photograph as proof of Trumper's superiority to the flat-footed batsmen of the present day: 'He was the boy who would have played the O'Reillys and the Grimmetts. There would have been no fiddling about with him.' 'Jumping Out', then, was taking on a new dimension, as a reference in the conversation of generations. And that conversation was livening up.

•

During his career, several batsmen had been likened in style to Trumper. Similarities had been discerned in his Sydney contemporaries Jim Mackay and Charles Gregory; the appellation of 'the English Trumper' had been settled on both R. E. Foster and Kenneth Hutchings; an elegant batsman from Perth, Ernest Parker, had been anointed 'the West Australian Trumper'. Melancholy fates awaited them all. Mackay's career was ended by a motorcycle accident, aged twenty-seven; Gregory and Foster succumbed to illness, aged thirty-two and thirty-six respectively; Hutchings and Parker were doomed to die on the Western Front.

The mantle was not bestowed indiscriminately, and, in cricket at least, seems to have required a physical resemblance. Charlie Macartney, impudent and irrepressible, was Australia's most exciting batsman after the war. But despite his strong personal kinship with Trumper, stocky Macartney was generally deemed too pugnacious for direct comparison, which he would have disowned anyway. 'I have never seen a batsman to equal Victor Trumper in brilliance,' he insisted. Aesthetes preferred slim, wristy Alan Kippax, an overt

Trumper copyist. As a boy he had followed Trumper to grade games with a scorebook in which he only entered his hero's runs. His mimicry extended to folding his shirtsleeves beyond the elbow, the Trumper way. The name of Trumper was also invoked in other sports, usually when practitioners demonstrated a sense of style or dash. Rugby five-eighth Tom Lawton, jockey Keith Voitre, golfers Joe Kirkwood and George Duncan, tennis players J. O. Anderson, John Bromwich, Daphne Akhurst and Suzanne Lenglen: all were likened to Trumper during the 1920s and 1930s.* *The Bulletin* even described Coil, a much-garlanded turn-of-the-century blue kelpie from Cootamundra, as being 'to the dog world what Victor Trumper was to cricket'.

In the mid-1920s, the Trumper name began rippling through cricket anew, with the appearance of a teenage prodigy. Captain of Balmain District Cricket Club was Arthur Mailey – no longer the dreamy drifter of before the war, but a journalist, cartoonist and raconteur as well as Australia's first-choice leg spinner. It was he who in Sydney's *Sun* alerted the public to his fifteen-year-old clubmate, Archie Jackson, then receiving an initial exposure to senior competition. 'I am not going to compare him with the glorious Victor Trumper at this stage,' wrote Mailey, 'but if wealth of common cricket sense and ability is an asset, then the boy's future is assured.'

Jackson was too young to have seen Trumper. Instead he had imitated Kippax – the tracing of a tracing, as it were. In due course Jackson would work behind the counter of Kippax's Martin Place sports store, too. But rhapsodies for his batting came chiefly from those with memories going back before the war. Not only was

---

* Duncan also attracted the admiration of George Beldam, who provided the illustrations for his *Present-Day Golf* (1924). In the same year, the golf correspondent of *The Australasian*, 'HC', said that one figure towered above the game: 'That man is George Duncan, the great Aberdonian golfer, and he deserves in all respects to be considered the Victor Trumper of the links. From an Australian gallery's point of view, surely no greater praise than that is possible.'

LIKE TRUMPER.

ARCHIE JACKSON.
"How like Victor," said Charlie Trumper, brother of the dead champion, when Jackson was compiling a delightful 183 for Balmain against Gordon on Saturday, "I was just about to say the same thing," replied Arthur Mailey.

Heir Today: *Daily Standard*, 13 October 1931.

Jackson a pretty bat, but in person shy and modest, a sportsman to his fingertips and a total abstainer to boot – an heir to Trumper in all respects. Doc Evatt, now the Labor member for Balmain, became his unofficial patron. He was praised by Tom Garrett and Charles Bannerman, and became a favourite of J. C. Davis, who was first drawn to Balmain by the advice of a friend: 'He looks to be Victor reborn.' Davis was transfixed.

Jackson was more of a prodigy than Trumper had been. Aged sixteen, he topped the Sydney grade averages; aged seventeen, he made hundreds for New South Wales against Queensland and Tasmania; aged nineteen, he made a ravishing 164 on his Test debut against England at Adelaide Oval. Clem Hill now thought him 'the nearest to Trumper I have seen'. Victor's brother Charlie agreed. Again Mailey counselled against direct comparison, while allowing an indirect one: 'My advice is this – let him work out his shots in his own way, and work out his own methods. You didn't need to tell Victor Trumper how to play bowlers. Cricketers are born not made.' The comparison so exercised readers that Davis found himself asked to adjudicate in *The Referee* in December 1929 as to which of Jackson and Kippax resembled Trumper more profoundly. He peered discriminatingly through his *pince-nez*:

> From the points of view of stance and polished style, Kippax
> is more like Trumper; and in some of his strokes he is more like
> Trumper. But in the variety of high-class scoring strokes, in the
> mastery of placing particularly between the bowler and cover-
> point, and in the disposition to use high driving on either side
> of the wicket, the palm goes to Jackson.

Not that Davis was quite ready to countenance a rival to Trumper, whom he praised in familiar terms: 'The master's bat made music to the tunes he loved, not to those his less gifted pals might have loved. It is always so with genius. And a genius Trumper was.' But he concluded broad-mindedly: 'Lucky is the country, lucky the state to have produced a Trumper, a Kippax, a Jackson.' Watching Jackson practise in October 1931, Davis fell into a virtual swoon: 'On Thursday, as one viewed him from a distance making his strokes at the net, it seemed as though Victor Trumper had come back to the old scenes.'

Tragically, Jackson's day was already done: the following month he collapsed in Brisbane, coughing up blood. Now the likeness to Trumper took on a darker complexion: installed in a Blue Mountains sanatorium, Jackson was diagnosed with tuberculosis. At his death in February 1933, he, too, was borne to his resting place by teammates through dense crowds, and his memorial funded by public subscription. Trumper's second coming had been a bittersweet affair. It had also, in a sense, already been overtaken by events.

•

In November 1928, Ben Travers was sitting in the Members Stand at the SCG watching Marylebone play the state side preparatory to the summer's Ashes – the same game, as it happens, in which Herbert Fishwick immortalised Walter Hammond. For the sport-crazy Aldwych farceur, it was the trip of a lifetime – 'a cricket-lover's nirvana'.

Suddenly, Travers recalled, there was a 'striking incident'. As a batsman played a sumptuous cover drive, a local devotee leapt to his feet with a shout of: 'Trumper!' 'He was pulled violently back into his seat and for the moment appeared in danger of being lynched,' the playwright remembered. 'This was near blasphemy.' *This* was twenty-year-old Donald Bradman.

With 87 and 132 not out, Bradman made sure of his Australian selection. In his second Test, like Trumper, he made a century, provoking further comparison, overheard by former Australian prime minister Billy Hughes: 'The experts around me that day compared him with Trumper, some holding he was not in the same class, others strongly contending that he was Trumper's equal.' This series, of course, was simply a prologue to the saga. Within eighteen months Bradman had compiled the highest scores in Test and first-class cricket history on opposite sides of the world, and broken the records for runs in a home summer and runs on an Ashes tour previously held by . . . Victor Trumper. The beamish boy from Bowral was the world's most lauded cricketer. Yet in some circles there were only two cheers. When the NSWCA decided for the first time to place an illustration on the cover of their yearbook in 1930–31, it was not of the man of the moment, but of the man of the previous moment: the line drawing of Trumper jumping out to drive would remain for the next twenty-five years. Why?

In some respects, Bradman was an ideal sequel to Trumper. He followed in the same tradition of autodidactism. He was instinctively enterprising with the bat, innately modest in person. 'Australia has unearthed a champion, self-taught, with natural ability,' stated Clem Hill. 'But most of all, with his heart in the right place.' Trumper's daughter was even sought out for approval of Bradman's 1930 records. 'We think Bradman is marvellous,' she told newspapers. 'Mother is especially excited. She has watched Bradman's progress with pride.'

Yet partly because the parallel between Trumper and Jackson was already so robust, it grew simpler to define Trumper and Bradman by contradistinction. Trumper was the lyric, Bradman the epic; Trumper was the Athenian, Bradman the Spartan; Trumper's age was identified with Edwardian brio, Bradman's with Fordist productivity. In retrospect, Bradman tends to be sentimentally identified with the Depression. At least as he emerged, he associated more readily with the project of modernism: Bradman 'the record breaker'; Bradman 'the run machine'. In the interwar years, Australians took pride in the maturation of their industries and expansion of their markets. Bradman radiated a comparable industrial efficiency, his statistics homologous with human progress and national potential.

Cricket, however, was a game, its heritage commonly seen as pastoral, its relations conservative, its inclinations romantic, its time spans long and gradual – it embraced rational and positivistic ends uneasily. Stupendous scores on doped wickets in the 1920s, when Victoria twice exceeded 1000 and Bill Ponsford twice exceeded 400, had already caused mutterings. 'This is the age of machinery,' protested Pelham Warner, 'but you cannot turn such a beautiful and subtle game as cricket into an affair of machinery.' Monty Noble saw the public succumbing to statistical delusions: 'Nowadays, far more notice is taken of batting averages than is good for the game. It is not how many runs a man makes, but how he makes them.' Bradman, then, occasioned immediate misgivings. When a 'correspondent from the country' asked him to rank Trumper and Bradman in *The Sun* in October 1930, Arthur Mailey described their eras as too difficult to compare, but left little doubt about his preference: 'It is fashionable now to break records. Ponsford started it and Bradman is finishing it with a vengeance. Bradman could never do the things Trumper did, and Trumper probably never wanted to do the things Bradman is doing.' He accepted Bradman haltingly: 'Trumper's batting was refined, cultured, and never undignified. Some of Bradman's strokes are crude by comparison, but, perhaps, more effective. The value of a batsman depends, I suppose, on the number of runs he scores. When making comparisons under the heading of value we must sacrifice artistry and grace for effectiveness.' *Perhaps. I suppose. The heading of value.* The concessions to modernity were grudging, and the issue, as Mailey acknowledged, ultimately evaded: 'Trumper was satisfied with a century. Bradman is not. That makes Bradman a more valuable batsman, but not greater, than Trumper. I am doubtful whether I have answered my country friend's question satisfactorily, but giving it in tabloid fashion I might say that Victor Trumper was a great batsman and Donald Bradman is a great run-getter.'

Bradman brought out, in fact, a certain unevolved Victorianism in cricket's aesthetic. His scores, huge, repetitive, homogenous, seemed distastefully out of proportion, almost inhuman: had Ruskin not warned that 'to banish imperfection is to destroy expression, to check exertion, to paralyse vitality'? Confronted by the objective reality of Bradman's runs, an elite of critics found grounds for subjective dispute, reasserting other criteria of evaluation: beauty, audacity, capacity in adversity, skill on poor wickets. Bradman quickly overshadowed Trumper's runs and steadily occluded his reputation. Yet in another respect, Bradman also ensured Trumper a continued relevance, as a counterpoint, as an alternative.

Unease around Bradman was not confined to his batting; his individualism disturbed the hard-won *status quo ante* of players and administrators. His profile and commercial heft soon rivalled the game's. The Board of Control looked askance at a twenty-two-year-old publishing his life story, especially as the serialisation of *Don Bradman's Book* (1930) in London's *Star* breached the clause of his tour contract forbidding 'any work for, or in connection with, any newspaper' – their decision to dock Bradman a third of his tour fee's 'good conduct' bonus, £50, presaged tense relations with cricket's new star. Needless to say, there was widespread public support for Bradman in the dispute – after all, he was the hero of the hour. But for those who wished to find fault, Trumper's legendary reticence and unworldliness offered a comparative standard. None observed the irony of Trumper's image adorning the publication of the association that had once suspended him; nobody wished to be reminded that Trumper had refused to tour England rather than accept the board's dictates. For this process was less about Trumper than it was about Bradman, whose relations with administration deteriorated so markedly over the next two years that he publicly countenanced abandoning the game in order to honour a contract to write for Associated Newspapers. In October 1932, Australian cricket faced a crisis the like of which it had not experienced in two decades.

Deep-seated misgivings about Bradman now found expression in a four-part series in the *Sydney Mail*, ostensibly adjudicating 'The Greatest Batsman of All Time'. Author Eric Barbour had been the finest flower of Sydney private school cricket before the war, scoring nearly 10 000 runs and taking nearly 500 wickets for Sydney Grammar, where his father George had been headmaster. George had also had a stint as Board of Control chairman, making close friends of establishment figures such as J. C. Davis and Frank Iredale, and Eric had imbibed many of their attitudes to amateurism and commercialisation. After the war he had put a medical career ahead of adding to a score of first-class matches, becoming instead a respected cricket pundit and pedagogue. His coaching manual, *The Making of a Cricketer* (1926), exhorted students of the game to be 'clean-living, clean-thinking and clean-talking'.

In the first three instalments of his series, Barbour ran the rule over Bradman, Trumper and W. G. Grace. While loyally saluting Bradman's run-scoring feats, Barbour deprecated his style: 'He plays many shots with a cross-bat; he frequently drives off his right foot; his defensive play, especially on the leg stump, is cramped and ungraceful.' Barbour ascribed this enunciation of 'efficiency, not artistry' to Bradman's rural upbringing, which had deprived his batting of metropolitan burnishing:

> Don Bradman grew up in a country centre, never saw Trumper bat, and did not see Kippax until he was himself a member of the N.S.W. side. His style has had to be his own, formed by experience

Victor Trumper : "The grace and beauty of his stroke play have never been equalled by any other player." — Dr. E. Barbour

Photograph by George Beldam, by courtesy of Mr. W. A. Oldfield.

"The Greatest Batsman of All Time"

Victor Trumper

By Dr. Eric Barbour

VICTOR THOMAS TRUMPER was born at Sydney on November 2, 1877, and died on June 28, 1915, in his thirty-eighth year. Some of the members of our present Australian eleven were not even old enough to be taken to see him bat, but those of us who had the inestimable privilege of seeing him and playing with him in his prime will keep his memory green till the Great Umpire has sent the last of us to join him in the pavilion.

EDUCATED at Crown-street school, Trumper in his boyhood showed a natural grace of style and a degree of skill that perhaps was not as rapidly recognised in those days as it would be to-day. In 1897 his appearance in Sydney grade cricket, or electorate cricket as it was then called, was an auspicious opening for a phenomenal career, for in eight innings, three of which were not out, he compiled the amazing aggregate of 1021 runs. J. R. M. Mackay exceeded this in 1905-06 with 1041, but had thirteen innings, and of those who have since then reached the thousand mark Bardsley had fifteen innings and Andrews seventeen. The first indication that the outer world had of the appearance of a new star in its firmament was in 1898, when he scored 292 against Tasmania and followed it with 253 against New Zealand. But this shy and unobtrusive youngster then found, as others had found before him, that to break into the Australian eleven was about as difficult a job as cracking a Bank of England safe. It was only the power of public opinion that forced him into the 1899 team for England as fourteenth man. Those who wished to exclude him must subsequently have looked foolish, for from the time of his arrival in England he began a career of meteoric brilliance that has made him the most picturesque figure in the history of Australian cricket and the most gifted exponent of the batsman's art that the world has ever seen.

NOT that his greatness was always reflected in actual figures, there are many, both in England and in Australia, whose figures, over a long period, are superior to those of Trumper. He had his good seasons and his lean seasons, but, whatever his results, he was always the "Nonpareil," the unequalled. To-day is the material age of figures and records. In cricket, athletics, swimming, and horse-racing we see the same tendency. Trumper lived and played in days when no one, least of all Trumper himself, bothered his head about records, aggregates, or averages. Almost invariably he threw his innings away after reaching a century, and often long before, if the winning of the match for his side were not in question. He played cricket first and foremost for the joy of it; he loved the thrill of cracking the ball like a pistol shot, and the exultation

of daring and seemingly impossible shots lured him more than the size of his score. A batsman so adventurous, so care-free, and so regardless of the scoring book could not avoid frequent failures; but even his failures were greater than most men's successes, for twenty runs from Trumper remained in the memory longer than a hundred from most of his contemporaries. I shall quote a few of his outstanding performances, beginning with the 1899 tour of England. On this tour, although he just struggled into the side, he was third in the aggregate with 1556 runs. His 135 not out in the Lord's test sat all England talking, and he followed it with 300 not out against Sussex, the record score for an Australian in England at that period. Returning to Australia, he batted brilliantly for 165 against South Australia. A score of 230 against Victoria was his most notable contribution in the following year, when he again headed the aggregate in Sydney grade cricket.

A Triumphal Tour

HIS triumphal tour of England in 1902 must rank as the peak period of his career. In one of the wettest summers on record he scored 2570 runs, including eleven centuries. What the size of his aggregate could have been had he wished we can only conjecture, for it has been said he risked his wicket away after reaching three figures. The speed of his scoring and the artistry of his stroke play amazed the English critics, who lost no time in enthroning him in place of their erstwhile idol, Ranjitsinhji. In a succession of innings, of which every one was a gem, it is not easy to select the greatest, but some of them may be mentioned. In the historic fourth test at Manchester, dramatically won by Australia by a margin of three runs, Trumper opened with a glorious 104, on a wicket soft after rain, and, as Wisden relates, "without a mistake of any kind."

The three articles which have traced the careers of Don Bradman, the late Dr. Grace, and the late Victor Trumper will be followed by a fourth, to be published next week. It will be a summing up, and we think that no cricketer will challenge the conclusions of Dr. Eric Barbour as to which of the three is entitled to be regarded as "The Greatest Batsman of All Time" and the relative positions occupied by the others.

'The Greatest': Barbour's Trumper.

and tested by results. The unprecedented success that has come to him is a wonderful tribute to the mind that devised it. Indeed, there will be many who will say that if Bradman's style differs from that of the old masters, then the old masters must have been wrong. Without subscribing to such bolshevism, we can at least pay the tribute of admiration to this extraordinary youngster, who from his cricketing cradle has done everything for himself and has achieved such marvellous results.

The rub was revealed when Barbour considered Bradman in relation to the board. While Barbour approved Bradman's 'quiet philosophic detachment' and 'inscrutable smile', he regretted that Bradman had 'shown the tendency to commercialise his outstanding success to a degree that has not been attempted by any of his predecessors in Australian cricket'. This was 'hardly in keeping with cricket tradition'; indeed, it smacked of the 'professionalism' tainting rugby league:

> There are many hundreds of people, some closely associated with the game, who are only too ready to give the wrong advice to a young player on these matters; many of them will say, 'Get as much out of it as you can while the going is good; cricket will not keep you when you are old and stiff.' But there are many thousands who think differently, and they include practically all the real men of Australian cricket. Cricket, fortunately, is not yet in the position of League football, nor do we wish it to be ... The essential point is that no player is greater than the game itself, and it is unfair for any one player to be treated differently from others merely because his performances are greater.

On the issue of Bradman's present stand-off, Barbour opined that the board had dallied too long, but also that its stipulations required compliance – for him a conclusion rooted in filial piety. 'The Board of Control has for many years had the sympathy and support of the majority of the cricket-lovers of New South Wales,' he recalled. 'They stood behind it in that most critical year of 1913 [sic], when the point at issue was whether the game should control the players or the players the game ... Criticise it as we will, there is no denying the fact that the Board is the governing body and its decisions must stand.' The more so, Barbour felt, because the board formed a rampart against vulgarising, American-accented materialism:

> Cricket is either a game or a business. If it is a game, let it be managed and administered as a game, and kept in the proud position it has occupied for so many years. If it is going to degenerate into a business, with the moral standards and box-office criteria of Hollywood or the Chicago White Sox, let us admit it forthwith and have an immediate choice by every player between amateurism and professionalism.

> I am aware that many will contend that this digression is beside the point when discussing the greatness of a batsman; my own view is that the personal factor must be considered, as the attitude of a player to the game may have a great bearing on the comparative value of his performances. Further, the question of example for young players must be taken into consideration, for the greatest batsman of the day can do no wrong in the eyes of the younger generation.

Writing a fortnight later of Trumper, Barbour left all the foregoing out of account. Trumper's belief in the players' entitlement to the spoils of Ashes tours; Trumper's distaste for and resistance of the Board of Control; even Trumper's involvement in the foundation of barbarous rugby league: all these were forgotten. Instead, Barbour appropriated Trumper for amateurism. 'He played cricket first and foremost for the joy of it; he loved the thrill of cracking the ball like a pistol shot, and the exultation of daring and seemingly impossible shots lured him more than the size of his score,' claimed Barbour.

> A batsman so adventurous, so carefree, and so regardless of the scoring book could not avoid frequent failures; but even his failures were greater than most men's successes, for twenty runs from Trumper remained in the memory longer than a hundred from most of his contemporaries. I am quite sure that to him cricket was not nearly so serious a business as it is to the modern young man. It is impossible to measure the achievements of an artist by statistics and records.

In conclusion, Barbour argued against 'the material age of figures and records', confident that others shared his views: Bradman's 'quiet certainty and confidence' did not 'inspire the warm affection that seemed to belong to Trumper' with his 'easy-going and good-natured' character. Readers would have felt no surprise at Barbour's eventual conclusion: 'I am sufficiently old-fashioned to look upon batsmanship as primarily an art, and for that reason I still regard Victor Trumper in his prime as the greatest batsman that ever lived.' Perhaps in anticipation of disagreement, Barbour had recourse to Noble's old observation that Trumper had to be seen: 'Some of the members of our present Australian eleven were not even old enough to be taken to see him bat, but those of us who had the inestimable privilege of seeing him and playing with him in his prime will keep his memory green till the Great Umpire has sent the last of us to join him in the pavilion.' For those deprived of that 'inestimable privilege', evidence was provided: a reproduction of 'Jumping Out', this time borrowed from Bert Oldfield's sports store.

Though crisis was averted when Associated Newspapers waived its contract for Bradman's services, still graver events were in the offing. Two weeks after Barbour resolved to his own satisfaction that batting was an art, Marylebone arrived for a tour that made it look more of an ordeal. The Bodyline series would reset relations between the countries, leave Oldfield with a fractured skull, and Barbour with fractured ideals. With Alan Kippax, he poured his grievances into a screed, *Anti-Bodyline* (1933), denigrating the 'Bodyliner' as 'on par with a footballer who puts the boot in' – a scathing appraisal of England's amateur captain Douglas Jardine. By then, too, Barbour was facing deliberation of the Great Umpire, in the form of the colon cancer that killed him in January 1934.[*]

It was a challenging time to love cricket, as Richard Binns worried in *Cricket in Firelight*: 'The survivors of a period which did so much to raise cricket to its highest levels must, like ourselves, be concerned for the future well-being of the game. No sensitive cricketer's ear can be deaf to the harsh notes that have crept into the harmony of cricket during the last two or three years . . . which need to be resolved.' For one writer, such assuagement was a long-term project.

•

If not the solo inventor of 'the Golden Age' as a descriptor of cricket before World War I, Neville Cardus was, as it were, its patron.

---

[*] Trumper appears to have sustained Barbour to the last: his final published work, printed posthumously by the *Sydney Mail* in February 1935, was a further lengthy tribute to his hero: 'Bat Magic: The Art of Victor Trumper'.

Most writers slip into nostalgia only as their careers evolve. Cardus was rheumy-eyed almost as soon as his career began, even about cricket he had not seen. The opening chapter of his first book, *A Cricketer's Book* (1922), recounts arriving early for an Australian practice session at Lord's and slipping into 'a reverie' of 'the great days of cricket' – specifically the inaugural Ashes Test of 1882, six years before his birth:

> I lost grip on events. It seemed that I sat there till the ground was almost deserted, till over the field came a faint mist, and with it the vague melancholy of twilight in a great city. Time to go home, I thought . . . a great match . . . great days . . . great men . . . all gone . . . far away . . . departed glory . . . A hand of someone touched my shoulder and I heard him say: 'The Orsetralians are on the way, and they'll be in the nets at four o'clock. Nice in the sun, isn't it?'

Departed glory: a common sensation in postwar England, and Cardus knew how to sheet blame home. It was the waning of amateur influence that had left cricket 'steeped neck-high in mediocrity' and under the sway of his archetypal lookalike professional 'Bloggs of Blankshire'. What a contrast to the cricket of before the war, so 'symbolical of the age's prestige'. What a contrast to Trumper: 'The manly chivalry of Victor Trumper, whose bat was always a banner in the air, will move us like poetry long after his performances have been buried out of sight under the dump of statistics which summer by summer are piled up prodigiously.' Unlike Binns and Carew, Cardus seldom addressed war directly; nor, unlike such belletrists of ruralism as E. V. Lucas and A. G. Macdonell, did he identify cricket with a village idyll. But his longing for a better time, a pristine bygone age of pedigreed amateurs and yeoman professionals, became an analog of national decline, disillusion and loss.

Cardus first gave this better time a name, tentatively and without capitalisation, in an elegy of Trumper in *The Guardian* on 24 July 1926: 'Trumper's winged batsmanship was seen in the golden age of cricket; he was, at his finest, master of some of the greatest bowlers the game has ever known.' Most readers would have understood the concept instinctively. The British Empire claimed a sort of lineal descent from great days past, from 'golden ages' of Greece and Rome. Not long before, too, Britain had attempted to roll back time by returning the Empire to the gold standard – a disastrous caprice that rendered much imperial industry uncompetitive by bloating the value of sterling, but which enjoyed popular appeal as an assertion of economic virility. Cardus had not sole licence on the expression 'golden age', which enjoyed a number of variations around this time. But only he applied it so sweepingly, and with such occasionally magisterial condescension.

'It is not the fault of the professionals that since the War they have not had before them the example of amateur style as we knew it in the golden age,' Cardus claimed in *Cricket* (1930), his contribution to Longmans' English Heritage Series. 'But the professional batsman in the lump, despite a superb and honourable skill, too often lets us know from his cricket that he learned to play in a world where a drab struggle went on persistently, and where every penny had to be hoarded, and where to be spendthrift was to be a sinner.' Trumper, by comparison, was 'enrobed in purple', 'a conquistador', 'a Saladin cleaving the silken cushion with his scimitar'. And just in case this was thought fanciful, Cardus flourished the most modern of empirical proofs: 'Look at the photographs of him, doubting young Thomases of the skeptical present, and see how far he would venture beyond the crease's rim at the sight of a well-tossed ball; his bat is held up behind him punitively, he is leaping to the ball, his every muscle responding to the demands of the will to power and victory.'

By the mid-1930s, Cardus was regularly capitalising 'Golden Age'; by decade's end, he was effectively quoting himself, referring to 'the period which I call the Golden Age of cricket', glow furbished by 'the genius of Trumper', connection reinforced by autobiographical recollections. And of the pantheon of cricket divinities that Cardus stocked to evoke his lost England, Trumper is the most interestingly perdurable, being from furthest away, and by springing straight from the writer's youth actually prefiguring many of the preferences he later formed, such as for the cricket of the public schools, for the abiding rivalry of Yorkshire v Lancashire, and for the civilising influence of Tonbridge's nursery of batsmanship. By dying almost simultaneously with the advent of the war that ended the Golden Age, Trumper also became its ideal personification, while his lingering ill-health could act as a metaphor of the era's fragile, doomed beauty.

The greater the loss and isolation, the brighter the past burned. It was in *English Cricket* (1945), a monograph written for William Collins' morale-boosting 'Britain in Pictures' series during his wartime sojourn in Sydney, that Cardus argued most fervently for 'the mighty convulsion of energy of genius which, between 1890 and 1914, hurled up all the peaks, the mighty ranges on which repose in unapproachable grandeur the masters of the Golden Age of Cricket'. Since then, thanks to the dwindling ranks of 'amateur players from the old social mint', the game had petrified under the sway of 'robot batsmen' involved in 'mechanical run-making'. Bradman? Cardus appreciated his 'spifflication of all bowling', but without the effusive warmth he reserved for Trumper: 'Efficiency, superb stream-lined efficiency! And don't mistake me, Bradman is often grand and exhilarating to watch. But if I were asked to compare him with Trumper I should say the difference is as that between the flight of the aeroplane and the flight of an eagle.' So while others rehearsed these themes, none couched them as persuasively or eulogistically as cricket's *homo aestheticus*, or condensed them to a phrase that tripped from the tongue so readily.

So captivating was the idea, in fact, that by the 1960s a wistful historicising of 'the Golden Age of Cricket' had begun, reinforced in books bearing the title by A. A. Thomson (1961), Patrick Morrah (1967) and Robert Trumble (1968). With the abolition of amateur status, cricket was losing its last connection to the idea of a gentlemanly vanguard. The trauma of war had given way to a more manageable but deeper ache. 'Of course, most of us have our own private Golden Ages, to which we look back as if remembering a lost world,' wrote J. B. Priestley, then in his late eighties, in the foreword to David Frith's *The Golden Age of Cricket* (1981). 'My own is roughly from 1910 to 1914, when I joined the Army and began to lose so many friends, when I entered another world, *which could never again be trusted* . . . Golden Ages, however different in other respects, have this in common: they will soon come to an end.' And when this particular *belle époque* needed to be reduced to a single image, there was only one for which to reach.

10

'WHAT A
LOVELY PICTURE!'

'On all the walls of all leading cricket club rooms there hangs
a picture, a picture of a batsman sweeping a ball to leg [sic], and beneath
it a simple plaque bearing the name "Victor Trumper".'
– 'Victor Trumper', episode of radio serial
They Were Champions, 3DB, 19 December 1953

In January 1947, the *Sydney Morning Herald* reported the death of
Lock Walmsley, president of the Sydney Musicians' Club, whose
orchestras had been playing old-time dance tunes in halls and cinemas
since before World War I. A much-loved character, he had prolonged
his penchant for the last word beyond death by recording his will on a
gramophone disc so 'they can't argue about that'. Having thus appor-
tioned his assets, Walmsley decided that he had one further thing

to add: 'I would like to record for posterity that Victor Trumper was the best batsman of the lot.' With that he proceeded to his grave.

For the demographic front was moving ineluctably. As Australia hosted England that summer in the first postwar Ashes series, barely a quarter of Australia's population were old enough to have first-hand recollection of Trumper. Those who still remembered did so ardently. During the Second Test in Sydney, England's Len Hutton played a brief, blazing innings of 37 in twenty-four minutes that brought the Hill to its feet. 'Those who were lucky enough to see this remarkable display must have grieved with me that such a super-lative innings was nipped in its golden prime,' wrote the *Herald*'s Bill O'Reilly. Not long afterwards, Hutton received a lengthy letter, signed simply 'Aussie', which he cherished evermore:

> Dear Sir,
>
> Both for myself and for a number of my Australian friends I want to extend to you our gratitude for the truly grand innings you played in England's second knock. It was a delight to the connoisseur of batsmanship, and brought to us again visions of the peerless Trumper, whom we saw in many of his matchless innings . . . Trumper was a glorious batsman, the acme of consummate grace and beauty when at his best – the gay cavalier of cricket, playing for sheer love of the game, his rapier-like bat flashing in carefree abandon and loveliness. Bradman does not compare with him as an artist.

Such aficionados were also conscious of their outnumbering. Revered former teammates like Noble, Darling, Trumble, Hill and Laver; journalists who had tended the Trumper legend such as Davis, Horan, Barbour, Poidevin, Knight, Trevor: all were gone by the time 'Aussie' sent his letter. Twenty years after Ben Travers had seen an SCG member decried for the blasphemy of comparing Bradman to Trumper, *Sporting Globe*'s Hec de Lacy sat in a crowd at the MCG during Bradman's testimonial match experiencing the opposite sensation:

> I saw both Trumper and Bradman, Trumper perhaps at that teen age when impressions and convictions are absorbed more readily than in the cold light of middle age. The superlative ease and grace with which Trumper did everything has often made me say of other champions, 'He's great, but he's no Trumper.' But for the life of me, I can't persuade my sons to accept Trumper, as I accept Trumper. Neither can any other father. Generations of cricketers are apart, and youth lives in the ever-bright present.

How, then, to revive Trumper for an audience that had mostly never seen him? Bradman was the game's benchmark, in quality and quantity. He had minted runs in such abundance as to be comparable only to himself, relegating Trumper's statistics almost to a historical footnote.

Nor were there heirs to anoint, no Kippaxes or Jacksons to speak of. The best that de Lacy's *Sporting Globe* could do, for example, was two teenagers. Vic Michael and Ray Flockton, two years apart, shattered school cricket records left and right in the late 1940s, but it was their provenance that attracted attention: they were alumni of Trumper's Crown Street School.[*] Both became useful cricketers; neither was a natural legatee of Trumper's. A 'new Trumper' was arguably less likely than a 'new Bradman'.

---

[*] Ray Flockton played thirty-seven first-class matches for New South Wales averaging 41; Vic Michael made 3735 first-grade runs for St George averaging 26.

"BOY" FLOCKTON NEW TRUMPER

By H. A. de LACY, who is touring with the West Indies cricket team.

SYDNEY, Sat.—Australian hero of the match between New South Wales and the West Indies undoubtedly has been so far young Ray Flockton, aged 21, and playing in the second big match for his State.

15 - YEAR - OLD MAY BE SECOND VICTOR TRUMPER

By a Special Correspondent

Being hailed as another Victor Trumper is a 15-year-old Sydney schoolboy who, at one stage of the current season, had an average of 581 for four innings, who took 42 wickets at an average of five, and who hasn't dropped a catch in any type of game for four years.

New Trumpers: *Sporting Globe* welcomes Ray Flockton (top), Vic Michael (bottom).

This, in fact, was to become a point in argument. In the early 1950s, Trumper's votaries began holding up his qualities against the austerity of the modern era. Cricket crowds were stagnating, competing attractions flourishing: tennis in Australia, which found a foil in the US, and football in England, encountering exciting opposition in Europe. Cricket responded anxiously, a ragged movement gathering beneath the banner of 'brighter cricket'. 'Cricket, and not just English cricket, needs an injection of culture and enterprise,' argued *Wisden*'s editor Norman Preston. Not surprisingly, Neville Cardus agreed wholeheartedly. Batsmen were afflicted by 'paralysis'; batting provided 'little in the way of delight' and at times was 'positively ugly'. 'Everyone really knows that first-class cricket is mainly a bore, a pretence, a decaying industry,' he opined. The affliction was 'undoubtedly psychological', although also sociological, insofar as cricket was 'under the influence of the period in which we are all living. Rationed batting. Standardised bowling.' To illustrate his point,

Cardus had recourse to a personal touchstone: he described gazing at Beldam's Trumper 'for the hundredth time' in 'the upstairs tea-room at Kennington Oval' and being interrupted in his reverie:

> A certain English batsman, vintage 1950, looked at this picture in my company and said: 'Was he really any good?' 'Why do you ask?' was my natural question. 'Well,' said this International, 'just look where he is – stumped by yards if he misses.' This sceptical England batsman had never in his life been so far out of his crease.

As the times militated against a new Trumper, thoughts reverted to the real one. Dr George McCleary was a specialist in maternal and child welfare who had begun his career as a 'sixpenny doctor' in London's slums and ended as a respected health bureaucrat leading the National Health Insurance Commission: a classical pianist and organist, he was a devotee of Gilbert and Sullivan, a scholar of Sherlock Holmesiana, and a fervent Trumper disciple. He dedicated his Ashes history, *Cricket with the Kangaroo* (1950), to Trumper, worshipfully reproducing 'Jumping Out' in a chapter dedicated to Australia's 'amazing genius', not merely unique now but unrepeatable:

> There may be those who hold that to apply the term 'genius' to a man because of his achievements as a cricketer is to violate the proprieties of language. If such there be, it may with confidence be inferred that they never saw the batsmanship of Victor Trumper. We who were so fortunate as to see it are getting on in years, and it is unlikely that any of us would cut much of a figure on the cricket field. But we all have this advantage over the people of the present generation: we saw the batting of Victor Trumper. What was it like? *It was like no other batting.* [my italics]

Nor need one have seen Trumper to echo this critique. Australia's two busiest cricket writers addressed the legacy in distinctive ways. Son of 'a dyed-in-the-wool Trumper fanatic', Dick Whitington became a handy opening batsman for South Australia before joining the first of many employers, Adelaide's *Mail*, in 1937. With Keith Miller he collaborated on a string of cricket books, which played on Miller's reputation as 'brighter cricket' incarnate, and in which Trumper appeared regularly as a kind of talisman. In *Straight Hit* (1952), for example, Whitington imbued the West Indians of 1951–52 with Trumper's spirit. Frank Worrell was 'likened to Victor Trumper'; Everton Weekes batted like a 'second Victor Trumper'; a superb catch by John Goddard would be remembered 'as old men today remember Victor Trumper's batsmanship'; Bob Christiani was described looking up at the print of 'Jumping Out' in the Members Stand at the SCG and saying 'with excited reverence, "What a lovely picture!"' Team members even paid Trumper homage by visiting his grave in Waverley Cemetery.

In *Bumper* (1953), Whitington devoted a whole chapter to Trumper, the 'dazzling chevalier' with his lesson for moderns. 'If ever cricket needs the Trumper flair and outlook it is now,' he concluded. 'Could we but instil and encourage that approach in the majority of the young batsmen of the future, cricket would soar back to its proper pinnacle in the world of sport.' In *Cricket Typhoon* (1955), Whitington recounted visiting a secondhand bookstore in Sydney's Elizabeth Street and chancing on *Great Batsmen*, Beldam's images a 'delight to the cricketing connoisseur'. Naturally his eye alighted on Trumper, the 'Nijinsky of the batting crease', dancing out 'with head held high and with direct eye, to drive as few have driven a cricket ball since he died':

The bat was held vertically behind the majestic head and the line of arm and shoulder was straight enough for one of Euclid's theorems. Though the ball had not yet intruded upon the picture, Trumper was yards along the pitch, his very intent breathing implacable purpose and defiant certainty of intent.

Jack Fingleton had been inducted in the Trumper legend by grade-cricket elders Davis, Poidevin and Barbour, and also his captains Hanson Carter and Alan Kippax. Mere mention of Trumper's name, Fingleton recalled, would bring 'a new light' into their eyes: 'As I walked home I used to wonder how one cricketer could so capture the imagination above all others. And the imagination, moreover, of men so steeped in the game that they were the severest of critics.'

Fingleton matured into an intrepid opening batsman for New South Wales and an energetic journalist for Sydney's *Daily Guardian* and *Sun* – a combination that courted the Board of Control's distrust during an eighteen-Test career. In particular he was blamed for leaking details of his captain Bill Woodfull's contretemps with MCC manager Pelham Warner at Bodyline's gravest extremity ('There are two teams out there. One of them is trying to play cricket . . .'). But Bodyline also became his great subject, told from close quarters in *Cricket Crisis* (1946), with a deferential nod to his mentors in the form of long rhapsodies of Trumper, especially as immortalised by Beldam: 'If a cricket lover never had the good fortune to see Trumper he could tell immediately by the Beldam photographs that here, indeed, was a classically artistic player.'

The chief focus of *Cricket Crisis* was Fingleton's teammate Bradman, especially Bradman's retort to Bodyline of backing away to the leg side to score on the untenanted off. Fingleton had disapproved. So, he claimed, had many teammates. It stoked a controversy.

In the *Herald*, Cardus praised *Cricket Crisis* as 'the most accurate and comprehensive examination' of the controversy. In his auto-biography *Farewell to Cricket* (1950), Bradman replied with caustic calculus: 'It may be well to remind readers that his [Fingleton's] last three innings against Jardine's men yielded 1, 0 and 0, whereupon he was dropped from the Australian team. In the same three innings I scored 177 runs at an average of 88.5. These figures scarcely give Fingleton any authority to criticise my methods.' Bradman further extended his computations to Trumper: 'I do not want to enter into a discussion about Trumper, but perhaps in fairness to myself I may say this . . . On a percentage basis, Trumper got one century for every 9.8 innings, where I obtained a century every 3.4.'

The exchanges commenced decades of coolness and mutual mistrust. Fingleton replied to Bradman on his own behalf in *Brown & Company* (1951) and on Trumper's in *Masters of Cricket* (1958), obliquely contrasting him with Bradman: 'Trumper was unique in that *nobody ever criticised him* as a cricketer or a man.' [my italics] Fingleton also contrasted the images available to posterity for appreciating each batsman. Beldam's stills of Trumper, he argued, were every bit as definitive as the various moving pictures of Bradman. 'All we have, so far as I know, are the several photographic stills of him at the beginning of an off-drive and at the finish and, also, of his stance at the crease,' wrote Fingleton. 'But these do portray his art. The two of him playing the off-drive are technically perfect in every detail – his feet, his shoulders, his head, his backswing, his follow-through with the proper transfer of weight and then, finally, the full flowing arc of the bat.'

'Technically perfect'? Bradman cavilled. He included 'Jumping Out' in his classic textbook *The Art of Cricket* (1958), but with a caveat that the hands were 'very high up the handle', rather than in the 'happy medium position' he himself favoured.[*] Was there even in Bradman's choice of title a response to his typing as a coldly mechanical batsmen? His approach might have looked scientific, Bradman seemed to be saying, but he could do 'art' too. Subtle disagreements; low-level skirmishings. The irony is that Bradman owned his own copy of 'Jumping Out', which hung alongside the gravure of Beldam's Ranji in the billiard room of his Adelaide home. But in their testy relations, Fingleton and Bradman made Trumper another area of sensitivity – and a lasting one at that.

•

Judgement in sport is bare, instant, unsparing – the score tells the tale. It is also, usually, decidedly perishable. As a proportion, only a tiny sample of feats and personalities endure across generations, and then in simplified form admired across a steadily widening distance. Victor Trumper was to prove a case in point.

Some wondered why no biography of him was undertaken, but they were not Australian. The English doctor McCleary, for example, had a taste for the novelist and biographer Rosaline Masson, especially her *I Can Remember Robert Louis Stevenson* (1923), a collection of vignettes of the writer. In *Cricket with the Kangaroo*, he yearned for 'a similar book about Victor', containing 'contributions

---

[*] Bradman's use of the photograph in the context of an instructional manual was not actually that unusual, in Australia or England. *The MCC Coaching Manual* (1955 and 1957) had used 'Jumping Out' and the follow-through photograph as the template for a straight drive: 'The start and finish of a straight drive; these two pictures convey a magnificent impression of freedom, power yet complete control.' Around the same time, it also featured in Jack Pollard's canonical *Cricket, the Australian Way* (1961, 1962 and 1969) ('Victor Trumper jumps out to drive in a shot that hangs on countless Australian dressing-room walls') and the official NSWCA coaching manual *Calling All Cricketers* (1954 and 1964) ('The late Victor Trumper: Moving Out to Drive').

from cricketers who had actually been in with him and could speak of his batsmanship from close personal observation'. The suggestion went unheeded.

In March 1960, Fingleton received chapters of an inchoate cricket book from an improbable source. Born in Port of Spain in 1901, C. L. R. James had been a scholarship boy at Queen's Royal College, a club cricketer with Maple CC, and an omnivorous junior reader of things English, from Dickens and Thackeray to magazines with their 'articles on great cricketers of the day, W. G. Grace, Ranjitsinhji, Victor Trumper, C. B. Fry'. Drawn into revolutionary politics in the US and UK, he had since written fiction, drama, Marxist theory and postcolonial historiography; he had dashed off *The Case for West-Indian Self Government* (1933) while living with Learie Constantine in the Lancashire village of Nelson; he had sojourned with Trotsky in Coyoacán, been detained by American authorities on Ellis Island.

Recently James had returned to his birthplace in Port of Spain to edit *The Nation*, organ of Trinidad's pro-independence People's National Movement, but also feeling 'increasingly aware of large areas of human existence that my history and my politics did not seem to cover', and looking back on his formative years: 'Me and my clippings and magazines on W. G. Grace, Victor Trumper and Ranjitsinhji, and my *Vanity Fair*, and my puritanical view of the world ... A British intellectual long before I was ten, already an alien in my own environment, among my own people, even my own family ... To that little boy I owe a debt of gratitude.' James had now written sizeable sections of a panorama of Caribbean cricket consciousness, which he was then calling *Who Only Cricket Know*. In the pages of *The Nation*, meanwhile, he was arguing strenuously for the West Indies to appoint their first permanent coloured captain,

Frank Worrell, for the forthcoming tour of Australia: to do otherwise would be a 'declaration of war and a defiance of the opinions
and attitudes and expectations of the cricketers and the cricket public the world over'.

James was a curious mix of dialectical materialism and rarefied
aestheticism. His cricket writing was indebted to Cardus, and in his
manuscript he genuflected to similar Golden Age idols. 'They and
their contemporaries were not only men of exceptional skill,' argued
James. 'They were what the modern audience finds so lacking in
contemporary players, men of dazzling personality, creative, original, daring, adventurous.' James' argument for Worrell's recognition
was actually couched partly in terms of his belonging to this line-
age, of elegant strokeplay and Edwardian brio: 'This is the authentic
fact. When Australian critics talk of Trumper, Kippax and the few,
half-dozen batsmen who have batted as if they were born to it they
include Worrell.'

Fingleton sent James helpful comments, to which James
responded with some of his own, including a question 'which I have
been asking for years'. That is: 'How is it that no one has yet written
a full-length biography of Victor Trumper? The best thing I have
ever read on him are two chapters in a book by M. A. Noble [*The
Game's the Thing*] . . . I continue to hope.' If it was an attempt to prick
Fingleton's interest, it failed. James was doubly gratified by his own
endeavours. Led by Worrell, West Indies fulfilled all James' hopes in
Australia; *Who Only Cricket Know* became *Beyond a Boundary* (1963)
and was acclaimed as a literary and intellectual *tour de force*. Yet the
first book devoted to Victor Trumper would be published not in
Sydney, not in London, not in Port of Spain, but in Bombay.

Vasant Raiji was born in Baroda, on the coastal plain of Gujarat,
five years after Trumper's death. Shortly before his first-class debut

as a teenager, he chanced on an article entitled 'The World's Greatest Batsman' in *Indian Cricket*, 'A Monthly Magazine Devoted to World Sport' published by the Cricket Club of India. It was the reprint of a tribute to Trumper by former Australian captain Herbie Collins from Melbourne's *Sporting Globe*; here, squeezed between advertisements for hotels, cars and furniture aimed at the upper reaches of the Raj, it struck Raiji forcefully. Collins' adoration of 'the most lovable personality that ever played cricket' led the young reader naturally to the effusions of Noble and of Cardus. Later he came across 'Jumping Out', when it adorned an article by Fingleton in the magazine *Sport & Pastime* in August 1952 extolling 'the greatest batsman known to cricket'. Such an image – why, Raiji thought, it must be 'the greatest in the gallery of cricket'.

For more obvious patriotic reasons, Raiji was also an enthusiast for Ranjitsinhji, concerning whom there was an extensive literature, biographical and autobiographical; he grew puzzled that 'on the crowded cricket shelf there is not a single book on Victor Trumper'. So, a practical man, in civilian life an accountant, he did his own, pulling together ten favourite essays on 'my hero', studiously seeking permission from all the publishers, names now with ancient echo: Rupert Hart-Davis Ltd, George G. Harrap & Co. Ltd, Hennel Locke Ltd et al. From *Great Batsmen* were reproduced Plates XXVII and XXVIII. *Victor Trumper: The Beau Ideal of a Cricketer* (1964) extended only ninety-six pages, and only 1000 copies were printed at six rupees each. But it would long remain the sole volume bearing Trumper's name, and Raiji regarded it as a success, in part because of the cherished acknowledgement of a complimentary copy he received from Sir Donald Bradman. So it was that Trumper inspired a book from a man who never saw him in a country he never visited.

From the land that had echoed with his name, however, nothing came – partly because nothing much has ever tended to, the stock of Australian sports biographies being paltry compared to sport's frequently asserted primacy in the national story. The 1950s and 1960s did see the emergence in the market of the life stories of cricketers, but the convention established was of firsthand narrative with the assistance of a ghost writer – and Trumper, of course, had long been a ghost cricketer. In a sense, too, the Trumper story already served satisfactory purpose in its mythic dimensions. It was hard to see how cricket would be better served by knowing more. Brief and circumspect appreciations of Bradman by Johnny Moyes and Anthony Davis aside, no writer sought to independently retell his story either. So Trumper receded into the past reverentially unmolested, a name in a book, a picture on a wall.

In February 1963, Sydney's *Sun-Herald* published a poignant story of two elderly occupants of the SCG's Ladies Stand watching the Fifth Test of the season's Ashes: Victor Trumper's eighty-five-year-old widow, Annie, and Charlie Macartney's seventy-two-year-old sister, Clara. Like many from the period, the Test petered out sleepily, and the writer quoted Annie's pointed commentary: 'I wish present-day batsmen would use their feet more and jump down the pitch . . . It would make cricket much more exciting.' This allowed the obvious inference: 'No doubt her views are prompted by the bright play she saw in the "good old days" of cricket and especially by the magnificent cover driving of her late husband which has been captured in a grand picture.' There was no need even to reproduce 'Jumping Out' – it could be summoned by a word.

Across the other side of the ground, David Moore was in the process of taking a different 'grand picture'. Australia's brightest photojournalist, Moore had just returned from photographing Asian sport for *Sports Illustrated*, from sumo and swordsmanship to fighting cocks and fighting crickets; now he was on a twelve-week assignment for the Time-Life Books Division Library of Nations volume on *Australia and New Zealand* (1965), and was drawn to a scene of his youth with an eye to its unspoken ritual and tradition.

Moore's photograph, 'Sydney Cricket Ground from the Hill – 1963', peeps between the bare shoulders of two spectators lounging by their esky on a wrinkled towel, a scene radiating soporific, late-afternoon heat. Yet every eye is trained in the same direction, on the same distant action and finite possibilities. Donald Horne had such austere hedonism in mind when he crafted his famous metaphor in *The Lucky Country* (1964) for the seriousness with which Australians partook of their pleasures – the middle-aged man in the open-neck shirt solemnly enjoying an ice-cream. Meanwhile, over in that Ladies Stand sat Annie Trumper, almost half a century after the death of her husband, the ground's first hero, herself with two months to live – representative of the history that passes unrecorded daily, until someone in this forgetful country abruptly realises that it has gone.

The Lucky Country: David Moore's SCG.

•

In Australia, there would actually be Trumper fiction before much accretion of Trumper fact. Born in December 1911, Dal Stivens grew up in Blayney in the central west of NSW. Some of his earliest recollections involved his cricket-loving bank manager father, Francis, talking about Trumper with friends, and of the copy of 'Jumping Out' that hung in the family garage, probably the reproduction from the *Sydney Mail*. 'When Trumper Went to Billabong' (1944), mentioned in Chapter 5, was the first of thirteen laconic and whimsical cricket short stories written in spurts across three and a half decades. Trumper appears in no fewer than ten of these, sometimes just as a kind of gold standard or magic word. 'He was a beautiful bat,' avers the yarn-spinning miner in 'Indians Have Special Eyesight' (1945). 'He had wrists like steel and he moved like a panther. The ball sped from his bat as though fired by a cannon . . . There was a batsman for you.'

One of these stories achieved an audience probably larger than for any of Stivens' five novels. Having first appeared in *Meanjin*, 'The Batting Wizard from the City' (1950) was widely anthologised in the 1960s, including in a collection that for many years was a standard literature text for schoolchildren in Victoria and NSW; it also became a personal favourite of the historian Manning Clark and prime minister Sir Robert Menzies.[*] In it 'a willowy young man' calling himself 'Smith' materialises before a country game and offers himself as an eleventh player. He receives a grudging welcome, such is the team's foreboding about a fast bowler in the opposition known simply as 'the Demon'.

'The Demon', who runs in 50 yards (46 metres) and breaks

---

[*] *Favourite Australian Short Stories* (1963), edited by Colin Thiele, went through four editions over thirteen years. 'The Batting Wizard from the City' also appears in *Australian Bag* (1966) edited by P. R. Smith, and *Southern Harvest* (1965) edited by R. F. Brissenden.

stumps and limbs alike amid an odour of burning leather, lives up to his vaunts:

> His mighty thighs lifted like the pistons of the Melbourne Express, his boots hammered the ground like a mob of wild horses, angry blasts of air whistled through his nostrils . . . The ball left his hand like a red streak. The consensus of opinion afterwards was that it was on the off, but no one really saw it until it sped over the boundary, went through the blackberries with a crash, scaring out six rabbits and a black snake, and ended up in the middle of the creek.

'Smith', however, proves more than a match, nonchalantly hitting the ball here and there, to the escalating consternation of his captain:

> 'Play a straight bat at those or you'll be out!' yelled the skipper at the young fellow.
>
> 'Sorry, but I always play them that way,' says the young man, very polite.
>
> 'Always play them that way!' the skipper snarls. 'Who the hell do you think you are – Trumper?'

In the aftermath of Smith's delirious 150, the reader is inclined to believe that this might very well be the case:

> 'Mr Smith,' says Stonewall, 'I never saw anyone – not even on the Sydney Cricket Ground – play some shots better than you did today. I mean that. They were nearly in Trumper's class.'
>
> You could see the willowy young cove was embarrassed by Stonewall's talk because he kept looking at the ground. But the funny thing was the queer sort of laugh he gave when the skipper

snapped: 'Don't talk nonsense, Stonewall! No one's nearly in
Trumper's class.'

When 'Smith' departs at the end never to be seen again, the story
takes on a dreamlike quality. The team are the only eyewitnesses to
something extraordinary, but how to convey what they have seen?
The awe in the narrator's voice and the ornate touch he brings to
description echo the cricket lovers of the generation of Stivens'
father, with their tales, and their loyalties, and their solitary pictorial
icon. In Stivens' last cricket story, 'The Man who Almost Ruined
Cricket' (1979), 'Jumping Out' itself looks down from the wall of a
pub of a dusty inland town with 'homely sawdust on the floor and a
couple of spittoons', as a yarn evolves of another mythological fast
bowler who purportedly bowled at 'two hundred and twelve miles an
hour'. With every glance at Trumper's image, the story grows wool-
lier, and by the end a little actuality has been stretched a good long
way. Three-quarters of a century after its taking, Beldam's photograph had become part of cricket's misty dreamscape.

•

But would anyone chronicle the actual Trumper? Gestures were
made. Both Whitington and the prolific sports writer Jack Pollard
started 'biographies', only to abandon them. With Trumper's centenary in the offing, this vexed one man in particular. Before World
War I, solicitor Eric McElhone had played eleven seasons of Sydney
first grade with Waverley and University, and seven interstate
matches alongside 'not only the world's most beautiful batsman, but
a man of the highest character and principles'. A tall, formal, faintly
aloof figure who attended University fixtures as a life member, on

An icon evolves: clockwise from top left: adorning *Wisden Past and Present* (1931),
The Boys' Book of Cricket (1953), *Armchair Cricket* (1968), John Arlott's *A Picture of Cricket* (1955).

the subject of Trumper he proselytised inexhaustibly. To this there was a certain piquancy: Eric was also a nephew of unbending Billy, founder of the Board of Control that had so alienated Trumper and his contemporaries.

Eric McElhone was particularly aggrieved when in November 1973 the SCG Trust opened the Bradman Stand, a companion to the Noble Stand. As he wrote to the *Sydney Morning Herald*, Bradman had 'left his native state, NSW, early in his career'; Trumper, whose 'exquisite beauty' as a batsman had 'electrified pre-World War I cricket', was far worthier of perpetuation. That some readers might not have heard the name troubled him further, so McElhone wrote a painstaking tribute and posted a copy to the *Daily Telegraph*, drawing attention to a forthcoming anniversary of his hero's death. 'Could you find space in your valued paper to keep alive the memory of the famous batsman, Victor Trumper?' he asked above a shaky signature – the sports editor, kindly, did. He submitted a similar article to the *Daily Mirror*, and composed a lengthy address to the Waverley Historical Society, which he also forwarded to Jack Fingleton.

Fingleton had aged. His children were grown up, his marriage had failed, and he had recently suffered a stroke as well as the loss of several close friends, including Cardus. He was dismayed by the drift of the game, by on-field rancour and off-field realpolitik; in fact, he found little to like about the 1970s generally, full of 'queers and Commies' and the 'Australian Women's Lib who have done their sex, as I see it, much harm'. But what exercised him most of all, as ever, was Bradman, and Fingleton's decision to write a book about Trumper was at least as much as about his former captain. The headline disclosure in *The Immortal Victor Trumper* (1978) did not concern its ostensible subject; it was Fingleton publicly naming Bradman as the leaker from the Adelaide Oval dressing-room in 1933. 'I have always held it against Don that he did not own up and clear me,' Fingleton complained.

Fingleton's book was welcomed as a long-overdue tribute to Trumper, and as a companion to the eternal image. 'My favourite cricket photograph of all time is the famous one by George Beldam showing Victor Trumper moving forward to drive,' reminisced the celebrity interviewer Michael Parkinson in the *Sunday Times*:

My second favourite cricket photograph is the one Beldam took at the finish of the shot, with the bat high, the shoulders square on, the eyes searching the far horizon for the missing ball. In the sense that these pictures adorned my bedroom wall for many a year, it could be said that Victor Trumper was my first pin-up.

I am delighted to learn that the photographs had a similar effect on Jack Fingleton, who once argued that they should be hung in every cricket dressing room in the world.

Others were troubled by the uneasy mix of hagiography and obloquy. In the *Times Literary Supplement*, Alan Ross thought Trumper too idealised: 'Such goodness, unselfishness, self-sacrifice, nobility and modesty sound somewhat cloying. Had he no faults, vices, frailties of character? I hope he had, though Fingleton remarks on

Bradman v Trumper: Fingleton revives an argument.

none.' In *The Cricketer*, Gerald Pawle accused Fingleton of reviving his views of Bradman 'with intemperate zest'. Neither feature of the book obscured the thinness of the research – perhaps to be expected from a seventy-one-year-old author with a ninety-one-year-old 'mentor', as Fingleton referred to McElhone. They were too late to speak to Trumper's Test teammates or siblings; they accessed neither correspondence nor official records; sections were bent out of shape by prating digressions, not merely about Bradman and Bodyline, but also the issue of the moment, Kerry Packer and his World Series Cricket, which Fingleton despised, like 'all players of my genera-tion'. The chapter nominally allocated to the 1912 Big Six upheaval was mostly concerned with deploring modern Test cricketers, who had 'nothing to grumble about as they get the best of everything', who were indulging in 'too many gimmicks, too much "sledg-ing" and too much bad language', and for whom Fingleton foresaw 'a lonely old age'. On the threat Packer posed to cricket's sanctity, funnily enough, Fingleton stood shoulder to shoulder with Bradman. 'Whereas players of the Trumper era and my own knew the mar-vellous feelings of "mateship", the Packer players will miss all this, and will be generally shunned by established cricket,' he concluded. 'I wonder if they will then think that the money was worth it all. I doubt it.'

If nothing else, *The Immortal Victor Trumper* underlined the plasticity of Trumper's fame. In the 1930s, he had been the amateur alternative to a professional game; in the 1950s, he had been a thrill-ing alternative to a moribund game; now he was a pure alternative to a corrupted game. Again, he made an ironic recruit to the fold of 'the establishment'. Trumper's generation of Australian cricketers had aligned with private interests in the form of the Melbourne CC and been suspended it for it by authorities – exactly like Ian Chappell's

Australians. But that part of the story was long forgotten, and Eric McElhone wasn't about to remind readers of his uncle's role in it. What survived were the tale's symbolic and emotional attachments. Trumper was now a figure whose carefree leap, spotless flannels, modest bearing and open hand represented all that was wholesome about the embattled game's traditions.

But ready or not, the world was changing. Writing on the centenary of Trumper's birth on 2 November 1977, the *Sydney Morning Herald*'s venerable cricket writer Tom Goodman acknowledged that the Bradman Stand had come to stay but urged the SCG Trust to rename the Hill in Trumper's honour – a fitting tribute in this age of millionaires to the cricketer of the people. Among readers who wrote in support was Jack Mundey, the Builders Labourers Federation secretary whose 'Green Bans' had stayed the hand of numerous Sydney developers, who thought it necessary to repel cricket's pirates too: 'If we don't name the Hill now, who knows, in a few years, Ian Chappell or Tony Greig may be leading a campaign to have it renamed the Kerry Packer Mountain!' Time was shorter than anyone knew. Barely a year later, the pirates were loose in the SCG, fans cramming the Hill to cheer Chappell, boo Greig and strengthen Packer – it would be another thirty years before the name Trumper formed part of the built environment at his former home ground. And by then, the legend had changed again, in ways none could have foreseen.

'YOU KNOW THAT PHOTOGRAPH'

'Famous Victor Trumpet Bat Handed to SCG Trust'
– Headline in *Manly Daily*, 2 July 2015

If the year of Victor Trumper's birth had been a seminal stage in cricket, the year of his centenary was even more so. The irruption of private capital, the fissuring of the official administrative monopoly, the defection of disgruntled players to a rival promotional body, the atmosphere of experimentation, innovation and commercialisation: 1977 contained more shocks to the system than most entire decades. Driven by television and made for it, Kerry Packer's

World Series Cricket was also a shock to visual sensibilities. Even with the coming of the 625-line screen and of colour, watchers had remained accustomed to partaking of the spectacle from a reverent distance. Under the influence of Channel Nine, cricket began the progress towards the experience described in the opening paragraph of chapter 1, whereby the home viewer is offered a privileged access to the action from intimate proximities, to the accompaniment of a commentary soundtrack that advertises as it analyses, that holds every moment as special and makes every player a star. The access has other subtler restrictions: players off the field recede from view almost altogether, so rigid are their professional regimes, so controlling their media handlers.

Yet George Beldam's vision of Victor Trumper has worn well. Close to the action, the glimpse of an instant, the revelatory angle, the idealised vision: had Beldam been setting out to create a modern mass media trope, rather than merely a demonstration of a straight drive, he could hardly have succeeded more totally. It admits no doubt. It brooks no contradiction. It forms a closed loop: Google the name 'Victor Trumper', and one is directed straight to it, as though further elaboration is unnecessary. For the fifty or so years after its rediscovery in the 1920s, 'Jumping Out' was the unifying, verifying and stabilising influence on the legend of Victor Trumper, available to corroborate memory, to authenticate the assertion of his 'genius'. In the last generation, the photograph has succeeded the legend, and very nearly effaced it. The photograph was once of Trumper. Now it *is* Trumper, helpfully corresponding with a few fragmentary, half-remembered factoids concerning the subject – that he was daring, graceful and so on. The photograph looks the way Trumper is imagined, even if the way Trumper is imagined has been derived in large part from the photograph.

In fact, Trumper is luckier than most. But for George Beldam, he might well have been forgotten entirely. Who recalls Joe Darling, Clem Hill or Reg Duff? How to comprehend Ranji, an Indian who played for England, or Fry, a cricketer who played everything? 'M. A. Noble' is a stand at the SCG, 'Hugh Trumble' a café at the MCG. Only one other cricketer from as long ago has shown comparable historical staying power, thanks likewise to a strong visual identity – the spade-like beard is to W. G. Grace what the leap is to Trumper. But while they died only four months apart in 1915, Grace and Trumper endure quite differently. In England, Grace remains explicable as an eminent Victorian. Four extensive Grace biographies have been published in the last twenty years. Trumper belongs to Australian times blurrily defined, between Federation and Anzac. Nothing of note has been published about him for thirty years.

Yet it's partly this lack that has allowed his image such free play. If cricket has a version of what Walter Benjamin called the 'optical unconscious', 'Jumping Out' is among its most hallowed originating artefacts – and if it has become Trumper, it does not denote only Trumper. Few cricket photographs can have adorned so many book covers – histories, annuals, guides, surveys – and proven so versatile. In different contexts, it has stood for aggression and vitality, evoked tradition and continuity, announced the coming of summers and stood for the passing of time. On the programme for the Royal Shakespeare Company's production of *The Return of A. J. Raffles* (1975), Trumper's unnamed image symbolised both Edwardian gaiety and decadence: in this Graham Greene farce, an epicene Lord Alfred Douglas turns the homoerotic undertones of the relationship between Raffles and Bunny Manders into overtones (Douglas: 'So Raffles could bowl as well as he could bat? Was he bisexual too, Bunny?'; Bunny: 'Of course not. He never looked twice at a woman').

Stamp of quality: Rafty's Trumper.

Juxtaposed with a photograph of left-handed Babe Ruth on Beth Hise's *Swinging Away* (2010), it dramatised the shared heritage of cricket and baseball, 'blood brothers, separated at birth but genetically linked'.

In the main, of course, it has remained an Australian avatar. In March 1981, Australia Post released four stamps featuring cartoon images of sportsmen, a first in each sense, by veteran caricaturist Tony Rafty, who had cut his teeth on *The Referee* before World War II and been more or less a fixture in Sydney's *Sun* since. Trumper was older than the other subjects, jockey Darby Munro, billiards champion Walter Lindrum and tennis czar Sir Norman Brookes. But he was the only figure additionally elaborated by an action pose: it was as though Trumper without 'Jumping Out' was unimaginable. An interviewer from *Women's Weekly* visiting Dennis Lillee's red-brick home in Karrinyup in the mid-1980s noted 'a poster of the elegant batsman Victor Trumper above the bar'. And as Trumper leapt across the front page of the *Daily Telegraph* on the occasion of 1988's Bicentenary Test, Australian cricket was just about to take an unexpected turn – towards, as it were, the past.

One of the players in that match, Steve Waugh, had developed an almost fetishistic attachment to the game's traditions, embodied in the Australian cap. Like Trumper he was superstitiously attached to his own, and expected a similar allegiance of his contemporaries. As captain he would inaugurate the ritual of cap presentations to new players by distinguished elders. And when Australia took the field in the first Test of 2000, it was beneath green skullcaps modelled on Trumper's headgear in 'Jumping Out' – an initiative of Waugh's arising from a question on his mind about how best 'to link the current team with the past':

> Racking my brain, I was struggling for an answer until I thought
> of my favourite cricket photo – that famous shot of a classic Victor
> Trumper cover drive. But at this moment it was not the exquisite
> artistry or beauty of the stroke that got me, but the 'skull cap' on his
> head that ignited my imagination. It is a very different cap from our
> current day baggy green, but in many ways it is just as magnificent
> and has a definite aura.

This 'rediscovery' of the Australian cap unconsciously re-enacted the debate around its status in Trumper's time. In the late 1990s, Cricket Australia was busily asserting legal ownership of the baggy green by obtaining trademark protections, with prime ministerial assent. Yet in a moral sense, Waugh argued, the baggy green belonged to its wearers: 'The players "own" the Australian team traditions and to be able to partake of those rituals and traditions has meant you have been awarded the highest honour in Australian cricket.' In a way,

'Jumping Out' constituted a proof of their prior proprietorship.

Linking 'the current team with the past', then, concerned more than sentiment. At one stage during argy-bargy over the terms of their Australian Cricketers' Association's first memorandum of understanding with Cricket Australia, Waugh and his colleagues went perilously close to doing as Trumper and his colleagues, withdrawing their labour. In the rapprochement between the players and their governors, Waugh's generation regained the direct share of the game's revenues that Trumper's generation had lost. When Waugh announced his retirement at a press conference at the SCG three years later, *The Australian*'s Mike Coward linked him explicitly with the hero of a century earlier, noticing that 'just out of his sight-line was a photograph of the immortal Victor Trumper' – a suitable emblem of Waugh's rise from 'the depths of despair to the heights of glory in eighteen years'.

Other leading cricketers have tapped into the image's power, too. In December 2000, Waugh's female counterpart, Belinda Clark, held the pose for the magazine *Inside Sport*. The image, lightly tinged in sepia, complemented the thrust of a profile that praised her technical purity and amateur drive, drawing an implicit connection between her and an older imagined ideal of Australian cricket, although Clark anchored herself in the present by appearing in a coloured one-day uniform. The message, this time, was inclusive. The game's traditions were not the prerogative of a male elite – rather did they embody a spirit by which anyone could be inspired. In the first summer of his Test captaincy, Michael Clarke formed a more conventional and self-conscious link in the chain by appearing attired as Trumper on the front page of Sydney's *Daily Telegraph* ahead of the SCG's 100th Test, reinforcing the notion of a summer rite stretching back to ancient days.

The stock of mythology appeals to both sides of politics, too. When Ashton Agar made his unforgettable Test debut at Trent Bridge in July 2013, *The Age*'s liberal conscience, Martin Flanagan, invoked the shade of Trumper, who had likewise played 'without freedom or fear' as captured in an 'iconic photo of . . . him dancing down the wicket to drive, bat raised high, perfectly poised and wholly attacking'. Artist Jim Pavlidis responded with a vision of Agar filling a Trumper-shaped hole. When Phillip Hughes suffered his mortal injury eighteen months later, the *Daily Telegraph*'s acerbic conservative, Tim Blair, saw in Hughes elements of Trumper, in their applying 'unconventional methods to a sport founded on convention', leading lives 'gently at odds with the moods of their respective times' and causing 'extraordinary mourning' at 'the agonisingly premature circumstances of their passing'. Illustrator John Tiedemann positioned Trumper and Hughes at opposite ends of the same pitch.

These days in Australia, of course, the whole concept of 'cricket history' tends to be summed up in the person of Sir Donald Bradman, the last stages of whose life were a cascade of honours, preluding an immense posthumous idolatry. There is a degree of competition between legends for a finite amount of public and historic consciousness, and Bradman's fame has in part obscured Trumper's. Yet it has also left Trumper a definable niche. As we have seen, the cultivation of Trumper as the alternative to Bradman began almost as soon as the latter appeared, continuing through phases of contention, to a point where they have achieved a certain complementarity. Bradman fits snugly with an age fascinated by measurement and quantification, topping every average table, outlying every graph; Trumper's run tallies, by contrast, lie fathoms deep. Yet this is also a visual age, of which Beldam has secured for Trumper a sizeable corner, while of Bradman there exists no single, quintessential image. The most widely reproduced photograph of the Don, ironically, is probably that of him being bowled for o in his final Test innings. An additional irony is that it was Bradman who led, circuitously, to the boldest recreation of 'Jumping Out' yet attempted.

Amid the festivities for Bradman's ninetieth year in 1998, the Zimbabwean-born sculptor Mitch Mitchell produced a life-size bronze of Bradman in the follow-through of a cover drive, which Christie's sold for $75 000 to businessman Sir Donald Trescowthick. The auction house's specialist in rare books and sporting memorabilia, Michael Ludgrove, immediately saw potential for a Trumper sequel, but Mitchell declined, as did a second sculptor, Dutch-born Louis Laumen. After discussions with Cameron McIndoe of Fundere Fine Art Foundry, Laumen decided instead to make a clay model of W. G. Grace, whose sesquicentenary was approaching, with a promise to render it in bronze for any buyer. A natural complement for the Grace Gates at Lord's, it was duly acquired by, and cast for, the Marylebone Cricket Club. The entrepreneurial Ludgrove then re-entered the story with David McLachlan, whom we met in the introduction, as backer. Trumper the cricketer had participated in tours that were financial speculations; now Trumper the image was to be one as well.

How, wondered Laumen, was he to regenerate an original to work off in his studio of a man in a state the very opposite of repose? For a full sense of Trumper in the round, he studied all the photographs in *Great Batsmen*, and hired a professional life model with Trumper's lithe but broad-shouldered physique. The model excelled, posing intently, bristling with energy and commitment – and he needed commitment, being required to climb into a customised rig, perch his backside on a stool, slip his front foot into a stirrup and hold a used tube of Glad Wrap for hours at a time. And over the course of weeks, Laumen's initial hesitancy about the project gave way. Beldam and Fry had been right, he decided, about their images inspiring statues like 'those of ancient Greece in the days of the athletic prizemen'. In the way 'Jumping Out' conveyed the impression of one movement becoming another, Laumen thought, it had a marked classical component. The detail also excited him: the coat of arms on the cap, the cane pads, the slim bat (to the specifications of a bat of Trumper's from the Melbourne CC collection).

Federe produced two casts: the second, in fibreglass, now occupies the forecourt of the headquarters of Kookaburra Sport in Moorabbin. And if the first has disappointed the initial commercial expectations of its owner, it shimmers with a possibility absent from comparable works. With Laumen's Trumper anything could happen; with Mitchell's Bradman and Robert Hannaford's similar Bradman outside Adelaide Oval, both at the end of strokes, everything already has. In this respect, perhaps, they reflect the contrast between the legends of each player.

'Jumping Out' has also been rendered in chalk, china, etchings, oils, miniature silver, miniature bronze, tapestry, resin – the plates section of this book offers a selection. It's been merged into montages by the cartoonist Wally Fawkes and the sporting artist Bryan Membrey and appropriated for advertising by Haig and Hahn, while there's no knowing how often it has inspired the 'private art' of gifts and tokens – on coffee cups, coasters, T-shirts, ties, bookplates and business cards, it has the quality of a greeting, inviting recognition, establishing personal connection. Two pleasing examples are included: a Father's Day painting by Cricket Australia's former public affairs spokesman Peter Young for his niece's husband, and a block print by Canberra public servant Russell Ayres for a friend's fiftieth birthday.

Yours truly: bookplate, coaster, business card.

Two further creative adaptations merit mention for sheer improbability. About twenty years ago, musicians Tim Rogers and Rusty Hopkinson of the successful Australian indie band You Am I were chatting in a London hotel bar, recalling the inspiration that rock-poster artists on the west coast of the US had drawn in the late 1960s from Art Nouveau. The pair were fans of cricket as well as of psychedelic rock, and hit on Victor Trumper as an symbol of the Australian *fin de siècle*, making his name into a tour catchphrase. Confronted by tiny stages and crammed crowds, members of You Am I would shout to each other: 'Let's Victor Trumper this fucker!' The in-joke extended naturally to advertising their 1997 Australian shows as 'Victor Trumper's Ever Lovin' Pop & Soul Revue', with a poster featuring a line version of 'Jumping Out'. After all, Rogers thought, cricket and rock music went well together: 'Get on the front foot, hoick the bugger, and get on with it. Towel down, drive another coupla hundred mile, repeat . . .'

If cricket and rock can coexist, what about cricket and sex? In 2006, retired Monash University social scientist Ian Marshall published a historical novel based on the celebrated 1936 case of a twenty-six-year-old Anglo-Indian divorcee, Mabel Freer, who was refused entry to Australia because she had had an affair with a married Australian staff officer in Lahore, Lieutenant R. E. Dewar. In *The Undesirable Immigrant* (2006), Freer became Georgina Lock and Dewar became Peter Renwick, but otherwise Marshall hewed close to the facts of the controversy, which like the expulsion of Egon Kisch two years earlier revealed how capriciously Australia's notorious 'dictation test' could be applied: Freer was twice deemed undesirable because of her inability to take down a passage in Italian. In one aspect of the story, however, the cricket-loving author allowed himself some creative licence – he had Georgina and Peter consummate their relationship in a Beldam-adorned bedroom:

> The room to which Peter took me when we first made love looked at first like any other room in officers' quarters on any military station . . . The coverlet and the pillows on the spartan bed were arranged as though for inspection. But then I began to notice the differences. Above the bed – it's the memory I most retain of this room – I caught sight of the photograph for the first time, a huge blow-up of an original. Already I'd learned enough about cricket to know that this picture was somehow remarkable, a moment when a daring player had advanced into the unknown, bat raised behind

his head, to plunder the opposition, careless of the consequences.

'Victor Trumper', Peter said, when I looked questioningly at the picture. He was clearly embarrassed. This was hero worship he was never going to discuss with anyone else, let alone a woman, even though he was about to go to bed with her beneath the picture. 'He died young,' was all he said, and I didn't ask any more questions.

Staid, respectable Peter comes to life under the picture's influence. When Georgina sees him play an 'unimportant cricket match against a comically earnest Indian side', he bats 'with such a breathtaking grace it was as though another man had temporarily taken possession of him'; he even surrenders his wicket to a deserving bowler, in Trumper fashion. On her thwarted journey to Australia, Georgina is accompanied by a copy of 'Jumping Out' as a keepsake of her lover, although Peter's sister casts a more sardonic gaze on his choice of hero: 'Apparently Victor didn't handle life very well. Without a bat in his hands he wasn't particularly good at looking after himself . . . Self-interest has a place as well. That at any rate is how I read it.' And reading Trumper, as we have seen, is a decidedly personal matter.

•

From all this multiplication and manipulation of 'Jumping Out', one figure was conspicuously absent: its originator. Perhaps this was its own form of compliment – such was the image's seeming transparency, it was treated as a window on the past rather than a facsimile of it. This illusion also conveniently dodged issues of copyright, which in theory remained with the Beldam family.

This rankled with Beldam's youngest son. George Jnr had grown up idolising the father who had died when he was seven years old. He had first encountered George Snr's handiwork as a schoolboy, in a little instructional manual, *Cricket for Boys* (1937). 'The photographs in this book are of cricketers of a previous era,' said the authors, two Wellingborough schoolmasters. 'We have chosen them purposely, not because the batsmen were necessarily better than the famous cricketers of today, such as Bradman and Hammond – photos of whom can be seen almost daily in the papers – but because the correctness of their play in theory and practice has never been surpassed and in consequence they are ideal models for boys to copy.' *Never surpassed? Ideal models?* The phrases lodged in George Jnr's mind. He had no particular aptitude for photography – his gift was languages, which he studied at Oxford, eventually becoming a teacher of French and German. But he grew ever more frustrated at the lack of acknowledgement for his father's work. Even when the photographs were used extensively, in such books as Thomas Moult's *Bat and Ball* (1935) and Patrick Morrah's *The Golden Age of Cricket* (1967), their significance went unremarked. In *Great Batsmen* and *Great Bowlers and Fieldsmen*, Beldam had secured more than 1000 likenesses of more than 140 cricketers. But for these likenesses, the intimate visual record of the game before World War I would have been virtually non-existent.

After his mother died in December 1969, George Jnr and his wife, Cornelia, moved into the big, draughty family home in Worplesdon, near Guildford, still full of his father's glass-plate negatives stored in old Kodak boxes. Some were in poor shape. During World War II, a sizeable number had been damaged while in the care of the family solicitor in Lincoln's Inn Fields: specifically, water from firehoses after a raid in the Blitz had fused the plates together. George Jnr was unsure what to do, but wanted to do something.

Uncurated and uncatalogued as it was, this was a unique photographic archive. Among the surviving plates, George Jnr found many images that had never been published, including a startlingly clear picture of Trumper walking out to bat with Reg Duff in the 1905 Lord's Test. The fame of 'Jumping Out', he felt, was a mixed blessing: that there were so many other photographs was invariably forgotten; that royalties might be due seldom occurred to anyone. To both issues, George Jnr saw the solution as a giant book chronicling his father's oeuvre and re-establishing his reputation.

Reunited: Trumper and partner Reg Duff photographed by Beldam, Lord's 1905.

First outlined in *The Cricketer* in February 1988, this would prove a mountainous labour of filial love. Nobody, for example, was prepared to help George Jnr separate the fused plates. When he tried himself, with a hammer and chisel, some shattered – including, he sadly told the collector John Hawkins, 'Jumping Out'. Transferring the plates to film was likewise a protracted process, unaided by software to counteract their tendency to darkness. George Jnr wanted to include each Chevallier Tayler print from *The Empire's Cricketers* alongside the corresponding Beldam photograph, thereby establishing his father's patrimony of what after many years had become a pricey collectable. But complexities multiplied and production costs mounted, George Jnr trusting no publisher to finish anything to his standards, and deciding to print at his own expense in Hong Kong.

At last in December 1991, *The Cricketer* publicised the imminent release of *Third Man In: The Lost World of a Camera Artist*, whose 700 illustrations would restore George Beldam to 'his rightful place in cricket history'. Alas, it left him deeper buried than ever. When George Jnr excitedly opened his first copies, he found them of lamentable quality, the reproductions indistinct. Then he was unable to recover the film of the book and go elsewhere. A scheduled launch at Burlington Gallery was cancelled; but for a handful of copies, the book was pulped. George Jnr died in Worplesdon in October 1996, life's desire unfulfilled.

The pieces were picked up by George Jnr's widow, Lia. She was hardly cut out to manage such a unique inheritance. A Swiss-born fashion model, she was known anonymously to millions as the nude figure who rises from a bath at the Overlook Hotel to embrace Jack Nicholson in Stanley Kubrick's *The Shining* (1980), with spooky consequences. But while neither schooled in photography nor fussed by cricket, Lia was determined to honour her husband's name. She struck a deal with veteran sports photographer Bob Thomas under which Popperfoto would preserve, index and market images from the collection; she partnered cricket-book dealer Michael Down in reviving *Third Man In* as *Great Cricketers: The Age of Grace and Trumper* (2000). Down, a retired nuclear engineer, ran an imprint, Boundary Books, in a picturesque Cheshire farming village, Goostrey. Carefully selecting a Spanish printer, Boundary successfully published 500 regular editions and forty-eight special editions which if they did not restore George Beldam to his 'rightful place' in the pages of cricket history at least elevated him from a footnote. Though they never played a game together, no great batsman has ever had a more faithful partner than Victor Trumper his photographer.

•

Fitting permanent memorial still eluded Victor Trumper. After the SCG Trust abandoned its 1919 plan for a fountain in favour of donating the money raised to Trumper's widow, no monument existed other than the grave in Waverley Cemetery. In *Full Score* (1970), Neville Cardus reported that Trumper's plot 'in a churchyard outside Sydney is to this day covered by fresh flowers'. It was another of his fond imaginings: the grave underwent several phases of neglect, despite hosting periodic anniversary ceremonies and numberless private tributes.

For as long as they were able, former teammates came regularly. In *The Referee*, J. C. Davis documented a 1935 visit by a 'bare-headed' Hanson Carter, Jim Kelly and Jack O'Connor: 'The old pals moved away with one thought: "HE was a MAN".' Later came pilgrims. In the summer of 1952–53, fifteen-year-old St George junior cricketer David Frith took the long train and tram ride east from his home in Carlton, and dodged among the headstones for hours before locating what he was looking for. Standing in solitary contemplation kindled a growing passion for cricket, further fanned by gazing at the print of 'Jumping Out' in the home dressing-room at Trumper Oval and by trying to locate the initials Trumper was reputed to have carved in his old Crown Street schooldesk – the patterns of an ensuing lifetime as cricket's most dedicated visual and material historian.

Still they come, too, and from far away. Fifty years after Frith, twenty-nine-year-old cricket writer Dileep Premachandran converged on the same destination. He owed his induction in the lore of Trumper to the tales of a maternal grandfather in Mumbai, to Fingleton's 1958 essay 'Never Another Like Victor', and to 'Jumping Out': 'I don't believe there's another image that conveys the beauty of cricket quite like it. I never had the ability to replicate the stroke, so I did the next best thing.' That was on the final day of his first Australian tour: 'I visited Waverley Cemetery and spent twenty minutes by Trumper's grave – paying tribute to the two men who had shaped my life.' Premachandran is now the editor-in-chief of *Wisden India*; 'Jumping Out' forms part of the masthead of his weblog.

'Vic': Trumper's grave, Waverley Cemetery.

Since the mid-1980s, Trumper's grave has been tended by a local resident. Peter Brown joined the *Daily Telegraph* as a copyboy in 1967, and later became press secretary to Neville Wran. The week he moved to Bronte, he satisfied an abiding curiosity by visiting Waverley Cemetery, and has since returned monthly to look over Trumper's varyingly kempt plot. He has read extensively of Trumper and felt drawn to his reputation for elegance and chivalry. The setting, with Edmund Barton, Henry Lawson, J. P. Archibald, Henry Kendall and Dorothea Mackellar also among the interred, puts him in mind of Père Lachaise.

For decade on decade, however, the SCG went on featuring next to nothing about Trumper. For sixteen years it even misplaced the commemorative plaque bearing his name previously affixed to the Sheridan Stand, after that structure made way for the Churchill Stand in 1986: just in time for celebrations of Trumper's 125th birthday, it was located by a nimble SCG Museum staff member crawling the crevices beneath the Members Stand stairs. This lacuna perplexed another man, David Strange, an English teacher at Killara High School. Strange grew up in Mount Druitt, a poor neighbourhood, but in a household with a love of reading and of cricket. His maternal grandfather had seen Alan Kippax and Archie Jackson, whom he described in relation to Trumper. Strange read all the canonical works, and marvelled at 'Jumping Out'. Yet when he visited the SCG, the past went back no further than Bradman – it was, he thought, like commencing a history of cinema with *Citizen Kane*. Strange had myriad ideas for Trumper's commemoration – too many for a lifetime, really. But he grew fixated on a Victor Trumper Day involving celebrity teams using Golden Age gear on the SCG, about which he finally approached the chairman of the SCG Trust, Rodney Cavalier.

Cavalier was all ears. A pillar of NSW Labor during its 1980s primacy and probably the country's best-read sports administrator, he also thought the SCG historically deficient, and had his own thoughts on Trumper's remembrance. The Trust was weighing up plans for a new $70 million development on the site of the former Hill, succeeding the spartan concourse of the Doug Walters Stand. Cavalier believed it should be named for Trumper. As Strange petitioned Cavalier and Trust chief executive Jamie Barkley about *his* idea, Cavalier listened attentively – Strange thought he looked rather pleased.

That the new development would be called the Victor Trumper Stand was made official in June 2008. Again it had bipartisan support, as it were. Trustee Alan Jones, a conservative, was strongly in favour. So was NSW Labor's assistant general secretary Luke Foley, who provided an erudite submission citing Cardus, Fingleton, Noble and Mailey, further substantiated by the obligatory visual evidence: 'The classic photograph of Trumper leaping out to drive, taken by George Beldam, remains famous today. It has appeared in countless cricket books and at cricket ovals around the world.'

Officially the clinching argument in Trumper's favour was his association with all the ground's sports: in addition to cricket, he had played rugby and Australian Rules as a youth; he had then been the founding treasurer of the rugby league. (It was expedient in this context to omit that the clubs had kicked Trumper out after little more than a year – forgetting failures and peccadilloes is as much a part of the nourishment of legend as celebrating triumphs.) Yet its visual reinforcement was obviously no hindrance to the case for Trumper, even if it acted merely as a spur of enthusiasm. It is one thing to tell, another to show.

Four months after plans for the stand were announced, 'Jumping Out' leapt from the cover of the programme for Victor Trumper Day, which David Strange funded with sponsorship, donations and a $35 000 drawdown of his mortgage. A brass band and a street organ played period tunes. Vintage cars and a penny-farthing exampled period transportation. Actors portrayed turn-of-the-century characters, including Henry Lawson and Nellie Melba. Jason Hogan, playing Trumper, mimed 'Jumping Out' for photographers. The teams turned out in period costume, the first ball from retired Australian fast bowler Greg Campbell entailing a hasty no-ball call when it extracted the off stump of Wiggle Greg Page. Comedian Mick Molloy bowled the last ball along the ground to me.

Efforts were made during the day to explain Trumper to the unitiated. 'He had the fighting instinct of Ian Chappell, the grace of Greg Chappell, the inventiveness of Darren Lehmann and

Victor Trumper Day: an actor plays the title role.

the philanthropic spirit of Steve Waugh,' Strange told the *Sydney Morning Herald*. 'I suppose for Queenslanders like myself,' said Prime Minister Kevin Rudd on dedicating the Trumper Stand in December 2008, 'Trumper could be best described as a combination of Wally Lewis, John Eales, Michael Voss and Matthew Hayden.' But Rudd then seemed to realise that he had no need of such lumpy mash-ups. 'The Trumper legend for later generations is grounded in that great black-and-white photograph of him launching that powerful Trumper drive,' he stated. 'You *know* that photograph. It just sits in your mind and your memory.' And he was right.

•

The day before the Fifth Test of the Ashes of 2015, I spent part of the afternoon with photographer Philip Brown dodging about the outfield at The Oval, him with his camera, me with a vintage survey map of Kennington from London Metropolitan Archives and a copy of 'Jumping Out', in search of the same vantage as Beldam in 1905. Inevitably the backdrop had changed. The terraces of what was now called the Peter May Stand stretched unbroken. Thirty years after Beldam's visit, the Clayton Arms had been demolished for the social housing today called Kennington Park Estate; the pub had crossed to the other side of the road, been renamed The Cricketers in 1966, and lain derelict since its closure ten years earlier.

Yet Clayton Street stretched in the same direction, opening the same gap in the skyline. Refurbished as apartments, the building that once housed the Kennington Road School, visible in the far distance of 'Jumping Out', still stood; likewise the great gasometers. And between times the pitch square at The Oval had not budged an inch. At its eastern extremity, as we watched, Steve Smith was immersed in a session of throwdowns on more or less the spot where Trumper and Beldam had rendezvoused eleven decades earlier; when we returned from exploring the pavilion half an hour later, in fact, Australia's captain-to-be was still hard at work. We left him at it. The following day he made a hundred.

Has Smith heard of Victor Trumper, I wondered? Possibly. George Beldam? Definitely not. Never mind: he sort of knows them anyway.

Next man in: The Oval, 2015.

GUIDE TO SOURCES

Three biographies have been published of Victor Trumper: Jack Fingleton's *The Immortal Victor Trumper* (Collins, London, 1978), Ashley Mallett's *Trumper: The Illustrated Biography* (Macmillan, South Melbourne, 1985) and Peter Sharpham's *Trumper: The Definitive Biography* (Hodder & Stoughton, Sydney, 1985). Fingleton's working materials are at the State Library of NSW, MLMSS 5691/Box 21; the uncorrected proof referred to in the text was provided by Russell Jackson; David Frith was kind enough to send me his lengthy corrections, and also to draw my attention to Trumper's correspondence with Worcestershire CCC.

A fourth most useful compilation was published on the centenary of Trumper's death collating papers delivered at a seminar on his life, edited by its organiser, Ronald Cardwell. Particularly useful in *The Life and Times of the Immortal Victor Trumper* (Cricket Publishing Company, Sydney, 2015) are the contributions of Alf James and Jim Cattlin concerning Trumper's junior and grade cricket, and Cardwell's own analysis of Trumper's business career, but everything is readable and illuminating.

Particular of Trumper's feats and fortunes have inspired other works: Lionel H. Brown's *Victor Trumper and the 1902 Australians* (Secker & Warburg, London, 1981), John Hawkins' *Trumper's Team in Queensland 1906* (Christopher Saunders, Newnham on Severn, 2012), Gerry Wolstenholme's *Trumper Triumphant: His Final*

First-class Century in England, Blackpool 1909 (Red Rose Books, Bolton, 2002), and a compilation of newspaper articles about his last big innings, *Great Knock: Sim's Australians v. Canterbury, played at Lancaster Park, Christchurch, 27, 28 February, 2 March 1914* (Nag's Head Press, Christchurch, 1978). Trumper provides numerous chapters in various edited compilations, those of special note being Neville Cardus's appreciation in John Arlott's *Cricket: The Great Ones* (Pelham, London, 1967), and Ross McMullin's in Garrie Hutchinson's *Test Team of the Century* (HarperSports, Sydney, 2000).

George Beldam can claim principal ownership of the following works:

Great Golfers: Their Methods at a Glance (notes by Harry Vardon, James Braid, Alexander Herd, J. H. Taylor), Macmillan, London, 1904

Golf Faults Illustrated (with J. H. Taylor), George Newnes Ltd, London, 1904

Great Lawn Tennis Players: Their Methods Illustrated (with P. A. Vaile), Macmillan, London, 1905

Great Batsmen: Their Methods at a Glance (with C. B. Fry), Macmillan, London, 1905

Great Bowlers and Fielders: Their Methods at a Glance (with C. B. Fry, F. R. Spofforth, B. J. T. Bosanquet, R. O. Schwarz), Macmillan, London, 1906

Cricket Illustrated, Gowans & Gray, London, 1908

Golfing Illustrated, Gowans & Gray, London, 1908

The World's Champion Golfers: Their Art Disclosed by the Ultra-Rapid Camera, Photochrome Co. Ltd, London, 1924 (11 volumes)

Beldam also provided illustrations for:

Vaile, Percy A., *Modern Lawn Tennis: Illustrated by Explanatory Diagrams and by Action Photographs Taken Expressly for This Work*, William Heinemann, London, 1904

Tayler, A. Chevallier, *The Empire's Cricketers: Season 1905*, Fine Art Society, London, 1905

Broadbent Trowsdale, T., *The Cricketers' Autograph Birthday Book*, Walter Scott Publishing Company, London, 1906

Watts, Mrs Roger, *The Fine Art of Jujutsu*, William Heinemann, London, 1906

Duncan, George and Bernard Darwin, *Present-day Golf*, Hodder & Stoughton, 1921

Fry, S. H., *Billiards for Amateurs*, Hodder & Stoughton, London, 1922

The indispensable volume on Beldam's life and work, mentioned in the text, is *Great Cricketers: The Age of Grace & Trumper* (Boundary Books, Goostrey, 2000), compiled by George Beldam Jnr and edited by his widow, Cornelia. Beldam gave a professional appraisal of his work in an interview with Adolphe Abrahams in a series, 'Sports and the Camera', for *The Photographic News* (21 June 1907) and a historical analysis of batsmanship in 'Style and Progression: Influences at Work in the Batsman's Art', a chapter in *British Sports and Sportsmen: Cricket and Football* (*The Sportsman*, London 1917, pp. 100–09). Further biographical information is from 'A Chat with Mr G. W. Beldam' in *Cricket: A Weekly Record of the Game* (20 June 1901) and 'A Full Innings' by Roy Beldam in the *Peterhouse Annual Record 2005/6* (University of Cambridge), pp. 45–53.

CRICKET: BIOGRAPHY AND AUTOBIOGRAPHY

Batchelor, Denzil, *C. B. Fry*, Phoenix House, London, 1951

Bonnell, Max, *Currency Lads: The Life and Cricket of T. W. Garrett, R. C. Allen, S. P. Jones and R. J. Pope,* Cricket Publishing Company, Cherrybrook, 2001

Booth, Keith, *The Father of Modern Sport: The Life and Times of Charles W. Alcock,* Parrs Wood Press, Manchester, 2002

Bradman, Donald, *Don Bradman's Book: The Story of My Cricketing Life to August 1930*, Hutchinson, London, 1931

Bradman, Donald, *Farewell to Cricket,* Hodder & Stoughton, London, 1950

Brodribb, Gerald, *The Croucher: A Biography of Gilbert Jessop,* London Magazine Editions, London, 1974

Brookes, Christopher, *His Own Man: The Life of Neville Cardus,* Unwin Paperbacks, London, 1986

Cardus, Neville, *Autobiography,* Collins, London, 1947

Cardus, Neville, *Second Innings,* Collins, London, 1950

Cardus, Neville, *Full Score,* Cassell, London, 1970

Cashman, Richard, *The 'Demon' Spofforth*, UNSW Press, Kensington, 1990

Daft, Richard, *Kings of Cricket: Reminiscences and Anecdotes, with Hints on the Game,* Arrowsmith, Bristol, 1893

Daft, Richard, *A Cricketer's Yarns,* Chapman & Hall, London, 1926

Daniels, Robin, *Conversations with Cardus,* Gollancz, London, 1976

Darling, D. K., *Test Tussles On and Off the Field,* self-published, Hobart, 1970

Down, Michael, *Archie: A Biography of A. C. MacLaren,* Allen & Unwin, London, 1981

Ellis, Clive, *C. B.: The Life of Charles Burgess Fry*, Dent, London, 1984

Fingleton, Jack, *Batting from Memory,* Collins, London, 1981

Furniss, Harry, E. J. Milliken and E. B. V. Christian, *A Century of Grace*, Bristol, 1896

Frith, David, *Archie Jackson: The Keats of Cricket*, Pavilion, London, 1987

Frith, David, *Caught England, Bowled Australia: A Cricket Slave's Complex Story*, Eva Press, London, 1997

Fry, C. B., *Life Worth Living*, Eyre & Spottiswoode, London, 1939

Grace, W. G., *Cricket*, Arrowsmith, Bristol, 1891

Haigh, Gideon, *The Big Ship: Warwick Armstrong and the Making of Modern Cricket*, Text Publishing, Melbourne, 2001

Hill, Les, *Eighty Not Out: The Story of W. J. (Bill) Whitty of Tantanoola*, Laurie & Watson, Mount Gambier, 1966

Hutton, Len, *Cricket Is My Life*, Hutchinson & Co., London, 1949

Iredale, Frank, *33 Years of Cricket*, Beatty, Richardson & Co., Sydney, 1920

Jessop, Gilbert, *A Cricketer's Log*, Hodder & Stoughton, London, 1922

Laver, Frank, *An Australian Cricketer on Tour*, Bell, London, 1905

Lilley, A. A., *Twenty-four Years of Cricket*, Mills & Boon, London, 1912

Macartney, Charles, *My Cricketing Days*, William Heinemann, London, 1930

McCool, Colin, *Cricket Is a Game*, Stanley Paul, London, 1961

Mailey, Arthur, *10 for 66 and All That*, Phoenix Sports Books, London, 1958

Mitchell, Alan, *84 Not Out: The Story of Sir Arthur Sims, Kt*, Hennel Locke, London, 1962

Monfries, J. Elliott, *Not Test Cricket*, Gillingham, Adelaide, 1950

Moyes, A. G., *Bradman*, Angus & Robertson, Sydney, 1948

Myers, A. Wallis, *C. B. Fry: The Man and His Methods*, J. W. Arrowsmith, Bristol, 1912

Rae, Simon, *W. G. Grace: A Life*, Faber & Faber, London, 1998

Raiji, Vasant, *Ranji: The Legend and the Man*, self-published, Bombay, 1963

Raiji, Vasant (ed.), *Victor Trumper: The Beau Ideal of a Cricketer*, Vivek, Bombay, 1964

Root, Fred, *A Cricket Pro's Lot*, Edward Arnold, London, 1937

Rosenwater, Irving, *Sir Donald Bradman*, Batsford, London, 1978

Sissons, Ric, *Reggie: Five Years of Fame – The Story of Reginald Duff*, Cricket Publishing Company, Sydney, 2016

Tomlinson, Richard, *Amazing Grace: The Man who Was W. G.*, Little, Brown, London, 2015

Travers, Ben, *94 Declared*, Elm Tree Books, London, 1981

Trumble, Robert, *The Golden Age of Cricket*, self-published, Melbourne, 1968

Whimpress, Bernard (ed.), *Clem Hill's Reminiscences: The 'Unwritten History' of His Test Career, 1896–1912*, Association of Cricket Statisticians & Historians, Cardiff, 2007

Wilde, Simon, *Ranji: A Genius Rich and Strange*, Kingswood, London, 1999

Wilton, Iain, *C. B. Fry: An English Hero*, Richard Cohen, London, 1999

Wright, L. G., *Scraps from a Cricketer's Memory*, Derbyshire County Cricket Supporters Club, Derbyshire, 1980

CRICKET: HISTORY

Alcock, Charles and Lord Alverstone (eds), *Surrey Cricket: Its History and Associations*, Longmans, Green, London, 1902

Altham, H. S., and E. W. Swanton, *A History of Cricket*, 2nd edition, George Allen & Unwin, London, 1938

Bateman, Anthony, *Cricket, Literature and Culture: Symbolising the Nation, Destabilising Empire*, Ashgate Publishing, Farnham, 2009

Bonnell, Max and James Rodgers, *Golden Blues: Sydney University Cricket – 150 Years of the Club and Its Players*, Darlington Press, Sydney, 2014

Cannane, Steve, *First Tests: Great Australian Cricketers and the Backyards that Made Them*, ABC Books, Sydney, 2009

Chignell, W. R., *A History of the Worcestershire County Cricket Club*, Littlebury & Co., London, 1951

Derriman, Phil, *True to the Blue: A History of the New South Wales Cricket Association*, Richard Smart Publishing, Sydney, 1985

Fahey, Michael and Mike Coward, *The Baggy Green: The Pride, Passion and History of Australia's Sporting Icon*, Cricket Publishing Company, West Pennant Hills, 2008

Frith, David, *The Trailblazers: The First English Cricket Tour of Australia, 1861–62*, Boundary Books, Cheshire, 1999

Green, Benny, *A History of Cricket*, Barrie & Jenkins, London, 1988

Haigh, Gideon and David Frith, *Inside Story: Unlocking Australian Cricket's Archives*, News Custom Publishing, Melbourne, 2007

Howat, Gerald, *Cricket's Second Golden Age*, Hodder & Stoughton, London, 1989

Kynaston, David, *WG's Birthday Party*, Chatto & Windus, London, 1990

Lazenby, John, *The Strangers who Came Home: The First Australian Cricket Tour of England*, John Wisden & Co., London, 2015

Lemmon, David, *The Official History of Worcestershire County Cricket Club*, Christopher Helm, London, 1989

McCleary, G. F., *Cricket with the Kangaroo: Studies in Anglo-Australian Cricket*, Hollis & Carter, London, 1950

Mallett, Ashley, *Eleven: The Greatest Eleven of the 20th Century*, UQP, St Lucia, 2001

Montefiore, David, *Cricket in the Doldrums: The Struggle Between Private and Public Control of Australian Cricket in the 1880s*, Australian Society for Sports History, University of Western Sydney, 1992

Morrah, Patrick, *The Golden Age of Cricket*, Eyre & Spottiswoode, London, 1967

Moyes, A. G., *Australian Cricket: A History*, Angus & Robertson,
   Sydney, 1959

Mulvaney, John and Rex Harcourt, *Cricket Walkabout: The Australian
   Aborigines in England*, Macmillan, South Melbourne, 1988

Palgrave, Louis, *The Story of the Oval and the History of Surrey Cricket:
   1902 to 1948*, Cornish Brothers, Birmingham, 1949

Parish, R. J., & ors (eds.), *Centenary Test Melbourne 12-17 March 1977:
   Official Souvenir Publication of the Australian Cricket Board*, Australian
   Cricket Board, Melbourne, 1977

Plumptre, George, *The Golden Age of Cricket*, Queen Anne Press, London,
   1990

Pollard, Jack, *The Turbulent Years of Australian Cricket 1893–1917*,
   Angus & Robertson, Sydney, 1987

Ranjitsinhji, Kumar Shri, *With Stoddart's Team in Australia*, James
   Bowden, London, 1898

Robinson, Ray, *On Top Down Under*, Cassell Australia, Sydney, 1975

Sandiford, Keith, *Cricket and the Victorians*, Scolar Press, Aldershot,
   1994

Sandiford, Keith and Brian Stoddart (eds), *The Imperial Game*,
   Manchester University Press, Manchester, 1998

Sharpham, Peter, *The 1899 Australians in England*, J. W. McKenzie,
   Epsom, 1997

Sissons, Ric, *The Players: A Social History of the Professional Cricketer*,
   Pluto Press, Sydney, 1988

Smith, Rick, *Cricket Brawl: The 1912 Dispute*, Apple Books, Launceston,
   1995

Standing, Percy Cross, *Cricket of To-day and Yesterday*, Caxton, London,
   1902

Warner, Pelham, *How We Recovered the Ashes*, Chapman and Hall,
   London, 1904

Whimpress, Bernard, *Passport to Nowhere: Aborigines in Australian Cricket 1850–1939*, Walla Walla Press, Sydney, 1999

Williams, Jack, *Cricket and England: A Cultural and Social History of the Inter-war Years,* Frank Cass, London, 1999

Winder, Robert, *The Little Wonder: The Remarkable History of Wisden*, Bloomsbury, London, 2013

Yapp, Nick, *A History of the Foster's Oval*, Pelham, London, 1990

CRICKET: INSTRUCTION

Barbour, E. P., *The Making of a Cricketer*, Sydney & Melbourne Publishing Company, Sydney, 1926

Barnes, A. R, *Calling All Cricketers: A Cricket Coaching Manual*, NSW Cricket Association, Sydney, 1955, 1964

Benson, E. F. and Eustace H. Miles (eds), *The Cricket of Abel, Hirst, and Shrewsbury*, Hurst & Blackett, London, 1903

Bradman, Sir Donald, *The Art of Cricket*, Hodder & Stoughton, London, 1958

Felix, Nicholas, *Felix on the Bat: Being a Scientific Inquiry into the Use of the Cricket Bat; Together with the History and Use of the Catapulta*, Bally Bros, London, 1845

Fry, C. B., *Cricket (Batsmanship)*, Eveleigh, Nash & Grayson, London, 1912

Jessop, Gilbert, *Cricket and How to Play It*, Harrap, London, 1925

Marylebone Cricket Club, *The MCC Cricket Coaching Book*, The Naldrett Press in association with World's Work, Kingswood, 1955

Murdoch, W. L., *Cricket*, George Routledge, London, 1893

Noble, Monty, *The Game's the Thing*, Cassell, London, 1926

Nyren, John, *The Young Cricketer's Tutor and The Cricketers of My Time*, Effingham Wilson, London, 1833

Pollard, Jack (ed.), *Cricket, the Australian Way*, Lansdowne Press, Melbourne, 1961

Ranjitsinhji, Kumar Shri, *The Jubilee Book of Cricket*, Blackwood, Edinburgh, 1897

Rudd, Cecil and Edgar Witham, *Cricket for Boys,* James Nisbet, London, 1937

Steel, A. G., and R H. Lyttleton (eds.), *Cricket*, Badminton Library of Sports and Pastimes, Longmans, Green, London, 1888

Warner, Pelham (ed.), *Cricket: A New Edition*, Badminton Library of Sports and Pastimes, Longmans, Green, London, 1920

Warner, Pelham, *The Book of Cricket*, revised edition, J. M. Dent & Sons, London, 1922

CRICKET: LITERATURE

Ashley-Cooper, F. S., *Cricket Highways and Byways*, George Allen & Unwin, London, 1927

Berry, Scyld, *Cricket: The Game of Life*, Hodder & Stoughton, London, 2015

Binns, Richard, *Cricket in Firelight*, Selwyn & Blount, London, 1935

Cardus, Neville, *A Cricketer's Book*, Grant Richards, London, 1922

Cardus, Neville, *Days in the Sun: A Cricketer's Journal*, Grant Richards, London, 1924

Cardus, Neville, *The Summer Game: A Cricketer's Journal*, Cayme Press, London, 1929

Cardus, Neville, *Cricket*, Longmans, Green, London, 1930

Cardus, Neville, *Good Days: A Book of Cricket*, Jonathan Cape, London, 1934

Cardus, Neville, *Australian Summer*, Jonathan Cape, London, 1937

Cardus, Neville, *English Cricket*, Collins, London, 1945

Cardus, Neville, *The Playfair Cardus*, Dickens Press, London, 1963

Carew, Dudley, *England Over*, Martin Secker, London, 1927

Carew, Dudley, *The Son of Grief*, Arthur Barker, London, 1936

Carew, Dudley, *To the Wicket*, Chapman & Hall, London, 1946

Fingleton, Jack, *Cricket Crisis*, Cassell, London, 1946

Fingleton, Jack, *Brown & Company: The Tour in Australia*, Collins, Sydney, 1951

Fingleton, Jack, *Masters of Cricket*, Heinemann, London, 1958

Giridhar, S. and V. J. Raghunath, *Mid-wicket Tales: From Trumper to Tendulkar*, Sage Publications, New Delhi, 2014

Guha, Ramachandra, *Spin and Other Turns: Indian Cricket's Coming of Age*, Penguin, New Delhi, 1994

Horan, Tom (writer), Pat Mullins and Brian Crowley (eds), *Cradle Days of Australian Cricket: An Anthology of the Writings of 'Felix' (T. P. Horan)*, Macmillan, South Melbourne, 1989

James, C. L. R., *Beyond a Boundary*, Hutchinson, London, 1963

James, C. L. R., *Cricket*, Allison & Busby, London, 1989

Kippax, Alan and E. P. Barbour, *Anti Body-line*, Hurst & Blackett, London, 1933

Knight, Albert, *The Complete Cricketer*, Methuen, London, 1906

Martineau, G. D., *They Made Cricket*, Museum Press, London, 1956

Moult, Thomas (ed.), *Bat and Ball: A New Book of Cricket*, Arthur Barker, London, 1935

Moyes, A. G., *A Century of Cricketers*, Angus & Robertson, Sydney, 1950

Moyes, A. G., *Australian Batsmen: From Charles Bannerman to Neil Harvey*, Harrap, London, 1954

Moyes, A. G., *The Changing Face of Cricket*, Angus & Robertson, Sydney, 1963

Pycroft, James, *The Cricket Field: or, The History and the Science of the Game of Cricket*, Longmans, Green, Reader and Dyer, London, 1868

Stivens, Dal, *The Demon Bowler and Other Cricket Stories*, Outback Press, Collingwood, 1979

Thomson, A. A., *Cricket: The Golden Ages*, Stanley Paul, London, 1961

Trevor, Philip, *The Lighter Side of Cricket*, Methuen, London, 1901

Trevor, Philip, *The Problems of Cricket*, Sampson Low, London, 1907

Trevor, Philip, *Cricket and Cricketers*, Chapman & Hall, London, 1921

Whitington, R. S. and Keith Miller, *Straight Hit*, Latimer House, London, 1952

Whitington, R. S. and Keith Miller, *Bumper*, Latimer House, London, 1953

Whitington, R. S. and Keith Miller, *Cricket Typhoon*, Macdonald, London, 1955

Whitington, R. S., *Captains Outrageous?: Cricket in the Seventies*, Stanley Paul, London, 1972

CRICKET: PICTORIAL

Alcock, Charles, *Famous Cricketers and Cricket Grounds*, Hudson & Kearns, London, 1895

Allen, David Rayvern, *Cricket: An Illustrated History*, Phaidon, Oxford, 1990

Anderson, Duncan, *Echoes from a Golden Age: Postcard Photographs of Cricketers by Foster and Hawkins*, Boundary Books, Childrey, 2010

Bouwman, Richard, *Glorious Innings: Treasures from the Melbourne Cricket Club Collection*, Hutchinson, Melbourne, 1987

Chadwick, Adam, *A Portrait of Lord's*, Scala Arts and Heritage, London, 2013

Dunstan, Keith, *The Tapestry Story: Celebrating 150 Years of the Melbourne Cricket Ground*, Lothian, South Melbourne, 2003

Eagar, Patrick (comp.), *Caught in the Frame: 150 Years of Cricket Photography*, CollinsWillow, London, 1992

Frith, David, *The Golden Age of Cricket, 1890–1914*, Lutterworth Press, Guildford, 1978

Frith, David, *Pageant of Cricket*, Macmillan, South Melbourne, 1987

Fry, C. B., *The Book of Cricket*, George Newnes, London, 1899

Green, Stephen, *Lord's: The Cathedral of Cricket*, Tempus, Gloucestershire, 2003

March, Russell (comp.), *The Cricketers of Vanity Fair*, Webb & Bower, Exeter, 1990

Ray, Mark (ed.), *Long Shadows: 100 Years of Australian Cricket*, Random House Australia, Sydney, 2006

Simon, Robin and Alastair Smart, *The Art of Cricket*, Secker & Warburg, London, 1983

Taylor, Alfred D., *The Story of a Cricket Picture (Sussex and Kent)*, self-published booklet, 1923

Whitington, R. S., *An Illustrated History of Australian Cricket*, Lansdowne Press, Melbourne, 1972

Wilkinson, Jack (comp.), *Great Australian Cricket Pictures*, Sun Books, Melbourne, 1975

Williams, Marcus and Gordon Phillips, *The Wisden Book of Cricket Memorabilia*, Lennard, Oxford, 1990

GENERAL: PHOTOGRAPHY

Baldwin, Gordon, Malcolm Daniel and Sarah Greenough (eds), *All the Mighty World: The Photographs of Roger Fenton, 1852–1860*, Metropolitan Museum of Art, New York, 2004

Benjamin, Walter, *A Work of Art in the Age of Mechanical Reproduction*, Penguin, London, 2008

Berger, John, *Understanding a Photograph*, Penguin Classics, London, 2013

Bowers, Mike (ed.), *Century of Pictures: 100 Years of Herald Photography*, Penguin Viking, Camberwell, 2008

Crombie, Isobel, *Fred Kruger: Intimate Landscapes*, National Gallery of Victoria, Melbourne, 2012

Davies, Alan, *Eye for Photography: The Camera in Australia*, Melbourne University Publishing, Carlton, 2004

Gernsheim, Helmut (with Alison Gernsheim), *The History of Photography from the Camera Obscura to the Beginning of the Modern Era*, Thames & Hudson, London, 1969

Hannavy, John, *Roger Fenton of Crimble Hall*, Gordon Fraser Gallery, London, 1975

Klugman, Matthew and Gary Osmond, *Black and Proud: The Story of an Iconic AFL Photo*, NewSouth, Sydney, 2013

Lydon, Jane, *Eye Contact: Photographing Indigenous Australians*, Duke University Press, Durham, 2005

McCabe, Constance and Neal McCabe, *Baseball's Golden Age: The Photographs of Charles M. Conlon*, Abradale Press, New York, 1993

Morris, Errol, *Believing Is Seeing: Observations on the Mysteries of Photography*, Penguin, New York, 2011

Prodger, Philip (with an essay by Tom Gunning), *Time Stands Still: Muybridge and the Instantaneous Photography Movement*, Oxford University Press, Oxford, 2003

Solnit, Rebecca, *River of Shadows: Eadweard Muybridge and the Technological Wild West*, Viking, New York, 2003

GENERAL: HISTORY

Adams, Francis, *Australian Life*, Chapman & Hall, London, 1892

Atkinson, Alan, *The Europeans in Australia: A History – Volume 3, Nation*, New South, Sydney, 2014

Cashman, Richard, *Sport in the National Imagination*, Walla Walla Press, Sydney, 2002

Cashman, Richard and Michael McKernan (eds), *Sport in History: The Making of Modern Sporting History*, UQP, St Lucia, 1979

Comettant, Oscar, *In the Land of Kangaroos and Gold Mines: A Frenchman's View of Australia in 1888*, Rigby, Adelaide, 1980

Dobbs, Brian, *Edwardians at Play*, Pelham, London, 1973

Finch-Hatton, Harold, *Advance Australia!: An Account of Eight Years' Work, Wandering and Amusement, in Queensland, New South Wales and Victoria*, W. H. Allen, London, 1886

Froude, J. A., *Oceana, or England and Her Colonies,* Longmans, Green, London, 1886

Harper, Melissa and Richard White (eds), *Symbols of Australia*, UNSW Press with National Museum of Australia Press, Sydney, 2010

Jalland, Pat, *Australian Ways of Death: A Social and Cultural History, 1840–1918*, Oxford University Press, Melbourne, 2002

Jalland, Pat, *Changing Ways of Death in Twentieth Century Australia: War, Medicine and the Funeral Business*, UNSW Press, Sydney, 2006

Kinglake, Edward, *The Australian at Home*, Leadenhall Press, London, 1892

McKernan, Michael, *The Australian People and the Great War*, Thomas Nelson, West Melbourne, 1980

Mandle, William, *Going It Alone: Australia's National Identity in the Twentieth Century,* Penguin, Ringwood, 1978

Souter, Gavin, *Lion & Kangaroo: The Initiation of Australia*, Text Publishing, Melbourne, 2000

Twopeny, Richard, *Town Life in Australia*, Elliot Stock, London, 1883

White, Richard, *Inventing Australia: Images and Identity 1688–1980*, Allen & Unwin, Sydney, 1981

MISCELLANEOUS

[--------], 'Instructions for Using the Adams Videx Camera', Adams & Co, Charing Cross Road, London, 1907

Birkenhead, Second Earl of, *F. E.: The Life of F. E. Smith, First Earl of Birkenhead,* Eyre & Spottiswoode, London, 1960

Darwin, Charles, *The expression of the emotions in man and animals*, John Murray, London, 1872

Dennis, C. J., T*he Moods of Ginger Mick*, Angus & Robertson, Sydney, 1916

Ellis, Havelock, *A Study of British Genius*, Hurst & Blackett, London, 1904

FitzSimons, Peter, *Great Australian Sports Champions*, Harper Collins, Sydney, 2006

Galton, Francis, *Hereditary Genius: An Inquiry into Its Laws and Consequences*, Macmillan, London, 1869

Greenland, W. Kingscote (ed.), *Raymond Preston, British and Australian Evangelist: Life Story and Personal Reminiscences*, Epworth Press, London, 1930

Heseltine, Harry, *Vance Palmer,* UQP, St Lucia, 1970

Horne, Donald, *The Lucky Country: Australia in the Sixties*, Penguin, Ringwood, 1964

Hornung, E. W., *The Camera Fiend,* Scribner's Son, New York, 1911

Hornung, E. W., *The Collected Raffles*, Everyman Library, London, 1985

Housman, A. E., *A Shropshire Lad,* John Lane Company, New York, 1906

Hughes, Thomas, *Tom Brown's Schooldays*, Thomas Nelson & Sons, London, 1900

Lawson, Henry, *Poems*, with preface and chronology by Colin Roderick, John Ferguson, Sydney, 1979

McMahon, Darrin M., *Divine Fury: A History of Genius,* Basic Books, New York, 2013

Marshall, Ian, *The Undesirable Immigrant,* Temple House, Hartwell, 2006

Masson, Rosaline (ed.), *I Can Remember Robert Louis Stevenson*, Frederick Stokes, New York, 1922

Morris, Ronald, *The Indomitable Beatie: Charles Hoare, C. B. Fry and the Captain's Lady,* Sutton Publishing, Phoenix Mill, 2004

Musil, Robert, *The Man Without Qualities*, Vintage Books, New York, 1996

Myers, A. Wallis, *The Complete Lawn Tennis Player,* George Jacobs & Co, Philadelphia, 1908

Palmer, Geoffrey and Noel Lloyd, *E. F. Benson: As He Was*, Lennard, Luton, 1988

Palmer, Vance, *Intimate Portraits and Other Pieces*, Cheshire, Melbourne, 1969

Palmer, Vance, *The Swayne Family*, Angus & Robertson, Sydney, 1934

Souter, Gavin, *Company of Heralds: A Century and a Half of Australian Publishing by John Fairfax Limited and Its Predecessors*, Melbourne University Press, Carlton, 1981

Spencer, Thomas, *How McDougall Topped the Score and Other Verses and Sketches*, NSW Bookstall Co, Sydney, 1906

Stephens, A. G., *Victor Daley,* Bulletin Newspaper Co., Sydney, 1905

Taylor, J. H., *Golf: My Life's Work,* Jonathan Cape, London, 1943

Tennant, Kylie, *Foveaux*, Gollancz, London, 1939

Turner, Duncan, *A New Treatment of Consumption and Other Chronic Chest Diseases,* George Robertson, Melbourne, 1904

Wainwright, David and Catherine Dinn, *Henry Scott Tuke, 1858–1929, Under Canvas*, Sarema, London, 1989

Wallace, Catherine, *Catching the Light: The Art and Life of Henry Scott Tuke, 1858–1929*, Atelier Books, Edinburgh, 2008

SELECTED JOURNAL ARTICLES AND BOOK CHAPTERS

Allison, Lincoln, 'Batsman and Bowler: The Key Relation of Victorian England', *Journal of Sport History*, Vol. 7, No. 2 (Summer 1980), pp. 5–20

Alomes, Stephen, 'Australian Nationalism in the Eras of Imperialism and "Internationalism"', *Australian Journal of Politics & History*, Vol. 34, Issue 3, December 1988, pp. 320–32

'C. G. K.', 'Science and Art of Cricket', *Nature*, Vol. 73, No. 1882, 23 November 1905, pp. 82–4

Cashman, Richard, 'Symbols of Unity: Anglo-Australian Cricketers, 1877–1900', *International Journal of the History of Sport*, Vol. 7, No. 1, 1990, pp. 97–110

Cunneen, Chris, 'Elevating and Recording the People's Pastimes: Sydney Sporting Journalism 1886–1939', in *Sport, Money, Morality and the Media*, edited by Richard Cashman and Michael McKernan, UNSW Press, Kensington, 1981

Goodwin, Clayton, 'The Aura of Celebrity', *The Lancet*, Vol. 363, No. 9409, 21 February 2004, p. 668

Haigh, Gideon, 'Top Shot That', *Portrait*, No. 34, Summer 2009, pp. 4–7

Haigh, Gideon, '"He Opened the Windows of the Mind": How Victor Trumper Changed the Way Australians See Cricket', Jack Marsh History Lecture 2015, Sydney Cricket Ground, 21 January 2015

Hanley, Howard, 'Silent Voices from the Lord's Pavilion', *The Yorker*, Issue 45, Spring 2011, pp. 17–22

Holt, Richard, 'Cricket and Englishness: The Batsman as Hero', *International Journal of the History of Sport*, Vol. 13, Issue 1, 1996, pp. 48–70

Judd, Barry, '"It's Not Cricket": Victorian Aboriginal Cricket at Coranderrk', *LaTrobe Journal*, No. 85, May 2010, pp. 37–54

McAuliffe, Chris, 'The Game of Nationhood: Art, Football and
    Australian Federation', *Journal of Australian Studies*, Vol. 37, No. 4,
    November 2013, pp. 520–34

Manning, Greg, 'The Cricketer as Galahad: A Sketch History of the
    Myth of Victor Trumper', unpublished

Mondy, Dave, 'How Things Break', *Iowa Review*, Vol. 44, Issue 3, Winter
    2014/15

Phillips, Murray, 'Remembering Sport History: Narrative, Social Memory
    and the Origins of the Rugby League in Australia', *International
    Journal of the History of Sport*, Vol. 21, Issue 1, January 2004, pp. 50–66

Sharpham, Peter, 'The Origin of the Green and Gold', *Sporting
    Traditions*, Vol. 10, No. 2, pp. 21–8

Smith, Paul, 'Through a Glass, Brightly', *MCC Magazine*, Summer 2015,
    pp. 32–5

AUDIOVISUAL MATERIAL

Australian Cricketers on the Field in Cheltenham, British Mutoscope and
    Biograph Company (1899), NFSA Title No: 1141013

England v Australia 1905, *British Movietone Digital Archive*, www.
    movietone.com

Australian Cricketers Practice at Lord's, Pathé Super Gazette (1930),
    NFSA Title No: 18477, fragments of recovered 1905 footage included
    in 1930 film

Australia v South Africa, Test Match Cricket, Sydney, Pathé Animated
    Gazette (1910), NFSA Title No: 817530

The Last Innings of Victor Trumper: The Champion of Champions,
    Australasian Gazette (1915), NFSA Title No: 66836

That's Cricket, Australasian Film (director: Ken G. Hall) (1931), NFSA
    Title No: 11010

They Were Champions: Victor Trumper, radio serial broadcast on 3DB
    (December 1953), NFSA Title No: 246850

'Victor Trumper' from The Lucksmiths' album *Boondoggle*, Candle
    Records (1994), NFSA Title No: 743256

NEWSPAPERS, PERIODICALS AND ANNUALS

Australia: *The Advertiser, The Age, Albury Banner and Wodonga Express, The
    Argus, The Arrow, The Australasian, The Australian, Australian Review
    of Reviews, Australian Town and Country Journal, The Bulletin, Courier-
    Mail, Daily Standard* (Brisbane), *Daily Telegraph, Gundagai Times,
    The Herald, Inside Sport, Manly Daily, Meanjin, Mirror of Australia,
    Newcastle Sun, Northern Star (Lismore), The Queenslander, The Referee,
    Richmond River Express and Tweed Advertiser, Singleton Argus, Sporting
    Globe, The Sportsman, The Sun, Sun-Herald, Sydney Mail, Sydney
    Morning Herald, Table Talk, Wellington Times, West Australian.*

India: *Indian Cricket, Sport & Pastime, Wisden India*

New Zealand: *Christchurch Press, Young Man's Magazine*

United Kingdom: *Amateur Photographer, Athletic News, British Journal
    of Photography, The Captain, C. B. Fry's Magazine of Action and
    Outdoor Life, Cricket: A Weekly Record of the Game, The Cricketer, Daily
    Chronicle, Daily Express, Daily Graphic, Daily Mail, Daily Telegraph
    (London), Daily Telegraph (Sheffield), Derby Daily Telegraph,
    Edinburgh Evening Post, Evening News, Evening Standard, The Field,
    Golf Illustrated, The Graphic, Hull Daily Mail, Illustrated London News,
    Illustrated Sporting and Dramatic News, Manchester Courier, Manchester
    Evening News, Manchester Guardian, New Review, News of the
    World, Nottingham Evening Post, Sporting Gazette, Sporting Life, The
    Sportsman, Strand Magazine, Sunday Times, Times Literary Supplement,
    Vanity Fair, Voice of the Century, Wisden Cricketers' Almanack*

IMAGE CREDITS

Author's Collection viii, 12–13, 46, 47, 100 (both), 103, 266, 272, 278 (all), 285

Beldam Collection 132 (all), 137 (all), 139, 282

Andrew Bernard 226

Max Bonnell 54

Boundary Books 89, 91, 114, 134, 216

British Newspaper Archive 64, 78

Philip Brown 290

Cricket NSW 191, 201

Eadweard Muybridge Online Archive 93

Fairfax Photos 288

Steve Flemming 147 (right)

David Frith 69

John Hawkins 144

Arthur Mailey Jnr 170

Melbourne Cricket Club 3, 7 (both), 9, 15, 18, 25, 37, 95, 97, 147 (left), 154, 196, 225, 237, 264 (all)

Estate of David Moore 260

National Library of Australia 123

National Portrait Gallery xvi

Michael Ryan 182 (left)

Peter Schofield 182 (right)

State Library of Victoria 20, 166, 207, 230, 250

PICTURE SECTION

Author's Collection 3 (top and middle), 14 (middle left),
15 (middle right and bottom right)

Russell Ayres 14 (bottom right)

Beldam Collection 4 (all), 7 (all)

Andrew Bernard 9 (bottom)

Boundary Books 11 (bottom left)

British Library 8

Peter Brown 12 (top left)

Judith Dobie 14 (top left)

Hardie Grant 11 (bottom right)

John Hawkins 15 (top left and top right)

The Hindu 13 (middle right)

Ian Kenins 12 (bottom)

Marylebone CC 1 (bottom)

Melbourne CC 2 (bottom), 3 (bottom), 5, 6 (top),
10 (top left and bottom right), 11 (top left and top right),
12 (top right), 15 (middle left)

National Film and Sound Archive 2 (top right), 9 (top)

National Library of Australia 13 (top)

National Portrait Gallery 10 (top right)

Newspix 16 (bottom)

Jim Pavlidis 16 (top)

Tim Rogers 13 (bottom left)

Peter Schofield 2 (top left)

State Library of Victoria 1 (top)

Surrey CCC 6 (bottom)

Dave Thomas 14 (bottom left)

Balaji Venugopal 13 (bottom right)

Peter Young 14 (top right)

ACKNOWLEDGEMENTS

The origins of *Stroke of Genius* lie in a talk, the Jack Marsh Memorial Lecture, delivered at the Sydney Cricket & Sports Ground Trust in January 2015: '"He Opened the Windows of the Mind": How Victor Trumper Changed the Way Australians Saw Cricket'. I should therefore first doff my cap to Rodney Cavalier, former chairman of the Sydney Cricket Ground Trust, for his invitation, and to museum staff Leah Domanski and Anthony O'Carroll for making the presentation possible. The book was then put together in and around various contemporary cricket commitments, including an Ashes series scheduled for thirty days which lasted eighteen, enabling invaluable visits on Michael Down and John Hawkins, Lord's and The Oval, and the pleasure of connecting with descendants of the co-authors of *Great Batsmen: Their Methods at a Glance*: George Beldam's daughter-in-law Cornelia, and C. B. Fry's grandson Jonathan and his wife Marilyn. Throughout this period I was most generously hosted by Mike Atherton and Isabelle de Caires: as ever, I am in their debt.

For help too extensive to enumerate fully, I should like to thank: Marie-Louise and Russell Ayres, Andrew Bernard, Max Bonnell, Keith Booth, Neal Bryson, Andy Bull, Stephanie Bunbury, Colin Clowes, Liz Conor, Kaz Cooke, Dennis Coon, Jennifer Cornwall, Brad Diebert, Judith Dobie, Marty Donald, Elizabeth Edwards, Michael Fahey, David Frith, Glenn Gibson, John and Jeremy Goff,

Ramachandra Guha, Howard Hanley, Graeme Haigh, John Harms, Philippa Hawker, the Rt Hon John Howard, Russell Jackson, Ian Kenins, Damien Kingsbury, Louis Laumen, Reg Lynch, Chris McAuliffe, David McLachlan, Greg Manning, James Merchant, Mark Mordue, Wayne Owens, Jim Pavlidis, Dileep Premachandran, Mark Ray, Tim Rice, Tim Rogers, Christian Ryan, Peter Schofield, Graem Sims, John Spooner, David Strange, Roger Taylor, Dave Thomas, Richard Warlow, Robert Willcocks, Peter Young. S. Giridhar introduced me to Balaji Venugopal; Clayton Murzello was kind enough to put me in contact with Vasant Raiji. Important advice and assistance on matters of photography came from Bob Thomas, Patrick Eagar, Philip Brown, Paul Smith, Eric Evans and a correspondent at www.earlyphotography.co.uk who remained anonymous despite answering in great detail my many questions about the workings of the Adam Videx.

Whatever's wrong with *Stroke of Genius* is my fault; any credit I must share with the personnel of Penguin Random House Australia who cared mightily for the book at every stage. Ben Ball was an exceptional publisher. Rachel Scully, Jeremy Sherlock and Samantha Jayaweera were tireless helpmates through the immense design challenge of marrying text and image. Katie Purvis was an attentive editor. Writing is a lonely business; I warmly appreciated the company.

I further acknowledge the assistance of staff of the National Library of Australia, the National Museum of Australia, the State Libraries of Victoria, South Australia, New South Wales and Queensland, the British Library, London Metropolitan Archives and the Surrey History Centre, Siobhan Dee and Sean Bridgman from the National Film and Sound Archive, Audrey Snell at the All England Tennis Club, Neil Robinson, Heather Thomas and Robert

ACKNOWLEDGEMENTS

Curphey at Marylebone Cricket Club. Above all, felicitations to David Studham, Trevor Ruddell, Steve Flemming and April West at the Melbourne Cricket Club, who were tireless, tactful and brought to my attention much I may otherwise have missed. The burden of living with a tired and taciturn Trumper obsessive, meanwhile, was nobly borne by my wife Charlotte and daughter Cecilia. Thanks to them, and apologies for my endless preoccupation.